W9-BJA-061

THE COLLEGEHUMOR GUIDE TO COLLEGE

THE COLLEGEHUMOR GUIDE TO COLLEGE

SELLING KIDNEYS FOR BEER MONEY,

SLEEPING WITH YOUR PROFESSORS,

MAJORING IN COMMUNICATIONS,

AND OTHER REALLY GOOD IDEAS

By the Writers of CollegeHumor.com

Amir Blumenfeld • Jeff Rubin • Sarah Schneider
Streeter Seidell • Ethan Trex • Ricky Van Veen

With Contributions from Jakob Lodwick, Jay Pinkerton, and John Roy
Illustrations by Bill Brown and Patrick Moberg

New American Library

New American Library
Published by New American Library, a division of
Penguin Group (USA) Inc., 375 Hudson Street,
New York, New York 10014, USA
Penguin Group (Canada), 90 Eglinton Avenue East, Suite 700, Toronto,
Ontario M4P 2Y3, Canada (a division of Pearson Penguin Canada Inc.)
Penguin Books Ltd., 80 Strand, London WC2R 0RL, England
Penguin Ireland, 25 St. Stephen's Green, Dublin 2,
Ireland (a division of Penguin Books Ltd.)
Penguin Group (Australia), 250 Camberwell Road, Camberwell, Victoria 3124,
Australia (a division of Pearson Australia Group Pty. Ltd.)
Penguin Books India Pvt. Ltd., 11 Community Centre, Panchsheel Park,
New Delhi - 110 017, India
Penguin Group (NZ), 67 Apollo Drive, Mairangi Bay,
Auckland 1311, New Zealand (a division of Pearson New Zealand Ltd.)
Penguin Books (South Africa) (Pty.) Ltd., 24 Sturdee Avenue,
Rosebank, Johannesburg 2196, South Africa

Penguin Books Ltd., Registered Offices:
80 Strand, London WC2R 0RL, England

Published by New American Library, a division of Penguin Group (USA) Inc.
Previously published in a Dutton edition.

First New American Library Printing, March 2007
10 9 8 7 6 5 4

Set in Rotis SansSerif
Designed by Jaime Putorti

Printed in the United States of America

Dedicated To Our Parents:

Please Stop Reading Here

CONTENTS

THE COLLEGEHUMOR GUIDE TO COLLEGE

INTRODUCTION

The Ten Commandments of College

Student was searching for divine inspiration. Student walked high on the mountain of knowledge and came across God. Student asked God how to live life as a college kid should. And God said unto him, Follow these Ten Commandments and you shall be all that a college kid is. And Student thanked God, and it was good. And Student spread the Ten Commandments of College to all.

Thou Shalt Nap

I

And God gave unto Student a great gift, the gift of napping. God said to him, You shall spend half your day napping. You shall nap in class, in your room, and in your friend's room. And God said, If you don't nap, you will not be able to stay up all night drinking. And Student said, Nap I shall, and it was good.

Thou Shalt Get Sick All the Time

II

Now God said to Student, You must be sick all of the time. And Student said, Why? And God said unto him, You shall share drinks, stay up too late, drink too much, and make out with people you don't know. Therefore, God said, you shall be sick all year round. But God said, Blessed are the sick, for they have partied the hardest. And it was good.

Thou Shalt Write Witty Away Messages

III

Student asked, But God, how will I show everyone that I am funny? And God said unto him, Thou shall write witty away messages. God said to Student, You shall never just say you are in the shower, you shall say you are getting wet and wild . . . in the shower. You shall never say you are at class, you shall say you are sleeping . . . in class. God said, If you do not write witty away messages, I shall smite you. Blessed are the funny, for they will get many girls to be their friends but never hook up with them. And it was good.

Thou Shalt Wear a Hoodie

IV

And then Student asked God, How do I look like a college kid? And God said unto Student, You must wear a hoodie, for it is a useful garment. And you shall never wash it, either. Student asked God, What kind of hoodie should it be? And God said, You shall own one with your school's logo on it and you shall own many others of varying colors and creeds. And Student was pleased and God was pleased, and it was good.

Thou Shalt Shit a Lot

V

And Student asked of his bathroom habit and God told him, Student, you shall eat in the cafeteria and you shall shit a lot. And it will not be good shit, it will be the shit of the devil, for your ass shall burn for hours. Your school shall put laxatives in their food and you shall feel their pain. And Student began to weep, and God said unto him, Student, fear not the shit, for all your fellow students will be experiencing the same. And Student dried his eyes and thanked God, and God told him to use wet naps to ease the pain, and it was good.

Thou Shalt Eat Easy Mac

VI

Student asked unto God if there were any alternatives to the cafeteria, and God said to him, You shall eat a lot of Easy Mac. It is easy to make and you don't need milk or a stove. And Student said microwaves were forbidden by the RA. And God said to him, You shall hide the microwave under your bed with a towel on top. And Student asked, What if it is discovered? And God told him to stop being such a pussy, and it was good.

Thou Shalt Hook Up

VII

Student then asked of sex. And God said, Student, you shall hook up and be happy. You shall go home with random people every weekend and forget about them the next day. You shall see them at class and be awkward amongst their company. You shall exchange saliva at bars and parties and it will be good. And Student became gleeful, and God told Student to wrap it up because He knows where she has been, but Student does not, and it was good.

Thou Shalt Join a Club and Never Go to Meetings

VIII

Student inquired of his spare time and God reminded him that he should be napping. But Student said he wanted to do other things. So God said unto him, You shall join a club at the beginning of the semester, but then never go to meetings. And Student asked why he should not go to meetings, and God told him, Because the glee club is gay. And Student understood His wisdom, and it was good.

Thou Shalt Wake Up Confused

IX

God said to Student, There will come many a day when you shall wake up in the bed of another and not know where you are. You will not remember what you did last night and you shall be confused. You will see that you have nipple rings and a tattoo now and are covered in Sharpie. And Student was disturbed by this, but God said, You shall tell great stories about it to your friends someday. And Student understood, and God took a sip of a beer, and it was good.

Thou Shalt Gain Weight

X

And Student wished to hear the final commandment and God said he would not like it. But Student insisted, so God said unto him, Thou shalt gain weight. However, God said, you will not buy new clothes, so you will wear sweatpants a lot. God said, Student, you will watch a lot of TV and become fat. And Student wept profusely. But God comforted Student, saying, You will still get ass even if you cannot tie your shoes anymore. Student felt better, and God pointed to Student's chest, saying, Those will soon be bitch tits. And it was good.

FINISHING UP HIGH SCHOOL

Introduction

Your college experience doesn't start when you set foot on campus, and it doesn't start the first time you get to second base with someone whose last name you don't know. It starts your senior year of high school when you apply and get accepted to a real-life college or university.

After you've taken your SAT and your SAT II, high school is basically over and the real collegiate fun begins. By April, you'll run to the mailbox every day to look for acceptance letters and start to realize that the bigger the envelope, the better the news. The biggest scholarship offers actually come in huge wooden crates drawn by teams of oxen; the worst rejection letters come on a three-by-five postcard and says, "Wish You Weren't Here."

The next step is choosing the right college for you. Your parents are going to stress how important it is that you go to the college where you'll feel welcome and happy. They'll tell you that there is a college for everybody. This sounds like a lengthy and subjective process, but the college that's right for you is ALWAYS the one with the highest *U.S. News and World Report* rating that admits you. Great, that took like two minutes. Now, go add a couple of kills to your Halo record.

Once you choose the right college for you, you can pretty much give up on high school altogether. If you do any work, you're doing too much. Have your dad put wheels on your bed and roll you to school, but wait until around fifth period. Your teachers and guidance counselors will say that a few years ago, a senior completely blew off his last semester, got a 1.2 GPA, and his college acceptance got revoked. That's just a myth propagated by high schools everywhere to keep seniors interested in AP Government.

Even if you completely slack off, you'll still make it to graduation. Outside of Halloween and every theme party in college, graduation is probably the best event you'll ever attend while wearing a costume. You'll hear some self-righteous semi-successful local businessman talk about himself in his speech to the graduating class, and you'll sweat in your cap and gown. It's a little-known fact that graduation gowns were designed by a vindictive high school dropout who wanted to punish graduates. He cracked his knuckles and said, "Let's see how you like wearing a black polyester trash bag in June. Who's too dumb to pass Trigonometry now?"

At your graduation, just sweat, smile, and accept cards from your parents' friends. Open them immediately. If there's a check inside, groan and say, "Aw, Christ, now I gotta go to the bank. Thanks for nothing!" Crumple it up and throw it in their faces. After two or three cycles of this, they'll usually just give you cash.

The only other important thing about the end of high school is the prom, which is short for "promise me we'll get married if we do this." Prom is a great way to finish high school off with a semi-consensual bang. If you want to learn more about the prom, consult any movie made with actors in their early twenties playing high-schoolers. Yours will be pretty much like that except with more arguing over whether or not you can really stick that airplane bottle of Jack Daniel's up your ass if the chaperones come into the bathroom.

If worse comes to worst, remember that some people say that college is a five-year experience that begins with your high school senior year, so even if you don't get admitted to any university, you can still tell people you went to college for a year!

SAT Tips

1. The SATs penalize for wrong guesses, but they also reward for correct guesses. So if you're going to guess, get it right.

2. On your essay, remember to write in active voice where the subject is doing the action. For example: "Sally was doing Tim" is actively fantastic, whereas "Tim was being done by Sally" is just passively obscene.

3. Remember the Pythagorean Theorem. Yeah, it was funny when you used to call it the "Py-fag-orean Theorem"; enjoy working the night shift, hatemonger.

4. No matter what you get, remember, you can always lie to people and say you got a 2150.

5. You will be asked to find the area of slices of a circle, which really tests how prepared you are for college-level pie-baking classes.

6. If you think you're bored by the reading passages, imagine how bored the wife of the guy who writes them must be.

7. Like all sequels, the SAT II is worse than the original.

SAT Answer Sheet

Not everyone can get a 2400 on their SATs like we did, but that doesn't mean you can't make fun little designs on your answer sheet. See you at DeVry, Einstein!

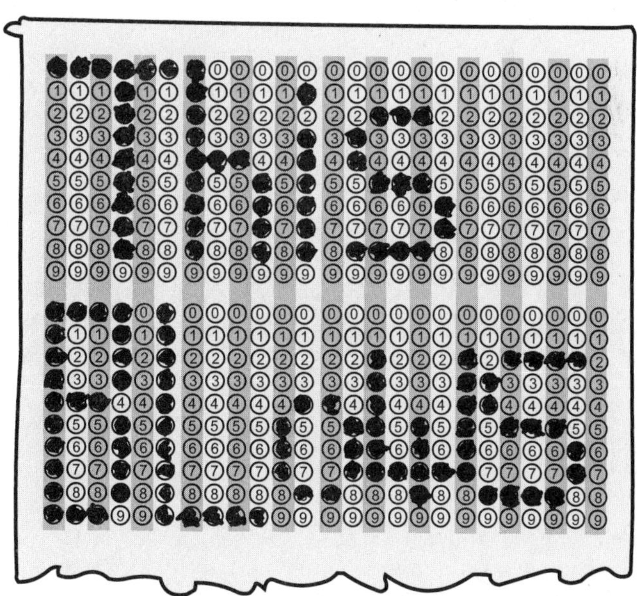

SAT Tip: #17 on the second verbal section is ALWAYS "c." Trust us.

Applying to College

Applying to colleges is one of the most boring aspects of senior year. In order to make the process slightly more enjoyable, try applying to a really crappy school and having fun with the application! Nothing spells "comedy" quite like getting a rejection letter from Appalachian State! Nothing spells "atherosclerosis" quite like an Indian third grader in a spelling bee!

Grades: Every application will ask for the courses you took in high school and the grades you received. For this application make up courses that sound funny, and for your grades, doodle different types of genitalia:

Intro to Awesome: *Picture of a dick*
Street Fighter II: *Picture of a vagina*
Chemistry: *Picture of a dick*

Short Answer Questions: Some applications ask you to answer some questions in a few "short, well thought out" sentences. For this application, you should answer in multiple choice:

"Which teacher, over your high school career, had the most positive impact on you, and why?"
A,B,B,C,B,D,D,B,A,B

Personal Statement: Most applications will have a personal statement. Something that really gets the admissions committee to know you as a person, not just as a GPA. But for this application, you should take the words personal statement literally:

"I got a personal statement for you: I lost my virginity to a vacuum!"

Next year, check that crappy school's admission rate in a student handbook. When it says 99%, smile proudly. You've made a difference.

Pretty ironic that they're called junior colleges, but nobody ever goes for a third year.

Dressing for the Prom

Many of us like to think of ourselves as "eccentric," but wearing something ridiculous to prom is the quickest way to make your date, and everyone else at your school, lose any shred of respect they had for you.

DO NOT WEAR THE FOLLOWING THINGS:

KILT

What's that, Braveheart? You like looking like a total idiot? Your date wants to go to prom, not the Highland Games.

WHITE TUX

Sir, we're ready to order. I'll have the guinea fowl and a Diet Coke, thank you. Dressing like a waiter is all well and good if you are a waiter, but this is a prom. You may want to stand out, but looking like you've got to get that order to table 14 pronto is not the way to do it.

LONG JACKET

Unless you were in *The Matrix,* you aren't cool enough to wear a jacket that goes to your knees. And don't even think about adding a top hat or cane unless you need it to walk.

TUXEDO T-SHIRT

Unless you're in some really cool, really famous band, this look is not for you. Your date will not appreciate the fact that she spent five hours getting ready for tonight while you played video games and slipped this gem on half an hour ago.

DRESS WITH COMBAT BOOTS

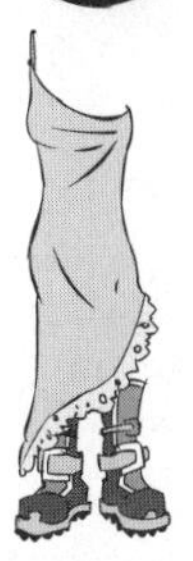

No . . . this is prom . . . The softball banquet is in the next room.

Everything I Needed to Know about Prom I Learned from TBS Movies

1. The ugliest girl in school will suddenly blossom into a beautiful swan on prom night. So go find a real beast and make her your date.
2. If you want him to respect you, you'll give it up in the backseat of his best friend's dad's car.
3. One normally reserved teacher will bust out and dance with a student. Everyone will crack up, but the laughs will temporarily subside when their affair comes to light.
4. Those flowers weren't cheap, so get your money's worth by putting them on Grandma's grave in the morning. She'll be dancing in Heaven, provided she's not burning in Hell.
5. Your formal wear won't keep you from looking like an ass if you do the YMCA.
6. This night is more important than your wedding, so treat it that way.
7. Your mom is taking such an interest in your prom because she loves you, not because she's trying to live vicariously through you now that she's old and fat.
8. Rent a limo so you can feel like your favorite celebrities: other middle-class kids going to the prom.

Free periods are awesome in high school but don't mean anything in college.
The same goes for varsity jackets and your parents.

Prom Night Sex v. Intoxication Chart

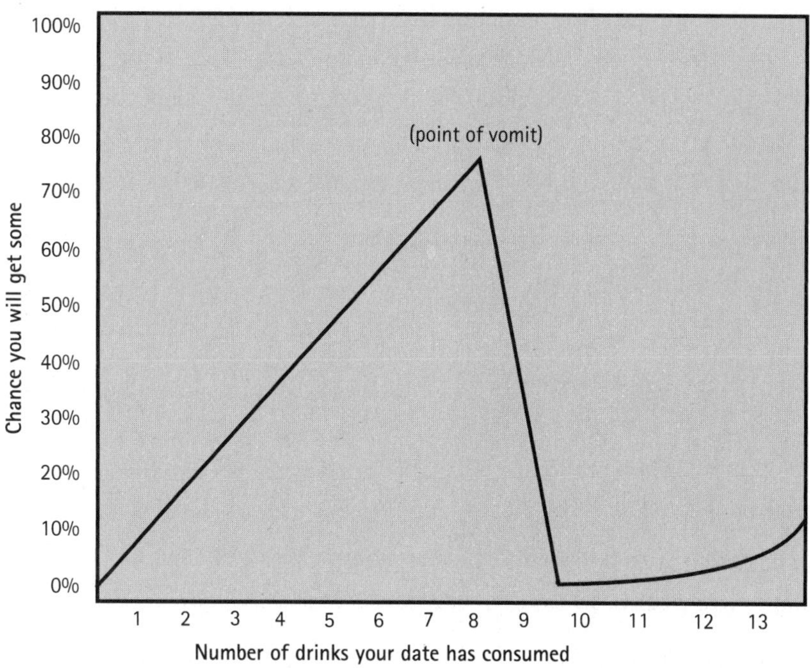

Prom Date Coolness indicator

Like the old saying goes, you're only as cool as who you bring to prom.

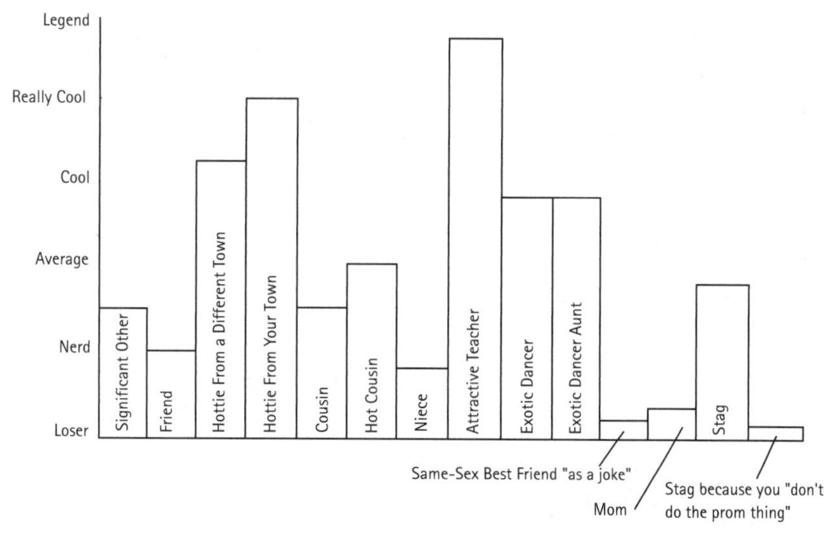

Senioritis

Most students know "senioritis" as a fictional disease referring to the growing apathy twelfth graders face as they complete the most meaningless portions of high school. However, senioritis used to be an actual debilitating illness. Just take a look at this excerpt from a 1943 medical journal:

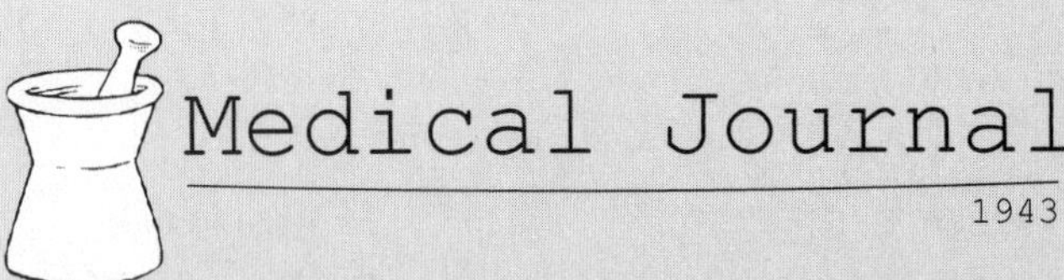

Just as appendicitis is an inflammation of the appendix, so too is senioritis an inflammation of the senior. This inexplicable malady causes a swelling of organs and bones in high school seniors, sending blood pressure so high that many of these students burst in the halls and classrooms as though they'd swallowed a grenade. A dirty Japanese grenade.

Now, this disease would be no problem if it only happened to, say, Japanese students in Japan, but senioritis is affecting everyday normal Americans with no prior health or medical conditions. The swelling process, from puffiness to explosion, takes only a couple of minutes, so the senior has no idea what is happening, and before he realizes it, it is too late. Late like Japanese dinner guests. Not like you would dine with one.

So what can be done about this new devastating epidemic? Well, with modern science being what it is today (close to nothing), there isn't very much that can be done. Teachers everywhere are lobbying for a three-year high school program that has juniors leaving straight to college, bypassing their senior year. However, this is a medical journal, not a logic journal, so we will stick to reporting about scientific facts based on evidence and data. For example, did you know that Japanese are genetically predisposed to ruin America? Buy war bonds.

Graduation Party Celebrating

"Graduation is one of the most important days of your life."

—Your Dad

"Graduation is one of the most important days of your weekend."

—The Truth

Time for a big graduation party to celebrate your many accomplishments during high school. Each great graduation party has a great punch that makes you think "What a long strange trip it's been" with each sip. Try our recipe.

Graduation Party Punch: A Recipe

1 pt. Male
1 pt. Female
Dash false sense of satisfaction
3 qts. repressed sexuality
5 Bottles any liqueur stolen from parents
Zest top-40 radio songs you won't like next year
1 case cheap domestic beer purchased by a hobo in exchange for a can of beans
2 tsp. Bad parenting

Mix all ingredients in home of That Rich Kid Whose Parents Always Leave Town. Strain through social awkwardness; remove clothing. Serve hot and sweaty in a younger sibling's bed. To spice things up, add cumin.

If he acts quickly enough, the homecoming king can usually order five to six beheadings before anyone notices anything's awry.

Graduation Thank-You Note

One of the best parts of graduating high school is the gifts. For some reason, people feel compelled to reward you with a gift for something that, if you're living outside of the Deep South, you're expected to do. When was the last time your dad said, "Good job today, Janet; you didn't drive into oncoming traffic; here's some leftover Halloween candy"?

The most important and frequently overlooked facet of this gratitude is the thank-you note. Write one for every gift you receive; it will separate you from the teenage rabble, your bad teenage mustache notwithstanding.

If this is still too much work for you, here's a template, you lazy bastard.

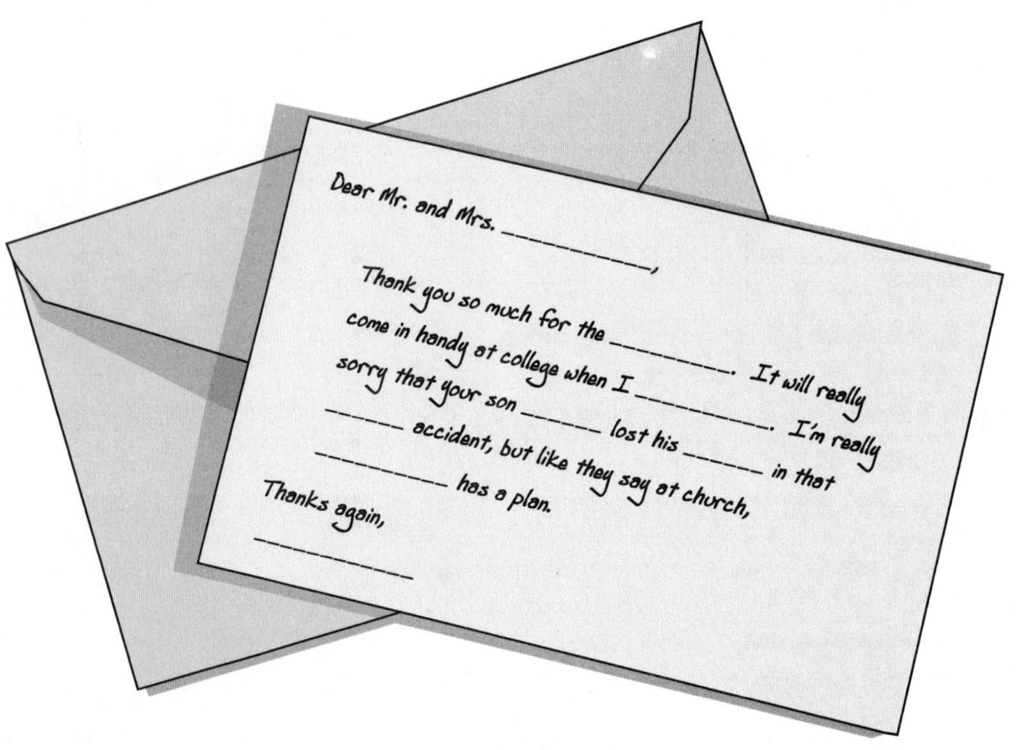

No one is going to believe that you're not going to the prom because it's "gotten too commercial." Nice try, Marx.

Central High School: The Best of What's Around

Senior Bios

5

Crowly, Melissa

Quote: "Er'body in da club get tipsy!"

Future Plans: Haverfield Community Rehabilitation Center

Hansen, Jeremy

Quote: "Never put off for tomorrow what you can get done today."

Future Plans: (Student failed to file future plans on time)

Jameson, Johnathan

Quote: "Life moves pretty fast—if you don't stop and take a look around once in a while you may miss it."

Future Plans: Professional Ferris Bueller Quoter

Nederlandt, Orenthal

Quote: "Never settle for second best!"

Future Plans: Silver Medalist at 2012 Olympics

Taking a Girlfriend to College

When you go to the pool, do you strap a cinder block around your neck? Of course not, you save those valuable blocks to make shoddy shelving in your college apartment. Then why would you go to college with a cinder block made of exploding, burning concrete that attracts angry hornets tied around your neck? Because that's what you're doing to yourself if you go to college with your high school relationship intact.

No high school relationships last throughout college, so why bother even trying? Here's a list of everything you could be doing, but you aren't:

WHAT YOU COULD BE DOING: Meeting new people and friends.
WHAT YOU ARE DOING: Talking to your girlfriend in the hallway until 4 a.m., reassuring her you aren't mingling with other girls.

WHAT YOU COULD BE DOING: Going to parties and getting wasted.
WHAT YOU ARE DOING: Talking to your girlfriend in the hallway until 4 a.m., reassuring her you aren't going to parties and meeting new people.

WHAT YOU COULD BE DOING: Making out with new babes. College babes.
WHAT YOU ARE DOING: Not getting any younger.

WHAT YOU COULD BE DOING: That hot girl down the hall.
WHAT YOU ARE DOING: Throwing your life away.

SO DON'T BE A FOOL, STAY IN SCHOOL, AND LEAVE THAT GHOUL.

Note: We call girls "ghouls."

A Final Note on High School

SATs and ACTs don't measure your intelligence, they just measure how well you can take tests.

And that was our impression of stupid kids' moms.

"Fill in the ______."

2 MOVING IN AND ORIENTATION

Introduction

Packing for freshman move-in is a lot like being a Pilgrim, except instead of the *Mayflower,* you've got a minivan, and instead of teaching you how to plant maize, the Indians are all going to be your chemistry TAs. You're about to leave your old life behind, and your new one offers infinite promise. If you were a nerd in high school, you can still become a really cool guy in college if you go in with the right mind-set.

Lots of students get really nervous the night before their freshman move-in, which is totally counterproductive. You're not going to be confident and outgoing if you pee the bed the night before move-in, so starting a week before move-in day, you shouldn't drink any fluids. Abstinence is the only sure bet. More importantly, though, you should remember that EVERYONE is nervous. Lots of them are probably way more nervous than you are. You see that kid with the big sweat stains on his back? That's not the August heat; his kidneys just exploded. He'll still make fifteen new friends today. Talk to everyone, ask where they're from, and make a joke about how the dining hall food is "probably going to suck." You just made a new friend, slugger!

Even if you're not crazy about these orientation friends, don't worry; more often than not, the people you hang out with at the very beginning of college don't remain your good friends throughout all of college. I mean, you don't still hang out with all the other babies who were in the nursery when you were born, do you? Hell, you hardly even see those guys anymore, except for Todd and Blair. Just keep meeting people, and you'll end up with the friends you wanted. To be on the safe side, though, if you want to know the guy not to be friends with, the one who stands up during the get-to-know-you game and says, "I'm Drew, and I like SIXTY-NINING BITCHES," is a pretty good choice.

Another great benefit of move-in and orientation is that the social strata of college are not yet fully formed, so you can hook up with people who are ridiculously out of your league. Even if you spot the most gorgeous girl you've ever seen, if you talk to her and manage not to say anything blatantly racist, she will probably be saying to herself, "Maybe retainers ARE cool in college . . . I really don't know. . . . I'd better go down on him to make sure." We know what you've made sure: that you just got your boner mopped, champ.

In fact, there's only one surefire way to not make friends during orientation: talking about how cool you were in high school. Yeah, even if everybody's impressed that you had four varsity letters in marching band, they're probably not going to believe that your nickname was "Lord of the Bench Press." Names like that are generally reserved for people with three-digit weights. Also, if you made the mistake to continue dating your high school boyfriend or girlfriend, don't limit your potential friends pool by telling everyone about him or her as soon as you meet them; you guys will be broken up by Thanksgiving. And don't say, "Oh, no, we're in love. . . ." because oh, no, you're not . . .

Finally, your parents probably took a day or two off of work to move you in, so be nice to them. It's a scientifically proven fact that every single freshman thinks he or she has the MOST embarassing parents on the PLANET. However, the most embarrassing parent on the planet is a dad who wears a baseball cap with fighting gamecocks that hardly even matches his "Too Funk to Druck" tank top. Kind of puts things in perspective, doesn't it? Still, you should smile for your parents, tell them you love them, and say, "We should probably go to Target and the grocery store before you leave."

You've arrived. Literally.

Before you steal something, you should always stop and ask yourself, "Do I really need this?" The answer will always be "Yes." You'll find a place for that twenty-five-foot Budweiser banner in your dorm room.

Pre-Move-in Roommate Conversation

Before freshmen move into their dorms they receive a letter in the mail that tells them their future roommate's name as well as phone number. These pre-freshmen open their letters, hoping to God their roommate's name doesn't sound Arabic and their area code isn't from the "poor side of town." Then it's time to call your future roommate and get some major details squared away before move-in day.

A *typical* conversation will go something like this:

YOU: Hi, is Oswald there?
OSWALD: This is he.
YOU: Oh hey, I'm your roommate.
OSWALD: Do you want a microwave and a TV?
YOU: Yes. You bring one and I, the other.
OSWALD: Best friends for life?
YOU: No doubt.

An *atypical* conversation will go something like this:

YOU: Hi, is Oswald there?
OSWALD: Hi, is Oswald there? I mean, is Oswald here?
YOU: Umm, what?
OSWALD: Yes, he IS and he ISN'T HERE.
YOU: I'm sorry, I think I have the wrong number.
OSWALD: Think again.
YOU: I . . . umm, is this Oswald?
OSWALD: YOU BRING THE MICROWAVE AND TELEVISION! I'LL BRING THE ATRIUM!
YOU: What's an atri—*dial tone*

Aren't you excited? You can use college-ruled paper and not feel like a poseur now!

Billy the Bigot

"What if my roommate worships the wrong god?"

Simple Dorm Furniture

Necessity may be the mother of invention, but poverty is the mother of building furniture from things you find in the garbage. Here are some particularly useful items:

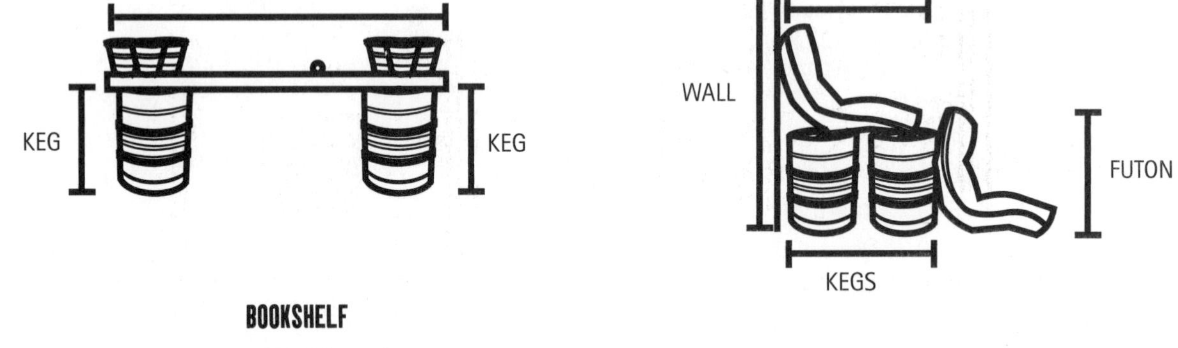

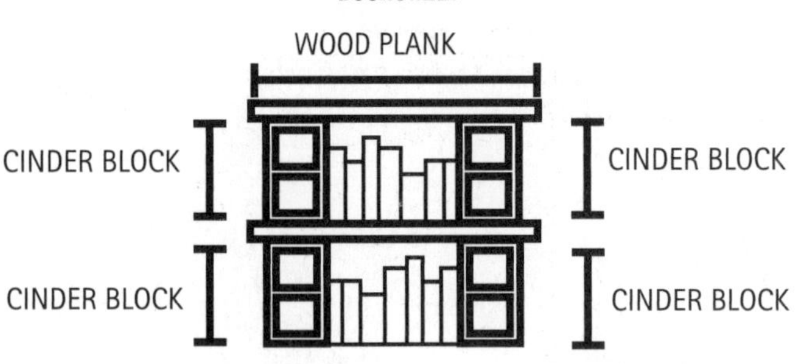

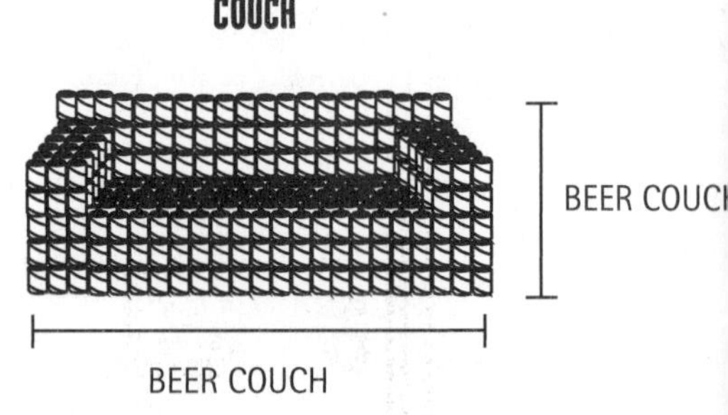

It's not really a bookshelf anymore if you just keep bongs on it.

Door Decorations

Many resident advisors get sick of their hall looking like the dank, fetid hole that it is. They will announce that everyone on the hall must decorate their door. Don't be like everyone else; do something different!

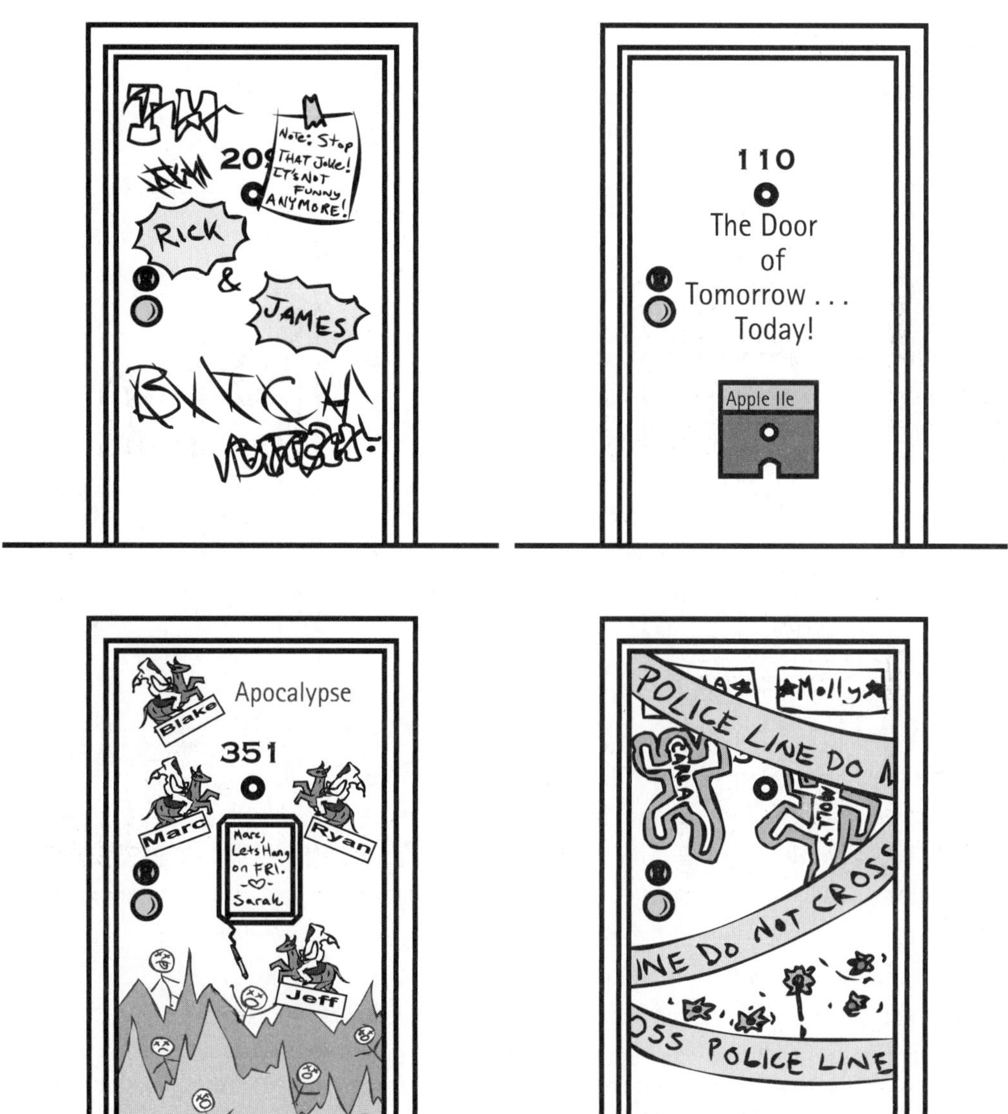

Top or Bottom Bunk:
The Most Important Decision of Your First Three Minutes of College

If your roommate arrives before you and takes the bottom bunk, chances are you can look forward to a year of painful falls and bitter resentment. However, just like poor people who play the lotto, there is always hope! Follow our simple three-step plan for a bed takeover and watch your roommate evacuate that bottom bunk in no time.

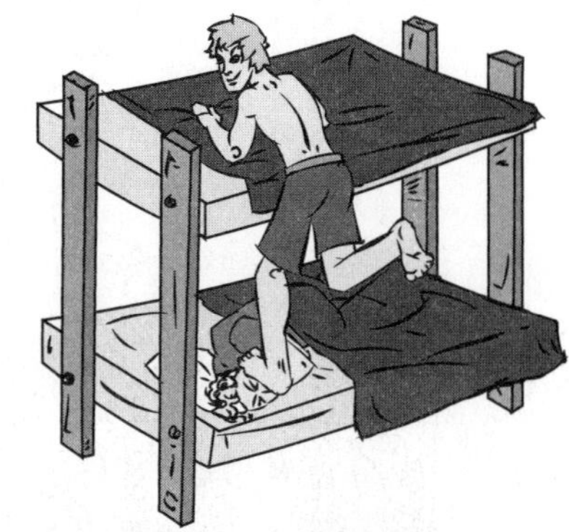

1. **The Big Foot:** When climbing up or down from your bunk, take special care to step on your roommate's head, hand, foot, etc. It's not a big foul, but it's irritating and will establish you as careless and clumsy. Also, knocking anything off a nightstand he may have is encouraged.

2. **The Curious Neighbor:** Nothing says "I might stab you" like watching someone sleep. The top bunk is perfect for a little over-the-edge spying. However, unlike most undercover operatives, you want to be spotted. When he asks why you are staring at him, just say, "You look so peaceful . . . so innocent." Note: Popping your head down when he is with a girl and asking a stupid question such as "When are you waking up tomorrow?" never hurts.

3. **The Waterfall:** How bad do you want that bottom bunk? Really bad? Good, you're ready for the final step. After a night of drinking, climb into bed and pee yourself. Don't worry, lots of kids do this in college, so your reputation won't be too hurt. The next day, when your roommate discovers himself soaked in your waste, explain the awful paradox you're in: you love to drink, yet you pee yourself every time you do! It's important to apologize profusely for the "accident" so your roommate doesn't catch on to your plan. After one or two soakings, you'll be sitting pretty on that bottom bunk.

Female Closet Wars

On move-in day, guys generally start rolling in at about noon. By stark contrast, freshmen girls camp out days before like Grateful Dead fans who don't realize that most of the band is now just plain old Dead. Why? They need to stake their claim to the shared closet. If a girl is even a minute late, if she shows up at 6:03 a.m. instead of 6 a.m., she's forfeited valuable garment real estate. The first girl's division of the closet says a lot about how their relationship will work out. Here's a translation:

Diarrhea runs in your jeans.

Dorm Room Shopping

When you go shopping to stock up your dorm room, it's important to take the right parent. If you take Mom, you'll end up with a well-decorated, boring room. If you take Dad, there's a good chance someone's losing a few pints of blood. If you go by yourself, make sure to bring something back for the other kids at the orphanage.

Mom's Haul

Dad's Haul

If your RA is heavy, try to be sensitive to that. Don't pin him/her up against a wall and call him/her a "fat fucking slob."

Dorm Contraband Search

Uh-oh, looks like you brought a bunch of stuff from home that your college doesn't allow . . . What to do? Don't send it back with Mom and "Uncle" Rodney, hide it! See if you can spot the following banned items in this dorm room!

- Microwave
- Halogen lamp
- George Foreman Grill
- Hot pot
- Bong
- Weed stash
- Keg
- Mexican day laborer
- Candles
- Incense
- Bald eagle

Answer Key:

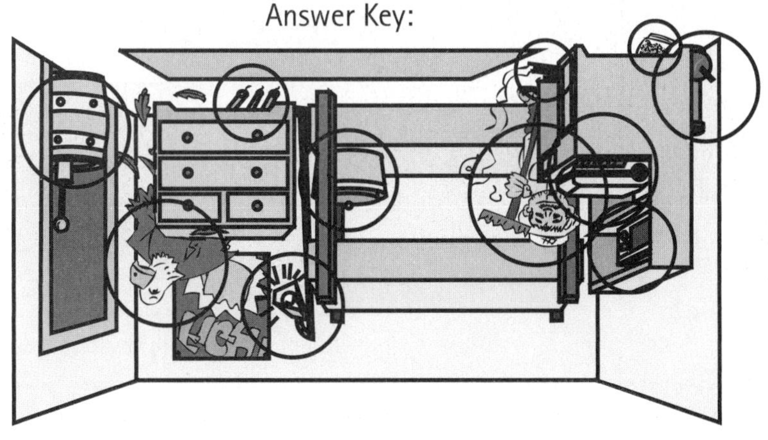

Make a Statement with Posters

"I don't drink yet, but I plan on starting soon . . . and HOW!"

"I like smoking pot, but I'm going to pretend I enjoy music more."

"I'm hungry for a great internship!"

"I like smoking pot."

"I'm cynical but I'm also funny . . . at least, to myself I am."

"Gay guys are disgusting . . . but I appreciate lesbians."

"I'm either black or Italian or want to be."

"I'm a Natty Light kinda guy."

"I was at the bookstore on move-in day."

"My appreciation of fine art is limited to this poster, plus I'm almost halfway through *The Da Vinci Code*."

"I'll lie about what base I've gotten to."

"I hope 'it' means marrying rich."

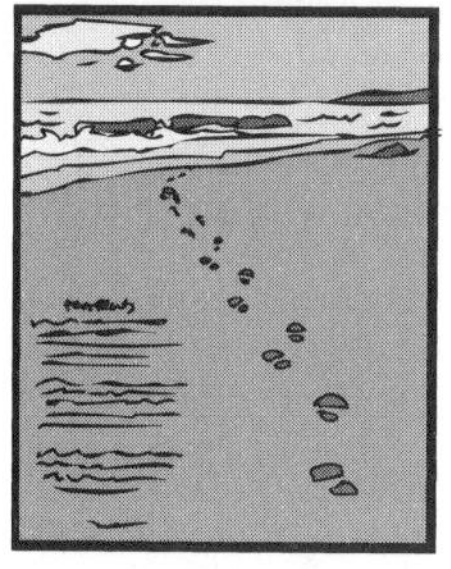

"Don't even get me started on Deuteronomy."

"I'm the kind of guy that hits on girls at Applebee's. 'Would you like to share an Apple-tiser?' That's my line."

My compulsively masturbating one-armed roommate single-handedly ruined freshman year for me.

Things to Take with You to College

Nothing on this list is a joke. Really pack this shit. If you laughed at the last sentence, go back to high school.

1. **Lots of socks and underwear.** Laundry sucks, and these are the things you run out of first. Plus, every organization at college gives away crappy T-shirts; nobody's ever handing out socks.
2. **A bottle of liquor that mixes well with soda.** The first night of school, everyone wants a drink, but nobody has older friends or the balls to use a fake ID. Bam! You've got liquid popularity. Plus, you can usually convince your dad to buy it for you now that you're a man.
3. **A filing box.** It sounds nerdy, but get one of these suckers and some hanging file folders. It costs ten bucks, keeps your desk neat, and keeps you from losing things in the fetid squalor of your room.
4. **A small, basic tool kit.** Nothing fancy, just a hammer, screwdrivers, dual bevel sliding compound miter saw with dual vertical rail guides and linear ball bearings, etc. Assemble furniture! Impress your friends!
5. **A good desk chair.** Your school's dorms will have flame-retardant desk chairs with names like the Spine Mangler that can be credited for their deft retarding of flames, but think about it like this: most of your time spent studying/IMing/downloading porn will be in your desk chair. Your ass will thank you.
6. **Pedialyte Freezer Pops.** You're going to use your newfound freedom to party way too hard in your first week or two. These are great hangover-busters because they taste good and rehydrate you quickly.
7. **A bedspread that won't match your roommate's.** If you're guys, there's no way to pull off matching bedspreads without looking gay. Yes, really.
8. **Surge protectors/power strips.** The typical college dorm room has roughly forty-seven things that need to be plugged in and exactly two wall outlets.

Decorate your room with stolen road signs. If someone says stealing a stop sign is irresponsible, reply, "If you can think of a more passive way to kill a stranger, I'd like to hear it."

9. **A big mug.** The most important dish you'll own in college. Ideally, it will fit at least two beers or a big rum and Coke for pregaming before parties, and it's also big enough to hold ramen and Easy Mac.

10. **Enough toiletries to last all semester.** You probably don't know this now, but deodorant, shampoo, razor blades, etc., cost real money. Buy them on your parents' dime instead of your own.

Roommate Warning Signs

It's tough to tell whether your new roommate is going to be a good person or not. However, if he says any of the following within the first couple days of meeting him, chances are it's going to be a long year:

"Actually, I collect DVD cases. All of the space and none of the fun!"

"If you wake up and I'm cutting your hair, don't freak out, that's just a thing I do."

"I sort of have my own private quiet hours that you should adhere to that differ greatly from the regular hall quiet hours."

"Sorry, I tend to yell when I play video games."

"I'm just trying to figure out what would be the best place for my drum set and alligator."

"Oh, you smoke pot occasionally? That's so weird, because I tell on people occasionally."

"Could you just say 'I love you' when you leave the room? I never had a dad growing up."

"How about we push these dorm beds together and make a king-size!"

Oh, man, so many people signed your high school yearbook. And you must really be fitting in at college if you're showing people that during junior year!

How to Become a Resident Adviser

1. Suck.

   Good work!

Orientation Friends

Most college kids handle making friends during orientation like they would a turn on *Supermarket Sweep*, grabbing as many as possible in a short amount of time. Thanks to this smash-and-grab mentality, you may find yourself with a crew of friends you don't really like. Don't worry, orientation friends can be swiftly tossed aside once you meet real friends in the weeks to come. Consult the following equation to figure out how long it will be until you can ignore The Greg-inator and pretend that conversation about shotgun v. handgun never happened:

$$\text{Days till you can ignore orientation friend} = \frac{(\text{Days you hung out with them}) \times (\text{Secrets they know about you})}{(\text{Times he annoyed you})}$$

Example: You and Matt "Dungeon Lord" Delman hung out for eight days, during which time you told him three secrets and he annoyed you six times.

$$\frac{8 \times 3}{6} = \text{4 days till you can ignore him.}$$

College Urban Legends

You've probably heard a lot of talk about certain college urban legends. Let us dispell some of them for you.

If your roommate dies, you get all A's. This is true—if you're smart enough to kill your roommate, you DESERVE those A's!

If you mix Coke and Pop Rocks, it will explode. This is false. You must be thinking of Coke and dynamite.

You should wash your hands after you take a crap. This is false. Human waste actually contains nineteen vitamins and minerals. One could even make an argument against wiping altogether.

The RA who "really doesn't care." This is true. His name was Derek. We loved him.

A girl broke a frozen hot dog off while masturbating with it. This is false. She grilled it first; otherwise it would have been way too cold to enjoy.

A girl sucked off the entire football team and had to get her stomach pumped. This is false. It was the basketball team, and she had to get her stomach stapled.

Off-Campus Housing

Off-campus housing, or OCH, is an integral part of becoming an adult. Getting your own place, or GYOP, is the final step toward becoming independent.

Suddenly you have to worry about toilet-paper supply, cleaning the kitchen, fixing a lightbulb, killing a mouse, disposing of old breads, and paying your rent on time.

You will realize how important it is to stay organized. Those large calendars that Mommy put up around the house are starting to seem like a good idea. File cabinets were clearly a "grown-up thing" but now seem more convenient than a second PlayStation.

It's a safe bet that the no-candles-in-the-dorm rule was a lot tougher to enforce in the 1500s.

Your damn arthritis will begin acting up. Phrases such as "Goddammit. Nancy! Get me my medicine, I can't even make a fist! Get me my fucking medicine or I'll club you with this here open palm! Nancy!!!" will become more common.

You will have bill collectors breathing down your neck. Damn kids and their damn tuition. Why don't they get a job? When you were their age, you worked three jobs just to help out your old man. How are you gonna retire at this rate? You still don't even have any real savings lined up!

Despite all this, living off-campus does have its perks: freshman girls. Nothing impresses them more than a dude with his own place. In the end, all the flooding bathrooms, shoddy electric wiring, bloodstained carpets, stray cats, and other joys are all worth it when a freshman girl crosses your threshold, gasping "Oh . . . my . . . God, this apartment is awesome." You're in.

A Final Note on Moving In

Move-In Day is one of the most memorable college experiences that involve boxes and your parents. Here are some others:

1. Move-Out Day
2. Ship-Your-Mother-to-Work Day
3. Boxing Day (Canada)

When your RA says, "I hate to do this," what he means is, "I hate that people hate me for doing this."

3 FRIENDS

Introduction

You remember when you were a little kid and your mom would set you up on playdates with neighborhood kids? Well, college is one big four-year playdate, except instead of a sandbox you've got a dorm, and instead of light beer you've got regular beer. (Your mom really shouldn't have let you drink when you were that young.)

Your campus is full of hundreds of potential friends who are also trying to make some pals of their own. With the right group of friends, college can be the best four years of your life. Way better than the first four years of your life, although breast milk is the best milk for me to get my suck on. This chapter is about friends: how to make them, how to keep them, and how to drop them like a ton of bricks. Seriously, everyone knows that a ton of friends falls faster than a ton of feathers.

With this in mind, as soon as you set foot on campus you should start accumulating friends as quickly as you can. If you thought student government elections were a popularity contest, just wait until the big game of "Who's Got the Most Friends?" The more friends you have, the more fun you will have. Period. Quantity over quality. You'll be spending about twelve hundred nights at college; ideally you would have twelve hundred friends and hang out with each one just once before moving on to the next. So get on board the friend ship, next stop: happiness!

Since everyone has a friend-making agenda, meeting people in college is easier than a cheerleader whose dog recently died, so there's no reason to be shy. You don't even need pickup lines; you can start out by complaining about the weather, about classes, or about other people. Sometimes it can even be all three! "Yeah, David is about as boring as Math 16A in the rain. Talk about lame."

After you make one friend like this, the rest just start rolling in, until you're in a small group of friends, or "clique." In order to ensure that your clique gets along with each other, it's important that all you guys have the same taste in music, fashion, and movies. Also, you want to make sure that everybody is of the same race. This is friendship we're talking about here, not a college brochure.

Being Cool in College

1. **Hair:** Do you put effort into making your hair seem cool? Don't. All cool kids put zero effort into their hair. When it's messy, you do nothing. When it gets long, you never under any circumstances PAY for a haircut! There is nothing more uncool than paying somebody to cut your hair. You can either do it yourself, or occasionally push the hair out of your face with your fist. Using fingers shows effort and that's simply uncool. Some people put a lot of effort into making their hair look unkempt; however, that effort shows and oftentimes you're left looking considerably less cool. Oh, and shave every third Tuesday, but not with a blade, with a stick.

2. **Clothes:** Hey, when did you buy that outfit you're wearing? Did your answer start with a "two thousand"? Because if so, you're not cool. The clothes you wear today should be the ones you wore in seventh grade. The smaller, the more worn down, the better. Is your shirt so thin you can see your nipples through it? Great. Now you're getting somewhere, nerd. The shirt you wore to sixth-grade PE is a great start. How about a sports team that doesn't exist anymore? Anything Quebec Nordiques or Vancouver Grizzlies = instant cool.

A good way to tell if your roommate is gay is if he's taken you aside and told you in confidence that he's a homosexual.

3. Demeanor: Do not speak loudly. No cool person speaks loudly. Say few, small words, but every once in a while drop a really big one just to show you've got the capability, but you're just too cool to use it. Example:

> GIRL: Hey.
> YOU: Sup.
> GIRL: I've never noticed you before. I like your shirt—PE, huh? It's cute.
> YOU: Sup.
> GIRL: I like your hair—is that effort I see?
> YOU: You know it ain't, bitch. Sesquipedalian.
> GIRL: * SWOOOOON *

4. Social life: In your free time you have two options. You can be a reader, which means you're cool because you read non-nerdy long books like *Gravity's Rainbow* or *Being and Time*. Or you can be a guy in a band. All you need to pull off that look is a guitar case.

Shakespeare once wrote, "To thine own self be true." However, you should focus on Shakespeare's more subtle philosophical points about dressing up as people and acting like characters. Cooler characters.

Friend Profiles

Hippie:

"You know, man, it's like everyone thinks they KNOW me just because I have these gnarly dreads, but I'm not your typical 'hippie' guy, ya know? I'm an individual. Sure, I play the bongo drums, but I've never even been to a Phish show —at least not since they broke up. Everybody comes up to me and asks me if I want to smoke weed like I'm some sort of pothead. Yeah, I smoke pot a few times a day, but I'm not really a stoner or anything."

Fat Frat Guy:

"GO STATE! I've got more school spirit than anyone in here and I'm standing next to the fucking school mascot, so that's saying something. I used to play starting tackle on my high school's football team, state champs back to back. Every time I go home all my old friends say, 'Wow, man, you've let yourself go.' They just don't get that when you're a Pi Kapp it's almost impossible to stay in shape. I mean, it's party tonight, party tomorrow night, and a sensible dinner. I'd get sick of it if I didn't like getting hammered and punching people in the face so much. GO STATE!"

Hipster:

"Isn't this ironic T-shirt rad? Isn't saying 'rad' ironic? You probably don't notice me because I'm always getting great indie rock and putting it on my iPod. I know it looks like a really old model, but that's because I was the first person in my entire school to get one. Oh, and you don't even want to try to talk to me about music. My favorite band is so underground it hasn't even been formed yet."

All my friends live on either the first, third, fifth, or seventh floor. Don't you find that a little odd?

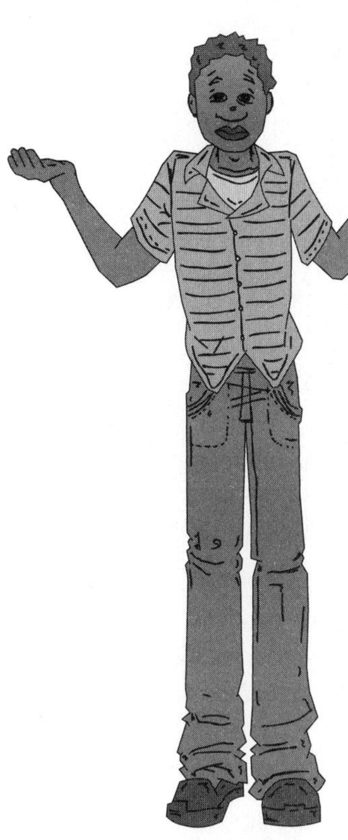

Black Guy:

"Being a normal black kid at college sure is tough. Everybody thinks I'm either a rapper or an athlete. I walk around campus and students ask me what position I play—I don't even like sports! At night people look at me like I'm some crazy gangster. We're in the same English class; you don't need to run away! Well, we know who's gonna get a rough peer edit now!"

Party Girl:

"I am NOT a slut. If I sleep with a few guys here and there, what's the big deal? This is college, right? I'm just a girl who likes to have fun! So what if I let Bruce (or was it James?) finger me a little on the dance floor last night? I was already twelve beers deep so I barely even felt it—no harm done! When my friends and I hit a party, you can tell all the guys are pumped to have us there. They're like, 'Oh yeah, this shit is ON!' I guess me and my bitches just get off on making people happy. Anyone up for a game of strip flip-cup?"

If your name is Mark, a good nickname for you would be Quotation Mark. Start memorizing movies, dick.

Asian Nerd:

"I get to class early to get a good seat. It's easier to walk quickly with this rolling backpack, and it holds my pouch of pencils and erasers. If getting straight A's and talking softly makes me a nerd, then so be it. I don't see anything wrong with staying in on Friday nights to finish up some calculus problem sets. We'll see who's laughing when I'm scoring grad-school fellowships left and right. Hello Kitty, good-bye college!"

Goth:

"You think you understand me? You understand NOTHING! It's just not easy, knowing every day when you wake up that it's going to be more disappointments. These Cure records and makeup can only hide so much of my pain; the rest just comes pouring out in the form of my blog: xxicutmyselfxx.blogspot.com. Current Emotion: sad."

One thing you definitely won't be needing the calculator on your watch for is tallying how many friends you have.

You:

"Man, look at me! I'm a complete original in every way. My style is different from everyone else's, but not in some freaky weird way. I do so many things that no one else does, like I dip my pizza in blue cheese. Who does that? Just me. Honestly, who wouldn't want to sleep with this guy?"

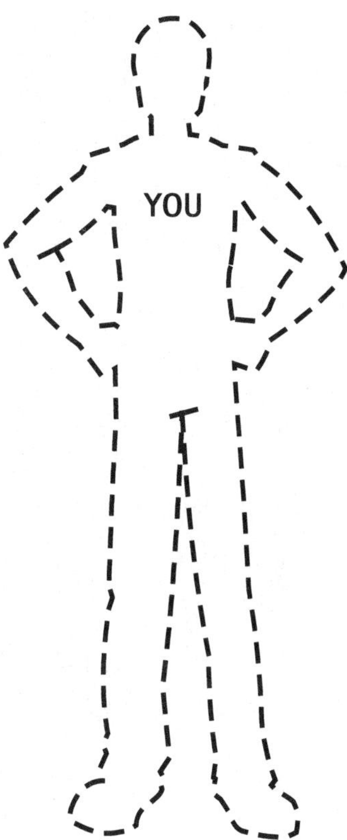

Freshman Hall Icebreakers

Making friends during your first two weeks at college can be overwhelming. You will meet so many new people and have to remember so many new names. In order to make sure you don't waste any brain space remembering people who aren't worth remembering, suggest to your RA that you play the following games in order to expedite the social outcasting of weirdos who aren't even worth meeting:

Jugglebug: The RA will ask if anyone in the hall can juggle. If anyone raises his hand, other residents will recognize that he is not worth knowing and not waste time learning his name.

By Hook or by Book: Your RA should ask everybody to list their ten favorite books of all time. As the lists are read aloud, if anybody includes the Bible, roll your eyes and cross him/her off your get-to-know list. That person is Lame 3:16.

The Name Game: Gather all the girls into one room and politely demand that they all change their name to "Jessica." Then tell them their agreement was a legally binding contract and refer to them all as Jessica for the next year. The only downside to this plan is that all Jessicas are bitches, so you will be living in the bitchiest hall of all time. As opposed to the bitchin'est hall of all time, which was Cheney Hall '95!!!!

Deathpit: A freshman hall can have as many as twenty residents. That's nineteen names you'll have to remember. Way too many. Put everyone on your hall in a 20' × 20' × 20' pit. Grease the sides so no one can escape. Residents fight until only you and one other guy are left alive. He'll shake your hand and say, "Hi, I'm Jack; we're lucky to be alive, bro." You'll smile and say, "I know. I always knew."

Enemies

Alvin the Chipmunk once said, "Keep your friends close, but your enemies closer." Theodore and Simon were none the wiser, but you can learn where they failed. How do you know if a friend of yours is actually an enemy? Just ask yourself these nine simple questions is how:

1. Is your "friend" close to completing a weather-control machine?
2. Does your "friend" wear a cape or, failing that, a top hat and monocle?
3. Does your "friend" have an anthropomorphic animal sidekick?
4. Does your "friend" reveal secret plans and then laugh menacingly?
5. Does your "friend" have powers that are perfectly evenly matched with yours?
6. Does your "friend" display hubris about never being brought down?
7. Is your "friend" constantly challenging you to a fight atop the Statue of Liberty?
8. Does your "friend" have his own minor-key music playing when he walks into a room?
9. Is your "friend" the only one aware of your true identity?

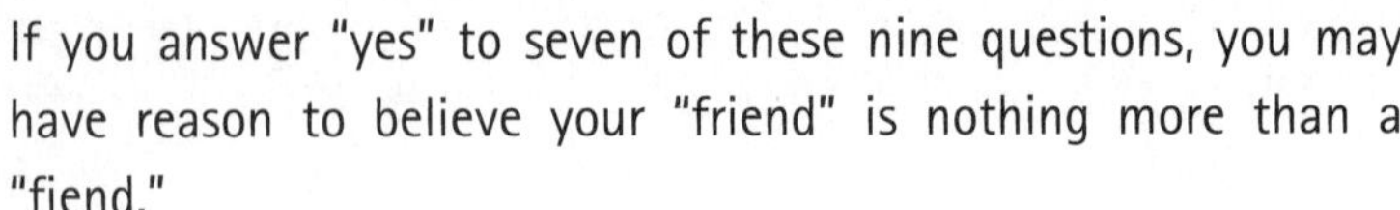

If you answer "yes" to seven of these nine questions, you may have reason to believe your "friend" is nothing more than a "fiend."

Role-Playing Friends

After you've established your core group of friends, you will need to fill in the peripheral role-playing friends in your social circle. These people aren't really "friends" as much as they are "acquaintances that you use for a very specific purpose." Collect them all!

The Friend with a Car: Everybody needs a friend with a car, because taking mass transit to your six-month-anniversary dinner just isn't romantic. In order for this friend not to feel used, start acting nicer toward him exactly two hours before you plan on borrowing his car, or ten minutes before stealing it.

The Rich Friend: You should have one friend who doesn't mind picking up the tab after dinner. The key is to "unknowingly" suggest the priciest restaurant in town for your meal. The other key is forgetting your wallet at home.

The Smarty-Pants: If you're interested in getting good grades with minimal effort, you are gonna need a genius friend. "Hey, let's compare homework answers tonight!" After that, you're one ether rag away from copying his hard work. "Oh man, how long have I been out, I don't even remember falling asleep . . ." Tell him to shut up and put his pants back on. It's not gay unless both people are awake.

The Responsible Friend: Also known as the "Guy Who Talks to the Cops." This responsible dude knows both where the hospital is and how to get there. His nickname is "Short Straight," but he is actually quite tall; he's just never lost a game of Yahtzee in his entire life.

The Corpse: "It's just that my buddy just died, and I've been having a really hard time getting over it." This buddy makes a handy excuse for things you don't want to do, with the added bonus that you never have to hang out with him.

Nonverbal Communication

Nonverbal communication: everyone does it but nobody talks about it. It's an unspoken bond between you and another student to acknowledge each other but to never exchange a word. Maybe you sat next to this person in a class or lived on the same floor freshman year? It's a real time-saver! If you were to actually say a verbal "Hi" to everyone you knew, that would take hours or even days, but that goes without saying.

I know and respect you. Unfortunately, I am also aware that you steal DVDs at parties.

Hello, we had class together where we spoke a few times. We probably should be friends but I don't have the time.

I am NOT gay, okay? Last night was a JOKE. You better not tell anyone . . .

I have no idea who you are but you seem to know me.

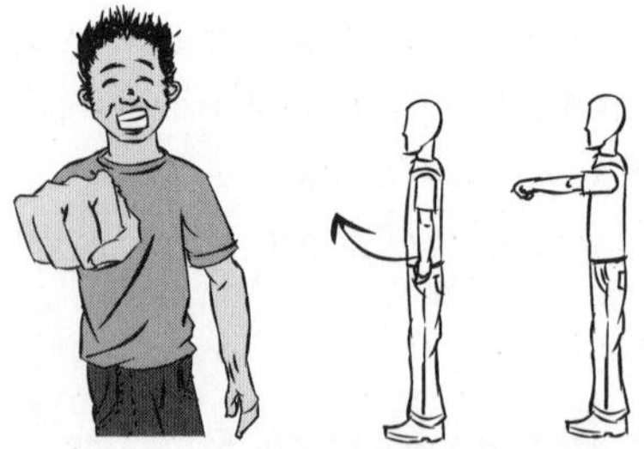

We'd be the kind of guys who call each other "Dawg" if I didn't secretly hate you.

Living with Your Best Friend

Requesting to live with a best friend during freshman year isn't just a bad idea, it's the worst idea of all time. And this book was written after the Vietnam War, so that's saying something.

"I know my best friend is great, so why would I want to share a dorm with somebody who may be a psychopath!?" you may be asking yourself. Because college is about the stories. If your roommate is a chronic masturbator, a vegan, or an Italian, these are fantastic fodder for great stories! You'll be regaling your friends with daily anecdotes that begin with "You'll never guess where my roommate masturbated today!" or "You'll never guess how my roommate put protein back in his diet today!" or "You'll never guess how my roommate pronounced 'meatballs' today!"

Also, living with your best friend freshman year will guarantee that you guys will hate each other by sophomore year. No matter how close your friendship is, it just takes a few months inside of a ten-foot-by-ten-foot room to transform the closest of lovers into the mortalest of enemies. Oh, "mortalest" might not be a word now, but by the end of the school year . . . watch out.

Staying Up Late

Now that you're in college, you can stay up all night. To sound cool while you do this, tell people, "I'll sleep when I'm dead," which, if you continue not sleeping, should be on Thursday.

Sauna Club

A popular male hall ritual is the "Sauna Club," in which the hall bathroom is turned into a sauna by turning on all the showers full-blast HOT and letting the steam collect. For a more relaxed atmosphere, bring in your dorm furniture so you can all have seats. When the RA asks how everyone's chair got warped from water damage, the correct response is, "The really shy kid did it. I forget his exact name. Why?"

Don't think you're fooling anybody. Saying a friend's thirteen-year-old sister "is going to be hot when she's older" means, "Your thirteen-year-old sister is hot."

Late Night Word Search

So many college kids enjoy "staying up all night, just talking about, you know, important stuff." These conversations seem extraordinary and unique at the time, but many of the same themes recur. If you can find and use the words in this word search, everyone will think you're smart enough to sleep with.

AGNOSTIC
CHOMSKY
COMMUNISM
CONSUMERS
EXISTENTIALIST
FREUD
KEROUAC
KUNDERA
KUROSAWA
MATERIALISM
NIETZSCHE
NIHILISM
POSTMODERN
SOCIETY
SPIRITUAL

Y A K F N C U P T I K E S Y M
T H E T N C I Z T U Q A P S Q
E O R S Z I A T N Y H H I S C
I A O I E U E D S C Q L R S R
C W U L A G E T C O A G I H L
O A A A S R U Z Z I N X T O Q
S S C I A G H H R S U G U C C
P O S T M O D E R N C E A F F
K R X N T D T J B H S H L P Z
J U D E Z A G R G E F R E U D
W K J T M B M S I N U M M O C
Z G N S N I H I L I S M Y P W
M T L I X V N V V D W N B I T
T C K X E U C O N S U M E R S
R I P E N P E Y K S M O H C L

"I'm suspicious that my roommate is stealing my socks.
Not because he has a lot of socks, but because he has a lot of homemade puppets."

Shortening Words

As a college student, you will lead a busy life. Between napping, class, eating, napping, and homework, we barely even have time to nap. For this reason, we look to save time whenever we can, even during our everyday conversations. Shortening words to quicker, abbreviated versions is a HUGE time-saver. Example:

"Whatever, I'm definitely going to vomit, but I obviously want a blow job."
That takes about four seconds to say. Doesn't seem so bad, until you see how much time you could have saved saying:

"Whatev, I'm def gonna vom, but I obvi wanna beej."
You just shaved off a second of precious time. Here's an even more abbreviated version for you experts:

"Wha, mef gont, biovi danna vomtabeej."
Amazing. Now go take a nap.

A Final Note on Friends

She said she wanted to be "friends with benefits." So where's my dental plan, slut?

When someone asks where you're from, it must suck to come from a town called "None of your business, faggot!"

4 FOOD, HEALTH, AND LAUNDRY

Introduction

In ancient colleges, students had to hunt down food and kill it themselves after their four o'clock Intro to Grunting. Things have gotten much more sophisticated in the years since; Intro to Grunting is now a master's level seminar.

College food is still something of a free-for-all, though. Most students are cooking for themselves for the first time and can't master the subtle art of taking their popcorn out of the microwave before it smokes and sets off the fire alarm again.

Instead of having your mom bring you big plates of warm food for dinner, you'll find yourself facedown in a pile of dirty laundry, thinking, "There's gotta be something I can cook with only salt and a somewhat moldy lemon. Maybe if I put them both on a cracker . . ."

It's these kinds of dilemmas that usually send you to the dining hall, or "cafeteria" for short. Your parents didn't really trust you to spend their money only on food, so they bought you an overpriced meal plan. You think that TGI Friday's has the worst $12 meals in the world?

You haven't even seen your dining hall's take on salisbury steak yet. It's so bad that the Earl of Salisbury himself once took a bite and said, "I'm changing my last name to 'Meatloaf.' "

Some nights you're just too tired of eating in the cafeteria and have to go out or make a delivery order. Anyone who's ever tried to make a delivery order knows that the second dirtiest combination of three words in the English language is "ten-dollar minimum." (The first dirtiest is just the word "cunt" written three times on a bathroom stall door.) You'll want some $6 pad thai, and you'll do whatever it takes to find another person who wants a $4 item. You'll bang on doors in halls you didn't even know existed in your dorm. You'll say things like, "Oh, wow, nice ski mask. You want to put down your ax and order a chicken satay?" In retrospect you'll realize that you probably should have just gotten a second pad thai and saved it for tomorrow night.

All of these terrible food-related decisions can lead to you being gravely ill for 85 percent of college. It's hard to envision a time period where you would be less healthy than your college years. Yes, the bubonic plague years were pretty rough, but did anyone ever have to say, "Dude, look at this rash. You think I should go to student health?" in fourteenth-century Europe? No, they didn't, because everyone knows that even then Student Health was only open from 6 to 8 a.m. on Monday mornings. What serf's got that kind of time? They always just told you you had an infection of the sinus humors, anyway.

Even if you take serious safety precautions like washing your hands every three or four days, there's a pretty good chance that you will contract some sort of serious illness that only still exists in college. How did you get scurvy? Guess your policy of "orange juice is just for mixin', not for drinkin' " wasn't as awesome as your fraternity brothers thought. When you come down with mono, known in college as the "kissing disease," be coy when people ask how you got it. A knowing smile and a wink goes a lot farther in people's imaginations than outright saying, "I probably shouldn't have licked that doorknob" ever will. The "kissin' cousins disease" is still incest and illegal in most states.

When you get sick, you will go to Student Health, where even if you're bleeding from a javelin lodged in your abdomen, they will helpfully inform you that it's "probably strep" and give you some mouthwash that will soothe your throat. You'll protest, but they'll tell you to stop trying to get out of class, weasel. You'll prove your point when you die of blood loss shortly thereafter, but at what cost?

This chapter is all about food, health, laundry, and the terrible decisions you will make regarding all three. Remember, when your mom told you a little vegetable never killed anyone, she wasn't talking about that small piece of broccoli that fell behind the radiator last semester. Oh, and it's a five-second rule, not a five-semester rule.

Is this a malignant melanoma or a chocolate chip? Phew, that was a delicious relief.

Barry McLinney on Dining Hall Food

(*Editor's Note:* We didn't eat at the dining halls much in college, so we brought in our friend Barry McLinney, who, in addition to having some great jokes about the dining hall, has done stand-up at several open-mic nights in his hometown of Akron, Ohio.)

Hey, CollegeHumor-heads, Barry McLinney here to give you the Barry McSKINNY on dining hall foods!

But seriously, folks, the dining hall is great. Some colleges have the all-you-can-eat options for meals. They call it all-you-can-eat and not all-you-want-to-eat because the food is so bad that nobody would want to eat it! Am I right? Am I right? I'm right.

Sometimes you go into the dining hall and they have sloppy joes. Sometimes—like EVERY DAY. Who is this Joe? And why is he so sloppy? Do you think neat people named Joe ever get their feelings hurt by this? Honestly, you can't make this stuff up!

But I'll tell you, the food at my dining hall is bad.

It's so bad, the estate of General Tso sued to get their name off the chicken!

Once I got a piece of fried chicken from the fat lady who works at the dining hall—you all know the one—and it had a feather on it. Can you believe it? It happened! I mean, who's running this place, a bunch of kids from our rival school in sports? Fuck those guys.

Did you ever notice the difference in the way men and women eat at the dining hall? When men go to the dining hall, they go with like three or four people. Women, they go with like NINE people! What, are they having a party or something? It's a miracle any of us can get along.

No, really, the food is bad, but the service is great. Every day, I go into the dining hall and see those bright scowling faces behind the counter and think, man, I really want some chicken fingers! But seriously, where else in the world can you see a Puerto Rican guy making sushi, a Mexican guy making pastrami, and an Italian spitting in your ratatouille! Hey, Alfredo, I'd like another bowl, please, and this time, less snot! Haha, only kidding, Alfredo; you know I love you.

Well, looks like my time's up. You've been a great audience; good night, dining hall!

Funyuns aren't a vegetable. Time to rethink that salad.

Your Dining Hall Menu

Le McMahon Dining Hall

Wednesday the Nineteenth of March, Two Thousand Aught 7

Aperitif

—Hand-picked vegetables stewed with water à la sink tap, presented in an aluminum steam tray. Seasoned with coarse-ground pepper and antiseptic window cleaner.

—Choice of poultry-infused soup, prepared in same pot used for clam chowder yesterday, or minestrone, lightly watered down, complemented by last Thursday's leftover spaghetti dish.

Pâtés

—A fine selection of overcooked and undercooked linguini accompanied by a delicate pâté de tomate, d'autres mots Heinz Ketchup.

Poissons

—We mix a fine chunk light tin of partial-white-meat tuna with a hearty helping of mayonnaise à la drum of SYSCO Food Distributors to make a delicious Salade Tunae.

Viande

—Grade C chicken breast marinated in refrigeration fluid, then slow-roasted in industrial microwave. Finished off with a caf-employee-sweat demi-glace and presented with miniature carrot niblets.

—Steak, chopped and seasoned with salt, pepper, salt, and salt, then rolled through grinder. Hand-formed into beef circles and cooked over a grill. Presented between a soggy bun, with wilted lettuce and browning tomato. Chef's Specialty.

Dessert

—Imported confections from around the state of New Jersey. Cookies from every stage of staleness. Ice cream product B15, available in 3 Flavariables.

Bon appétit!

College Food Pyramid

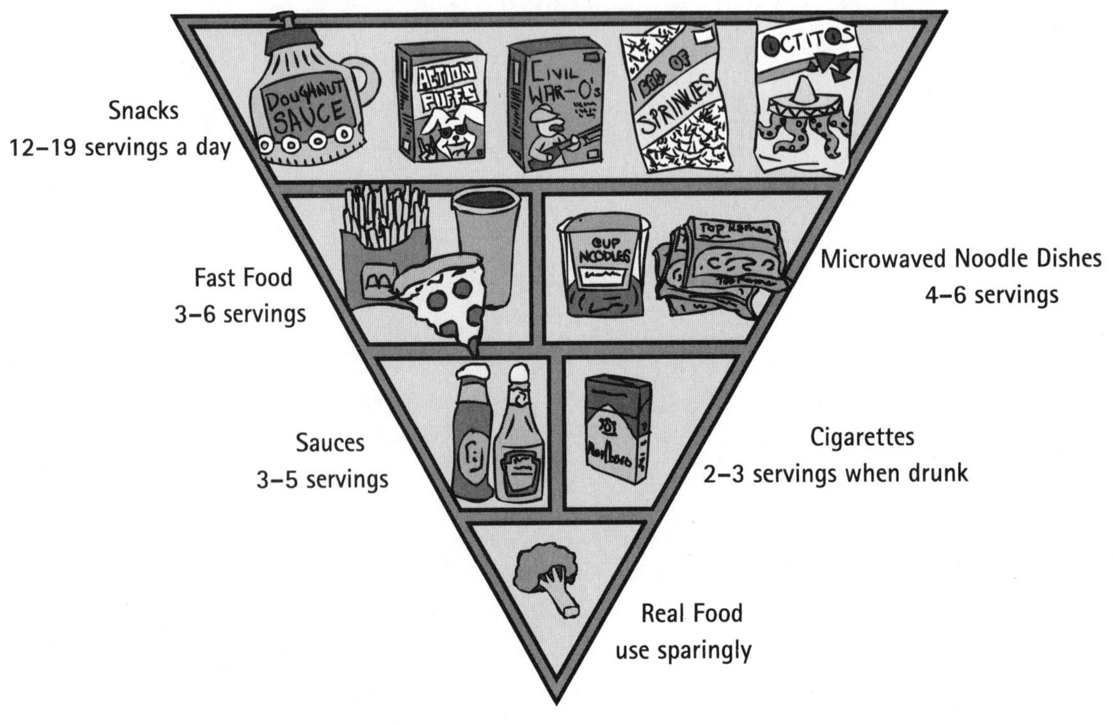

You can save a lot of money buying things online. That being said, your dairy products probably shouldn't come from the free section of craigslist.

Fundamental Truths of Food Delivery

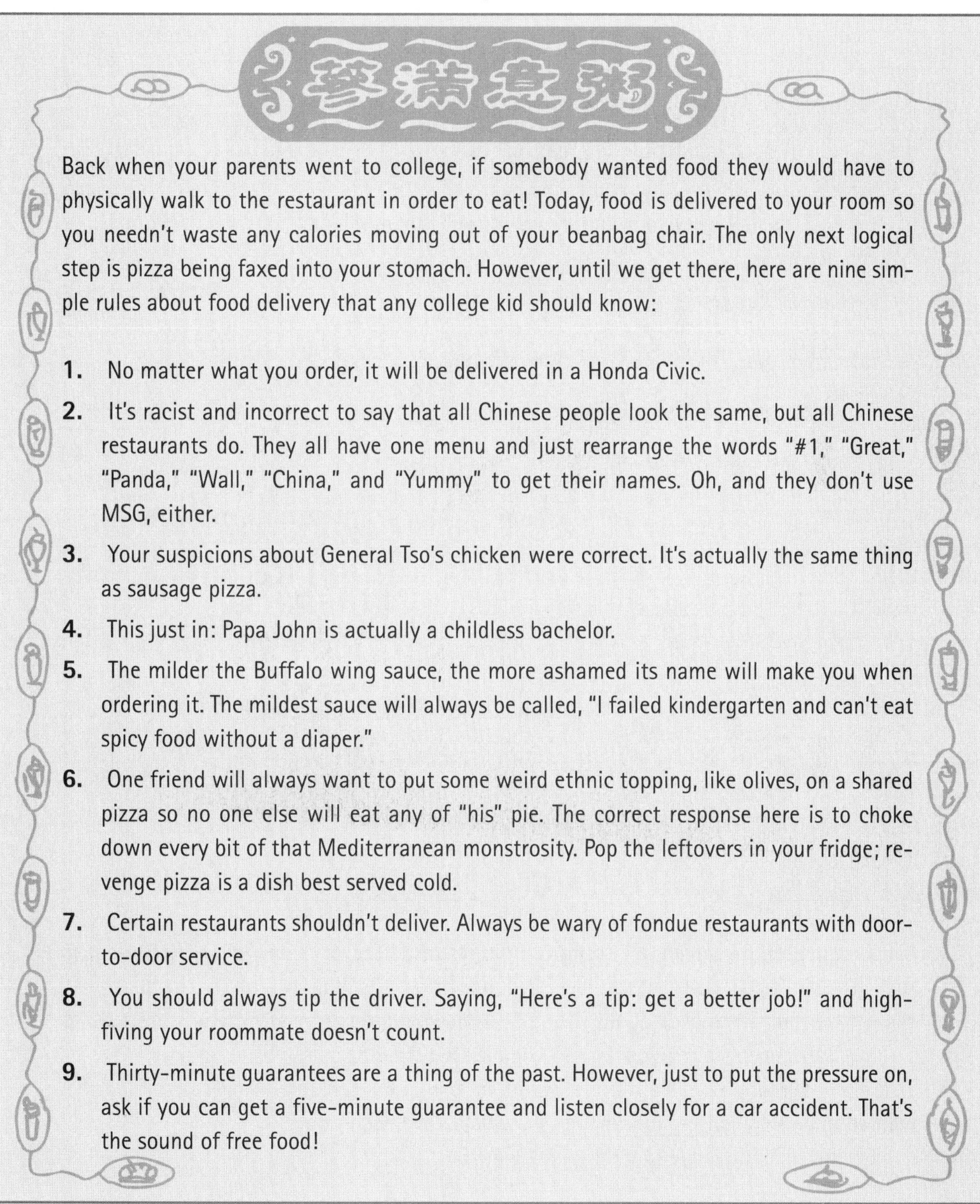

Back when your parents went to college, if somebody wanted food they would have to physically walk to the restaurant in order to eat! Today, food is delivered to your room so you needn't waste any calories moving out of your beanbag chair. The only next logical step is pizza being faxed into your stomach. However, until we get there, here are nine simple rules about food delivery that any college kid should know:

1. No matter what you order, it will be delivered in a Honda Civic.
2. It's racist and incorrect to say that all Chinese people look the same, but all Chinese restaurants do. They all have one menu and just rearrange the words "#1," "Great," "Panda," "Wall," "China," and "Yummy" to get their names. Oh, and they don't use MSG, either.
3. Your suspicions about General Tso's chicken were correct. It's actually the same thing as sausage pizza.
4. This just in: Papa John is actually a childless bachelor.
5. The milder the Buffalo wing sauce, the more ashamed its name will make you when ordering it. The mildest sauce will always be called, "I failed kindergarten and can't eat spicy food without a diaper."
6. One friend will always want to put some weird ethnic topping, like olives, on a shared pizza so no one else will eat any of "his" pie. The correct response here is to choke down every bit of that Mediterranean monstrosity. Pop the leftovers in your fridge; revenge pizza is a dish best served cold.
7. Certain restaurants shouldn't deliver. Always be wary of fondue restaurants with door-to-door service.
8. You should always tip the driver. Saying, "Here's a tip: get a better job!" and high-fiving your roommate doesn't count.
9. Thirty-minute guarantees are a thing of the past. However, just to put the pressure on, ask if you can get a five-minute guarantee and listen closely for a car accident. That's the sound of free food!

How Much Pizza Should We Order?

Foolproof plan for figuring out how many pizzas to order, when ordering for more than four people:

1. Tell everyone to hold up fingers for how many slices they want.
2. Add up all the fingers, and figure at least two more for some guy who is going to show up and want in. Now round up to the nearest multiple of eight (those are numbers like eight, sixteen, twenty-four, thirty-two for you comm majors). That's how many slices you need.
3. DON'T GET AHEAD OF US.
4. Divide by eight. This is your "base" number of pies.
5. Add one "safety pie" for good measure.

Enjoy! Goes best with everything.

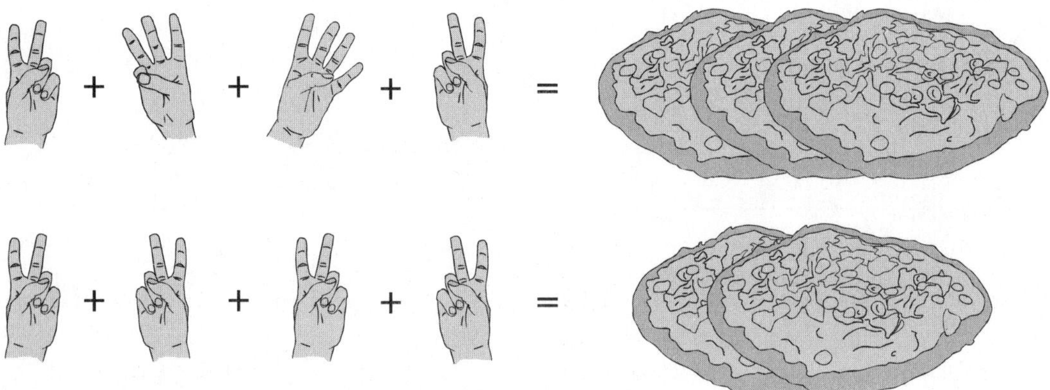

Splitting the Bill

For some reason, freshmen like to move in herds of fifteen or more. Urban legend has it that this trait initially evolved to evade predation by wolves that lived on college quads, although we think it's mostly about fitting in with a big group of your fifteen closest buds.

Inevitably, meals are going to be a complicated issue because you're going to have to split a bill fourteen ways. No waitress wants to ring up ten separate credit card bills. If she wanted to be a computer programmer, she would have been smart.

Empirical studies have found the following:

- 59 percent of college students don't carry cash and "just want to put the whole thing on my card."
- 31 percent of college students will have just gone to the ATM and only have twenties.
- 15 percent of college students have never gone to an ATM and only have nickels.
- 37 percent of college students forgot their wallets back in the dorm room, but will gladly "smoke out" the person who pays for their meal.
- 29 percent of college students claim that they're "good for it. Don't worry."
- 3 percent of college students are actually "good for it." So, worry.

Inevitably, someone will not pay his part of the bill, and then it comes down to the rest of the party overpaying or cheating the waiter on the tip. It will take a few months to figure out who this guy is. Please don't tell anyone we told you to do this, but when you figure out who the perennial underpayer is, you take him out behind the Applebee's, and you stab him. You don't have to tell him why. He'll know.

Freshman Fifteen

Calling it the "freshman fifteen" isn't fair to you, and it isn't fair to the weight you put on. Each pound you apply to your fattening girth is unique in its own special way. Pound for pound, this is the best breakdown in this book:

Pound 1: Welcome Week means free pastries. One pound cake, please.

Pound 2: You mean to tell me this dorm food is all-you-can-eat? No more deciding between onion rings or fries! It's "and" from here on in!

Pound 3: A free ice cream social to get acquainted with your on-campus association? I'll get acquainted with these sprinkles, thank you very much.

Pound 4: Oh man, free soda day at this YMCA booth. Don't mind if I Dew!

Pound 5: $1 Krispy Kreme donuts at that bake sale? Well, it's for a good cause. Here's $13—make it a baker's dozen, my good man.

Pound 6: The thing I love about Cheez-Its is, you can eat several boxes a day and not feel bad about it.

Pound 7: You bet me I can't eat ten hamburgers in one sitting? You're on.

You're not going to lose weight adding more veggies to your diet if they're all in "popper" form.

Pound 8: Okay, double or nothing.

Pound 9: I've heard of the milk gallon challenge before, but not with half-and-half!

Pound 10: $2 Burrito Wednesday is the greatest thing since $3 Burrito Tuesday.

Pound 11: Chocolate milk, chocolate syrup, what's the difference? I'll have one glass of each, sir.

Pound 12: Hmmm, doctor says my one-pound tumor is malignant. But what does he know? CHEEZ WHIZ FIGHT!!!!

Pound 13: Another birthday for some kid in the hall? I'm not one to turn down a cupcake . . . or two . . . or nine.

Pound 14: Finals week is so stressful; pass me the cookie dough log. No, the fried one.

Pound 15: Finals week is over! We can finally eat our textbooks!

Who Got Fat?

If you want a really cheap calzone, just buy two slices of pizza.

Creative Food Ideas

The best way to tell if a restaurant is worth eating at is to imagine it burning down in the middle of the night. Then, ask yourself, "Would anyone care the next morning?" Well, I'm sure the waiters at Ruby Tuesday would be pissed they had to get new jobs, and the manager at Bennigan's would probably have tons of paperwork to deal with, but most of your nearby chain restaurants are far from beloved.

So, rather than succumb to yet another night of large but mediocre dishes ("Man, I am FULL! That meal must have been GREAT!"), why not come up with some wacky meals of your own?

Ham and Cheese Wafflewich

Ingredients: Two Eggo waffles, some ham, a slice of Muenster cheese, maple syrup

Directions: Toast the Eggos until they're about three-quarters done. Remove them from the toaster and put the cheese on one and ham on the other. Put it all back in the toaster oven for a couple more minutes. When the ham is hot and the cheese is melted, take both Eggos out of the toaster, put some maple syrup on, and close the sandwich. I've truly saved the best for first. This sandwich is so good, it will make you wish you'd never cut your tongue out. We have started making them for our friends even when we are full, just so we can vicariously enjoy the syrupy satisfaction. If you don't have the ingredients on hand, we implore you to purchase them NOW. GOD, THESE ARE GOOD.

Raw-men noodles

Ingredients: One package of Ramen noodles

Directions: Ramen noodles are about as cheap as any other food out there, but if you're in a hurry, they can be problematic. You have to boil water, put the noodles in the water, and about a million other things before they're ready to eat. Instead, just unwrap the noodles, sprinkle some of the wonderful flavoring all over that crunchy white brick, and enjoy.

Blotting pizza isn't gay, it's healthy. Same with giving another man a blow jay.

"College"

Ingredients: Hamburger patties, hot dogs, macaroni and cheese, hot sauce, scrambled eggs
Directions: Cook everything and put it in the biggest bowl in your house. Eat it out of the bowl using a cooking spoon. Laugh at how irresponsible you are and what an easy life you live while your mouth is full of "College."

A friend of ours told us about "College" the other day, so we haven't actually tried it. But based on everything we know about guerrilla cooking, it is probably edible. "College" is the result of being responsible enough to have certain foods on hand without having the foresight to possess equally important components such as buns.

Cook This Meal and You Will Get Fucked

by Ethan

If you can cook, you will get laid. This is an immutable truth of the universe, and one that I took advantage of quite a bit in college.

Now, loyal readers, I'm giving you my go-to getting-fucked recipe. It was invented by the Greek gods of food and fucking, who then gave it to my mom. She gave it to me with a huge box of ribbed condoms and a wink. This meal is easy to make and quick to eat, which leaves you plenty of time to get fucked. Plus, it costs under thirty bucks for the whole thing, which is less than you'd pay for dinner at most decent restaurants, much less a decent prostitute, and you have the added bonus of already being in close proximity to your bed when you're finished. This makes boning easier.

Let's get started.

Wash your hands. With soap. Well. Don't worry; you'll dirty them again later.

Dessert
Chocolate Mousse with Toffee Topping

If you have to borrow a blender to make this, do it. It's worth the effort. It is hands-down the easiest thing in the world to make, and it has gotten me to at least third base on no less than seven occasions. You have to make this earlier in the afternoon because it has to chill in the refrigerator.

1 bag milk chocolate chips
½ pint heavy whipping cream
2 shots coffee liqueur (Kahlúa/Copa de Oro)
1 Heath Bar, crushed into bits

In a small pot, boil the cream, stirring frequently. When the cream reaches a boil, dump it, the chocolate chips, and the liqueur into the blender and blend until it's creamy with no chunks left. Pour the chocolate mixture into a martini/wineglass, champagne flute, or small bowl. Place in the refrigerator to chill for three to four hours. Before serving, top with Heath crumbles. Put your boner to work for you.

Entrée
Baked Salmon with Citrus Glaze

Sounds impressive. Looks impressive. Could be prepared by the dumbest kid in your high school class.

2 tbsp orange juice
2 tbsp orange marmalade
Tiny splash green Tabasco
Tiny squirt yellow mustard
2 nice salmon fillets

Preheat the oven to 350 degrees on bake. Mix all ingredients except the salmon together in a bowl and stir it well. Add some salt and pepper and a squirt of lemon juice if you've got it. Line a baking dish/pan with foil and place the salmon in it, skin side down. Spoon half of the glaze onto each fillet. Bake for fifteen minutes or until the thickest part of the fillets flakes when touched with a fork.

Side 1
Orzo

The pasta for people who prefer rice to pasta.

1/2 pound orzo
Handful raisins

Bring a pot of lightly salted water to a boil and pour in the raisins and orzo. Cook according to the directions on the orzo box, usually around ten minutes. Strain through a colander. The baller part here is that the hot water plumps the raisins, which add color and sweetness to the dish. That's the kind of extra step that will get you nailed.

And you're done. Spoon out some of the orzo and put the salmon on top of it. Split no less than a bottle of white wine. After eating the mousse, say, "Hey, we should probably start plowing." She'll be too full of food and wine to think it's anything other than a good idea. This could NOT have been any easier. You don't have to send me a check for my troubles, but I'd certainly appreciate it if you said my name when you came.

Turns out you can only park in the spot if you're already handicapped. There I go, putting the cart before the horse again.

And Now a Word on Eating Disorders by a Dad from the 1950s

Eating disorders? What kinda hippie shit is that? We have mashed potatoes and ham for dinner, young lady. Eat it.

SO YOU'VE DECIDED TO Eat a Live Boar

"Lousy boar! I'd eat you if I could!" Well, now you can!

What you need: A boar, a cage, a rope, a chain saw, a Twinkie, an appetite

What you do: Skip breakfast and lunch. Around 6 p.m. (your time), release the boar from his cage, but keep his left ankle tied down with the rope. If somebody knocks on your door asking what that boarlike racket is, insist that you are simply watching a nature show on TV and proceed to tell that person to leave you the fuck alone. If he acts wise, be polite. "Sorry, I didn't mean to yell, I just have a bad headache is all."

Great, they're gone. Turn the chain saw on and slice the boar into two halves. Eat each side like a bony flesh watermelon. Don't stop until you're sitting alone at the foot of your bed, rubbing your stomach next to a pile of bones. "What have I done?" you'll think. You've kicked ass, is what you've done. Now . . . how about that Twinkie?

As far as spices that sound like states are concerned, oregano is good, but nothing beats parsleyvania

And Now, Two Words on Sex in the Dorm Shower

Fucking gross.

Beer Pong Balls: A Closer Look

Science: Christianity's slutty daughter.

Beer pong is the dirtiest of all fraternity-based games, with mud wrestling a close second. What seems like good, clean, fun on the surface level, is actually infested with microbiotic germ colonies waiting to attack your entire immune system. Also, despite what you've heard, dipping the ball into a "water cup" does not help to disinfect; if anything, it introduces a whole new species of aqua germs onto the surface.

Using a microscope to inspect an average used beer pong ball, we were able to take some staggering photos of the surface magnified to one hundred times its normal size. Warning: The following image is not suitable for freshmen.

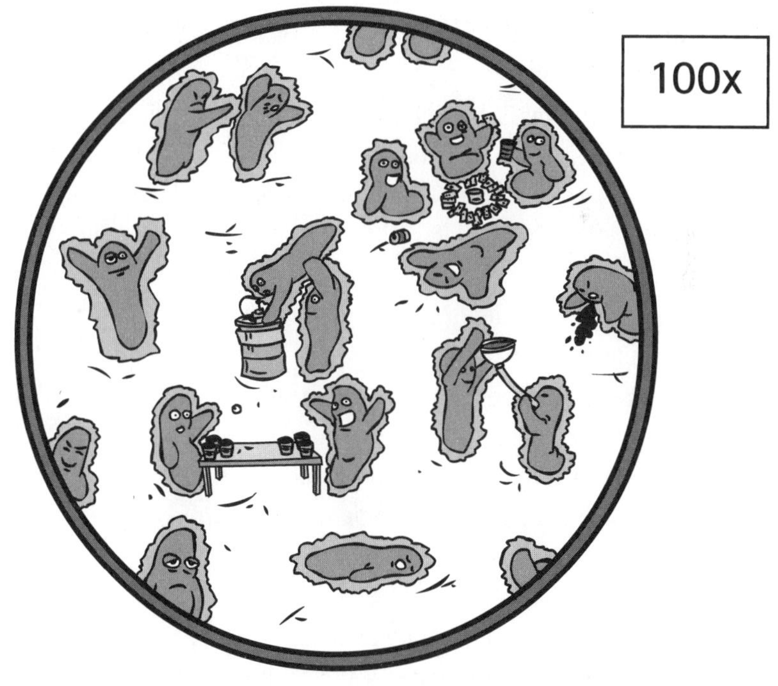

Colgate is only one of many colleges named after a toothpaste. Others include Crest College, The Ultrabright Institute, and Arm & Hammer Now With Whitening Peroxide University.

True College Stories—Cleaning, by Jay Pinkerton

If you're living in any kind of student housing with other people, you're eventually going to have to work out the cleaning. If you're unfortunate enough to live with four other guys like I did, cleaning will most likely be explored only in a strict hypothetical sense, like, "We should really clean one of these days," or, "I seem to have contracted botulism somehow."

As five guys coming from upper-middle-class families, we'd each been given boxes of dishes from our concerned moms, who feared the thought of their baby boys eating food with their bare hands off the floor. We consequently had a bounty of plates and glasses—all of which we crammed into the cupboard and tossed in the sink when we were done eating.

By the two-week mark, our sink overflowed. Cups and pans found their way to nearby flat surfaces—so as to reach them more easily, we presumed, when we eventually got around to washing them. The top of the stove, in the fridge crisper—as the real estate shrank, creativity took over. I remember hiding some glasses behind the curtains and feeling pretty proud of myself.

Eventually our promises to clean up were laid bare for the hollow, shamefaced lies they were, and the dishes were moved directly onto the floor, which seemed easier. The cleaning schedule on the kitchen wall had by this point gone from being marked up with notes and arrows ("Monday—JERRY, THIS MEANS YOU!!!") to being ignored entirely, the illusion that any of us were even remotely paying attention to it having long since been buried under an enormous pile of beer-smelling mixing bowls.

After four months, every one of the 12,571 dishes we owned was stacked in precarious filthy mountains in the kitchen. Like anyone faced with an unpleasant job, we rolled up our sleeves and adapted our lives around it. You could still root around for a fork or a plate when you needed one, after all, and clean it under the hose in the backyard. (Our one-dish-at-a-time washing technique was inefficient, but I'd argue that you really get the cleanest dishes that way—each one plucked out of a pile when needed, lovingly bathed in dish soap, and given the focus it deserves.)

After six months it became impossible to find the more useful items (forks, plates, cups) under the growing pile of useless dish detritus (whisks, woks, frying pans, Burger King collector's mugs, long-lost TV remotes). Essential dish staples found their way up to bedrooms, where they languished under beds, forgotten and unused.

We welcomed the challenge. It's one thing to pick a fork off a pile of dishes. It's another thing entirely to stick your arm into a sink full of rotting spaghetti noodles, old toast, and Tom Collins mix in search of a serviceable plate. Eating had become an adventure.

Anyone unfortunate enough to be visiting could expect to find one of us in the living room watching TV while lapping rum out of a saucer, or mangling a steak into smaller pieces with two giant stirring spoons. It's freeing somehow to sip at a beer mug full of soup, applauding your wisdom in freeing yourself from the tyranny of spoons entirely.

The lowest ebb was reached—for me, anyway—when I was forced to abandon dish technology altogether. I'd simply drop whatever I'd cooked onto the coffee table and rip it apart with my hands, cleaning up the mess afterward with some Lysol and a paper towel. Here we had enough dishes in our house to serve sixty people, and yet I'd find myself in my living room, barbecue sauce coating the lower half of my face, eating a chicken leg like a coyote. Something had to be done. That very week I began eating out all the time and didn't enter the kitchen for the rest of the semester.

Shower Sandals

Every hall has one student who figures he/she does not have to wear shower sandals because everybody else does. In economics we call this the "free-rider complex." This is the same reason that some people opt not to get the polio vaccine.

On a related note, every hall has one person whose feet begin resembling a swampy marshland toward the end of the academic year.

Here's a footnote for you: wear shower sandles.

How to Do Laundry

Other than frequent gypsy attacks, the scariest part of adapting to college is learning how to do your own laundry. Chances are, your mom has done your laundry up to this point. If your mom hasn't been doing your laundry, don't ever send her a Mother's Day card. Ever.

Laundry may be intimidating at first, but it's pretty simple. Just follow these steps:

1. *Whites and darks:* Separate, but equal. You already know that one wrong move here can turn your whitey tighties into pinky tighties. Not only are pinky tighties, like, totally gay, but it also doesn't rhyme. This is the most important step: start two piles, one for things that are white and one for things that aren't. Double-check your piles; it's easy for a white shirt or robe to sneak its way into the colored pile.

2. *Pocket pool:* Check all of your pockets on your pants; it's especially catastrophic if you leave your wallet or a pen in there for a whole spin cycle. People will yell, "Boo, inky-pants" while you walk around campus, and you're running out of quiet places to cry.

   While you're at it, make sure all of your socks are right side out, too. Otherwise, the ones you lose in the laundry room won't be clean. Some stuff, like wool sweaters, silk, and cashmere, doesn't go in the washer. Take these to a dry cleaner, where Chinese people will use ancient magic to defeat dirt and stains in a badly over-dubbed karate fight scene.

3. *Machinehead:* Wait patiently for a machine to open up, then jump in to claim it like an 1830s prospector. Put in your detergent (liquid is best because it won't leave white flakes all over your room) and select the right temperature. For whites, use a "hot/cold" setting. For darks, use a "cold/cold" setting. Also, if you ever see a girl leaning over a washer, sneak up behind her and say, "Mind if I throw in a load of white?" Suspension lasts one semester, but a good bit of harassment lasts forever.

Scented candles work well, but it's much cheaper to decide your favorite smell is "mildew."

4. *High and dry:* Once the washer does its business, it's time to dry! As any sitcom will tell you, there's always the hi-larious possibility that you will shrink your clothes down to a doll's size and then Alan Thicke will beat Kirk Cameron with a telephone for being such a troublemaker. The important thing here is to use enough heat to dry the clothes and get wrinkles out without shrinking things. A good policy is to pick a medium setting and just keep an eye on it. Throwing in some dryer sheets is also a good idea if you like your clothes to be soft or not smell terrible. Once the insides of your jean pockets or the elastic parts of your socks feel dry, they're done. Fold, wear, and enjoy!

SO YOU'VE DECIDED TO Break Your Own Legs

"Stupid legs! I wish I could break them!" Well, now you can.

What you need: A monster truck, a bandanna, a plank of wood

What you do: Put your bandanna on. Lie down on the street and place a plank of wood over your legs. Give the monster-truck driver a signal (perhaps a thumbs-up). He will drive the truck slowly toward you, then eventually over the plank of wood, crushing your legs. Your bones will break in several locations and you'll let out a primal shriek so loud it can only be compared to the noise level of a thousand rockets taking off at once. When the yelling subsides and your larynx is on fire with the pain of a million screams, stare into the sky and realize that you're lucky to be alive.

When you've had so many cups of coffee your pee is starting to smell like hazelnut, it's probably a good idea to switch to not peeing.

Laundry Pyramid

Nobody likes to do laundry. When packing for school, the most important thing is that you get the right ratio of threads to keep you out of the laundry room and out on the prowl. Here is your recommended dormly allowance for all of the major clothes groups:

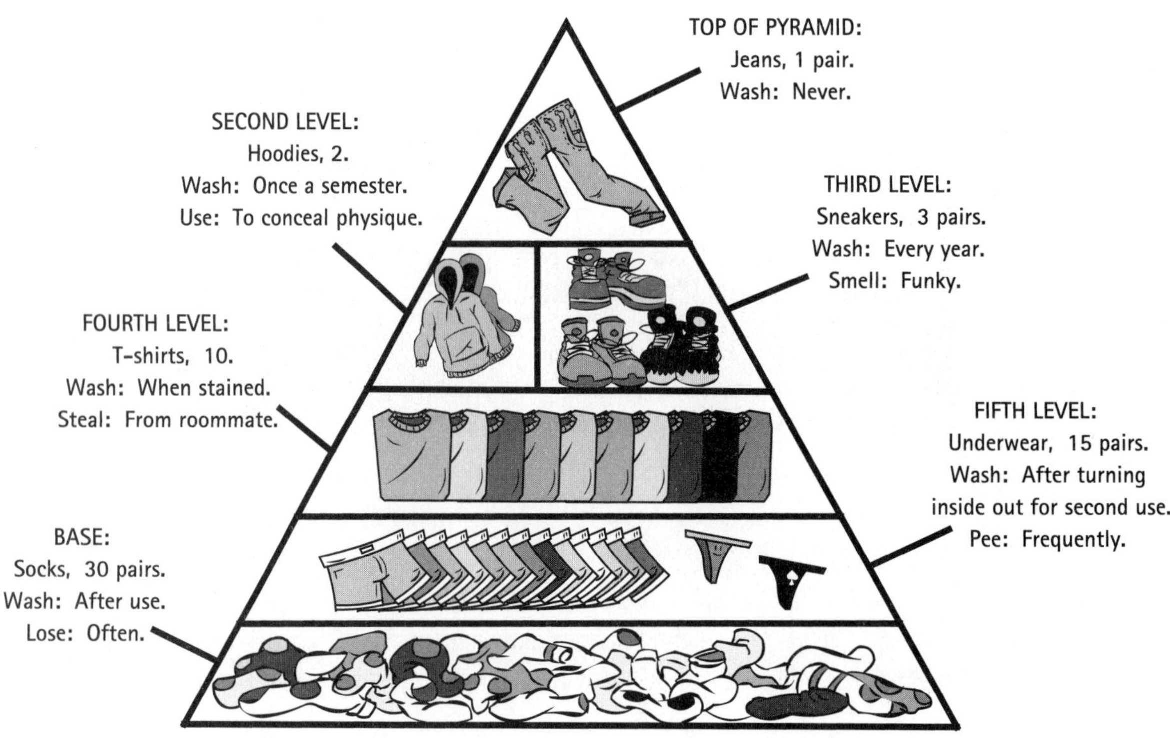

Every time you read a fortune cookie, add "in bed" to the end. Unless you read it in bed; then you should add, "Oh, fuck, the crumbs!" to the end.

Your Laundry Room

1. Girl stealing clothes
2. Guy hitting coin machine out of frustration and for fun
3. God Squadders folding other people's laundry
4. Vulture Pack waiting eagerly for a washer or dryer to free up
5. Guy who hasn't done his laundry in four months dragging bag in
6. Mystery bra and thong unclaimed for four months
7. Guy throwing someone's wet laundry on the floor
8. Couple discreetly making out
9. The spot where the smelly dirty kid next door should be doing his laundry
10. Girl doing her boyfriend's laundry while he enjoys the view
11. Chronic bed wetter washing his sheets . . . again! (Can be easily identified by following urine trail from fifth floor down.)

How to Fold a Shirt

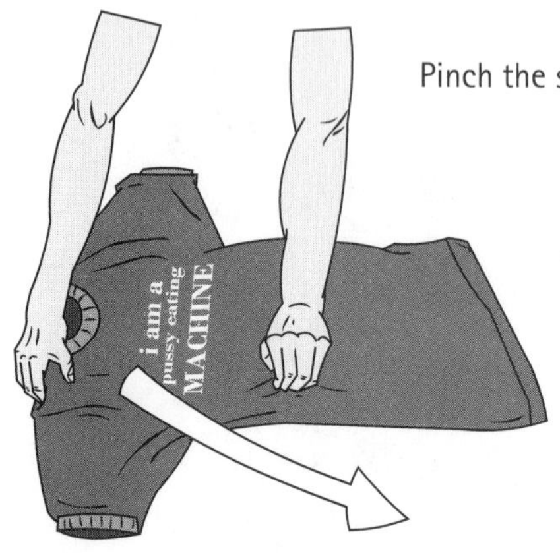

Pinch the shirt at the collar.

Pinch the shirt about halfway down from the first pinch.

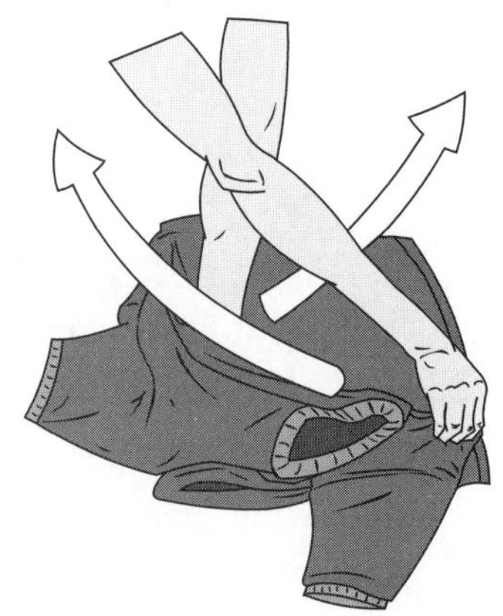

Lift up and cross over your hands.

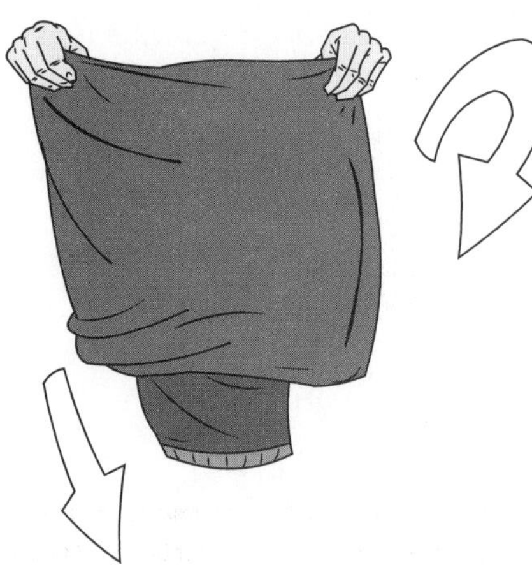

Pinch shirt with your hand, lift, and uncross your arms.

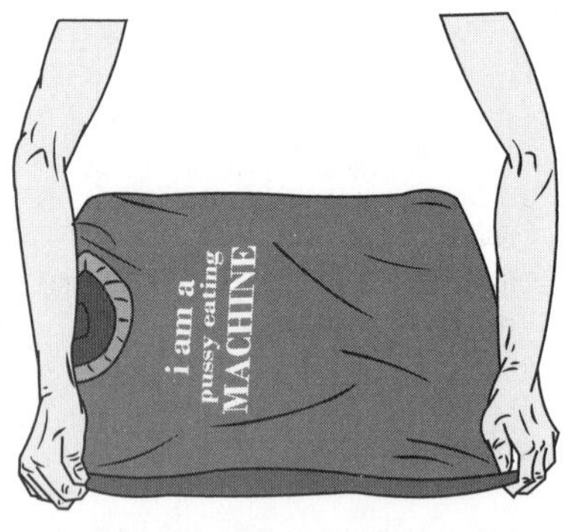

Fold the sleeve under the main shirt section. Fire maid.

Have it my way, Burger King? All right, one cheeseburger, please. Except instead of cheese, I want a layer of chicken fingers. Oh, and I'll take that for free.

A Final Word on Food, Health, and Laundry

There's no cheaper medicine than pills of "It'll go away on its own." Take every four to six hours, or until dead.

If I had to rank how much I enjoyed things I read on the toilet, "school newspaper" would come in just below "shampoo bottle" and just above "Chinese takeout menu."

5 ALCOHOL

Introduction

We all knew this chapter would come. If you're still in high school, you probably did a quick flip-through looking for naked boobs, then skipped right to this chapter. And here it is: the alcohol chapter.

Drinking in college is a paradox. On the one hand, everyone thinks it's the most important part of college. On the other hand, it is the most important part of college. Wait, that's not a paradox. PARTY! College is the only time in your life when, as long as you don't drive drunk, you can blame any crude, boorish, and semilegal action on being "so fucking drunk, dude, just so fucking drunk," and people will think it's cool. It's like you've been given a "get out of jail free" card that's made of cool, crisp, refreshing light beer.

Don't think that drinking is the only way to have fun in college, though. There are lots of fun things to do without alcohol. Well, those two sentences fulfilled all of our legal obligations, but we do have a few more helpful hints.

First, don't go to class drunk because you think it will be fun. Instead, it's everything bad about being drunk—the short attention span, the constant having to pee, and the thinking "Two more drinks and I might not even notice her scars . . ."—combined with the boring, draining elements of class. Plus, you'll probably be drunk enough to make your move on your professor who must totally want you because you get together every Tuesday afternoon from three to five. She's not that into you; those are called "office hours," champ, and the university makes every professor hold them.

Second, there will come a time when someone asks you to be the designated driver. It's only responsible to tell them, "No problem." Grab a 3-wood and rip a massive tee shot onto the fairway. Celebrate by drinking six beers. Sure, you can't get home now, but your buddies shouldn't have set you up for such a great pun. It would have been illegal not to follow through on that kind of setup.

Finally, everyone calls half-finished beers "wounded soldiers," but what do you call a guy with one leg, a Purple Heart, and half a Coors Light sitting at a bar? You call him "Sir," and then you recite the Pledge of Allegiance. Semper Fi, soldier . . . Semper Fi.

Alcohol is awesome! It makes people more attractive, jokes funnier, and the great cities of St. Louis and Milwaukee richer. Everybody wins, so crack a cold one and dive into our guide to drinking. Unless you're driving. Drinking and driving is seriously not cool. Actually, reading and driving is pretty irresponsible, too. Stop doing that.

Oh, and one last thing. No matter what your peer health educators tell you, if you're not drinking to get drunk, you're not really drinking.

Knowing a lot about wine can help you win a woman's heart. However, saying, "This box is a great vintage" while standing in a gas station just sounds pretentious.

SOME GREAT SHOTS AND DRINKS TO HELP YOU FEEL GOOD ABOUT YOURSELF

"Liquor" before "beer" only if your dictionary is printed incorrectly.

CREATIVE COLLEGE DEATH SHOTS

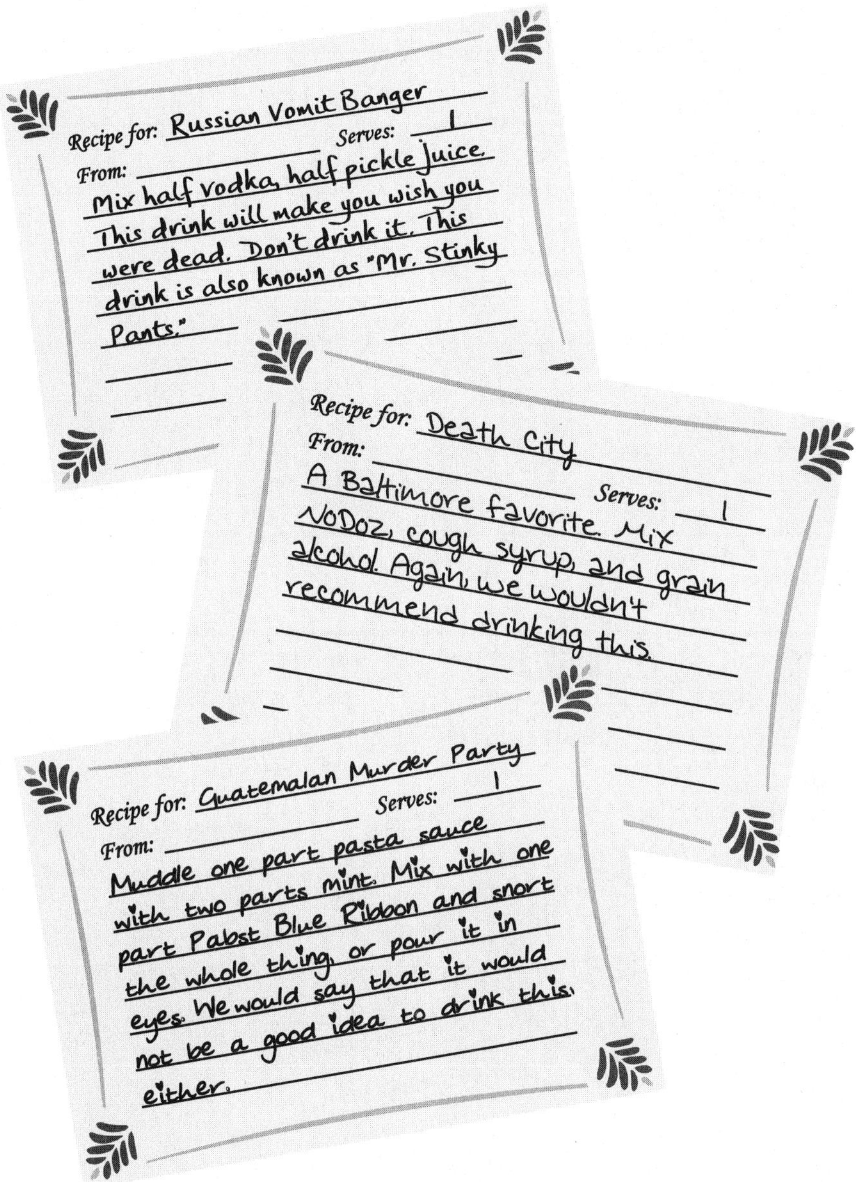

Drink Mixing Guide

	Tonic	Cranberry	Coke	Sprite	Ginger Ale	OJ
Vodka	☺	☺	☺	☺	☺	☺
Rum			☺			☺
Tequila			☺			☺
Whiskey			☺		☺	
Gin	☺	☺		☺	☺	☺

A Word of Warning

Mixing drink types is a pretty bad idea. Not to be confused with mixed drinks, mixing drinks means consuming different types of poisons out of order. Total party foul. Just remember the simple rhyme:

Beer before liquor, never been sicker.
Liquor before beer, you're in the clear.
Beer before wine, you're probably fine.
Alcohol before weed, lose the deed,
To your house, if you do coke before cantaloupe.
Oh my God, I'm so fucking out of it, dude,
I swear, I can't even breathe, let alone remember this fucking poem. Oh my God, call the cops. I cannot feel my own lungs.

If it's too long to remember, just put it to a catchy melody! Can we recommend "The Farmer in the Dell"?

Jell-O Shots

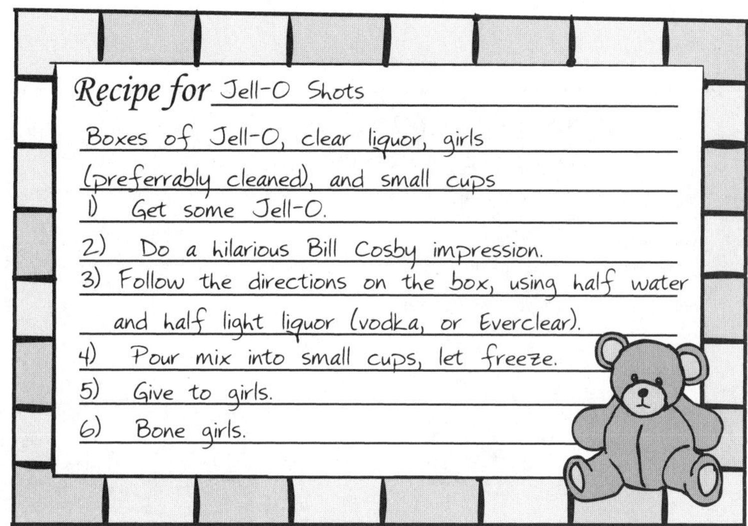

Jungle Juice Recipe

We don't know who invented jungle juice, but it's fueled just about every incident of streaking, every same-sex makeout, and every accidental death in the history of college. That's why we're proud to bring our secret recipe to you. Before you know it, everyone at your party will be pissing on your dog, lighting your DVDs on fire, and quietly enjoying some quality TV . . . naked.

5 Bottles Juicy Juice (fruit punch)
3 Whole oranges
1 Bottle Sprite
2 Bottles Everclear "Filtered Death" Grain Alcohol
(can be replaced by 5–7 bottles of regular liquor in a pinch)
2 Bottles vodka.

1. Cut oranges into half-inch slices. Take care to remove any seeds and/or imperfections from the fruit. Any bruised or rotten fruit should be immediately thrown away and replaced with fresh, pesticide-free fruit. Some may choose to save the peel to zest the jungle juice after it is made. This is a personal preference and we take no stance either way. Place the oranges in a neat row on your kitchen counter. You should have about fifteen to twenty slices.

2. Dump everything into a clean garbage can.

3. Serve.

Drinks for Sex

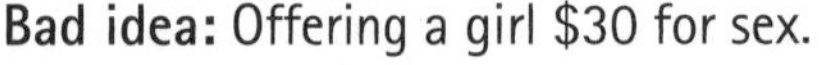

Bad idea: Offering a girl $30 for sex.

Good idea: Offering a girl $30 worth of drinks for sex.

College Beer Taste Test

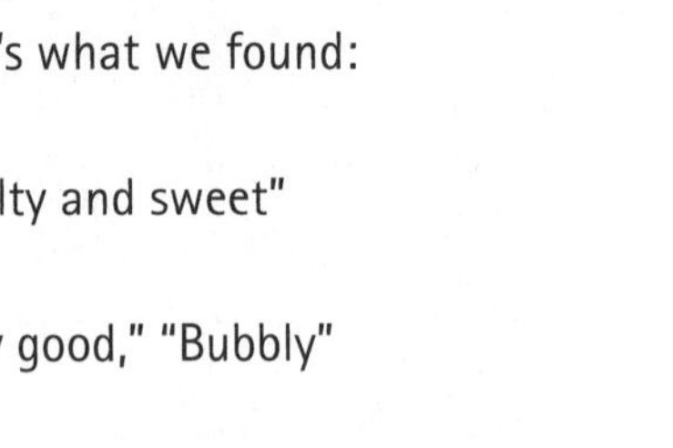

"Dude, I told you, I don't drink Natty; I'm classy. You got any Bud Light?"

Everyone hears about favorite cheap beers in college, so we decided to do a blind taste test of college beers to see what was the tastiest, and the coolest. Because you can't judge quality based on hilarious commercials!

We guessed what each beer was and gave it a score on a ten-point scale. Here's what we found:

Coors Light—7.3—"Crisp, refreshing," "Malty and sweet"

Miller Lite—7—"Light corn toasty," "Pretty good," "Bubbly"

Bud Light—6—"Watery, but crisp," "Tastes like a cheap beer should"

Budweiser—6—"Thicker," "Stronger aftertaste"

Natural Light—5.33—"This tastes like other beers do when they get warm."

Pabst Blue Ribbon—5—"Tastes like corn," "Skunky"

Natural Ice—5—"Soupy," "You can really taste the alcohol"

Heineken—4.3—"Thick," "Smooth, but not good," "Tastes like cold medicine"

Busch Light—4—"Only to get drunk," "Smells bad, tastes slightly worse"

Colt 45—3.6—"Sweeter," "Smoother," "Thicker"

Can of Clam Chowder—3—"Clammy," "A bit on the chowdery side"

Miller High Life—2.7—"Very bad," "Skanky corn," "The worst yet"

Olde English 800—0.67—"Gross," "Fucking gross," "Thick and shitty," "Disgusting"

We're not scientists, but the results of this study speak for themselves: beer is not a matter of personal preference; some beers are in fact objectively shitty. Also, you can use Olde E to remove paint from walls, but you probably shouldn't drink it.

Drunktionary

Ah, drunk people . . . will they ever say what they mean? Below you'll find some common drunk phrases and what they translate to in sober language. I hope this helps you gauge whether or not it's a good idea to let your buddy in the car when he claims he's "totally fine, dude."

(**Drunk Term** = Sober Translation)

I LOVE this song! = I KNOW this song!

Dude, all the chicks at this party are ugly = Dude, none of the chicks at this party will talk to me.

Man, I'm hungry = Man, if I don't eat right now I am going to be puking all over this bar . . . again.

You're really pretty = I'm going to be ashamed of it tomorrow but tonight is all about instant gratification, honey.

Want to watch a movie? = Want to come over to my room for some extremely creepy back rubbing and some equally disturbing neck nibbling?

I'm soooo drunk = I'm planting a seed in your head that will eventually grow into a beautiful tree, which excuses me from blame for my actions tonight.

I just, like, want to help animals, ya know? = I just, like, want to get in your pants, ya know?

You're my best friend, man = You're my only friend in arm's reach right now and I need someone to pay for this shot, man.

I don't want to ruin the friendship = You're a nice girl but you're very heavy and I'd rather pretend I value our friendship than spend tomorrow dreaming up ways to kill myself.

This is the BEST night of my LIFE! = This is the BEST night of my WEEKEND!

Let's take a walk, this bar is crowded = I prefer my hand jobs outdoors.

I'm totally fine, dude = I'm totally going to be needing a toilet or bucket in about five minutes, dude.

What's up, bro? = What's up, guy-whose-name-I-can't-ever-remember?

Who wants to dance? = Who wants to watch me stumble around the party, waving my arms, spilling my drink, and pile-driving my genitals into anything wearing a skirt?

Hey, did you get the notes from Bio? = Hey, I'm going to ask you about class because I'm too scared to ask you out.

I had, like, ten beers before I even came out = I'm, like, the kind of guy that lies about how much I drink.

Dude, I didn't even make it out of the dorms last night! = Dude, my girlfriend made me stay in and watch the *Gilmore Girls* Season 1 DVD with her last night!

Now, seriously, who wants to watch a movie?

Beer Bong Physics

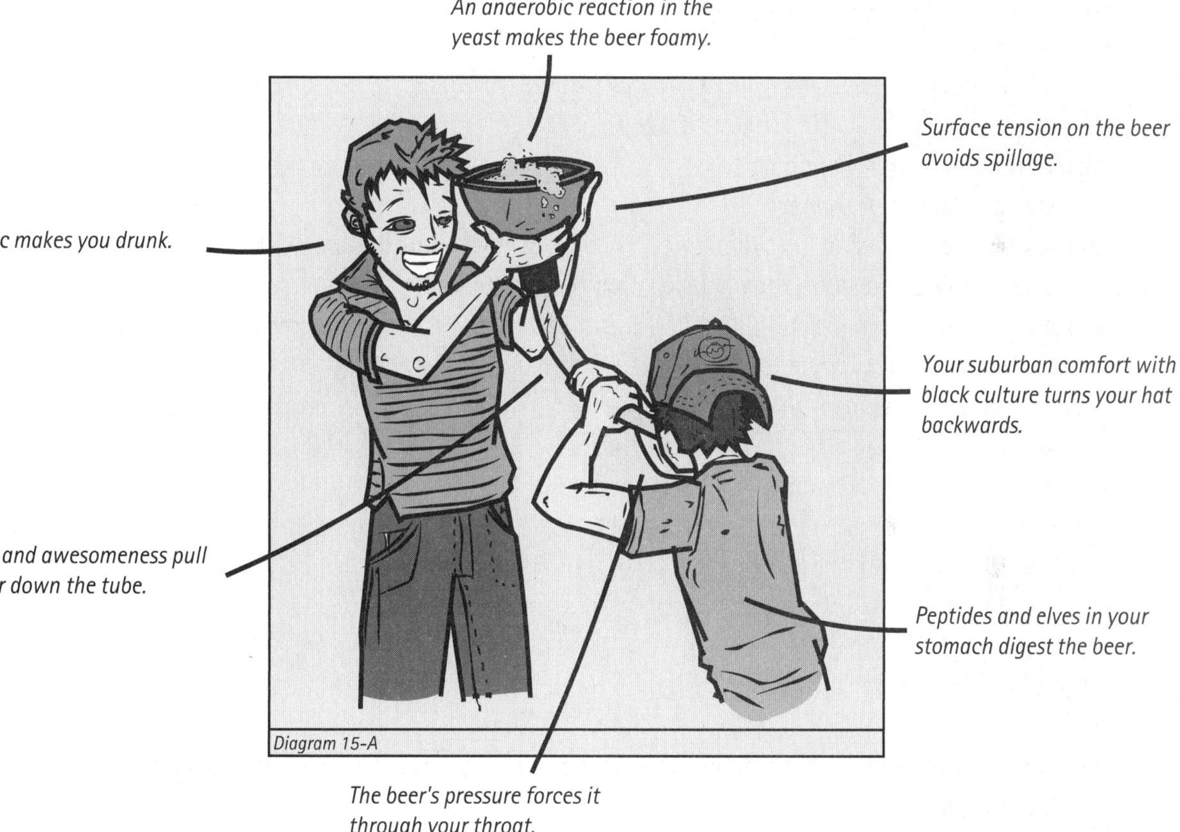

Diagram 15-A

If you want to make cool kids think you're not cool, next time somebody brings up Radiohead act like you've never heard of them. Then, a few seconds into their explanation, pause and say, "Oh, wasn't he on the *Clueless* soundtrack?"

Beer Goggles

Beer is a magical beverage. It makes you dance better, it makes you funnier, and it makes you not care about peeing your pants. But the infamous beer goggles can also make ugly people seem like the sort you'd want to hook up with, like in this picture:

Oh, and one other thing, that line about "I didn't know she was so heavy... it must have been the beer goggles!" doesn't work. They make ugly people more attractive, not fat people skinnier.

Oh, relax, if everyone who killed a hooker went to jail, there'd be no one to run the country.

Beer Pong Rules

The rules of beer pong, or Beirut (see below), vary widely from school to school. This can lead to major confusion if you are visiting a friend at a different school or trying to hustle Beirut games across the country to get enough money to pay off the mortgage on your frat house before the bank forecloses . . . like in the movie we're writing, *10 Cups till Destiny*.

BASE RULES

- Two teams, twenty cups, two balls, six beers, and you've got yourself a game. If you need to know any more about the standard rules, watch three seconds of a game and you'll understand.

OPTIONAL RULES

- *Elbow rule:* In order to thwart any advantage held by lanky players or cheating sorority girls, many beer pong matches are regulated by this rule, which requires that at no time during shooting may a player's elbow cross their end of the table.
- *Bitches blow:* At some sexist colleges, women players (the sport was integrated in 1972 by Lilly Carmichael of Ohio) are allowed to blow out a ball spinning around a cup. Also, yelling "Blow, BITCH!" at your female partner is knee-slapping funny and empowering.
- *Distraction:* Many schools do not allow distraction (such as dancing, depth perception throw-offs, or stabbings) unless the distraction is being perpetrated by a woman. And, boy, do those whores enjoy it or what!?
- *Airball:* There are two popular rules for an airball. (1) The airball costs the shooting team a cup, or (2) the shooter must take off his or her pants until he or she sinks a cup.

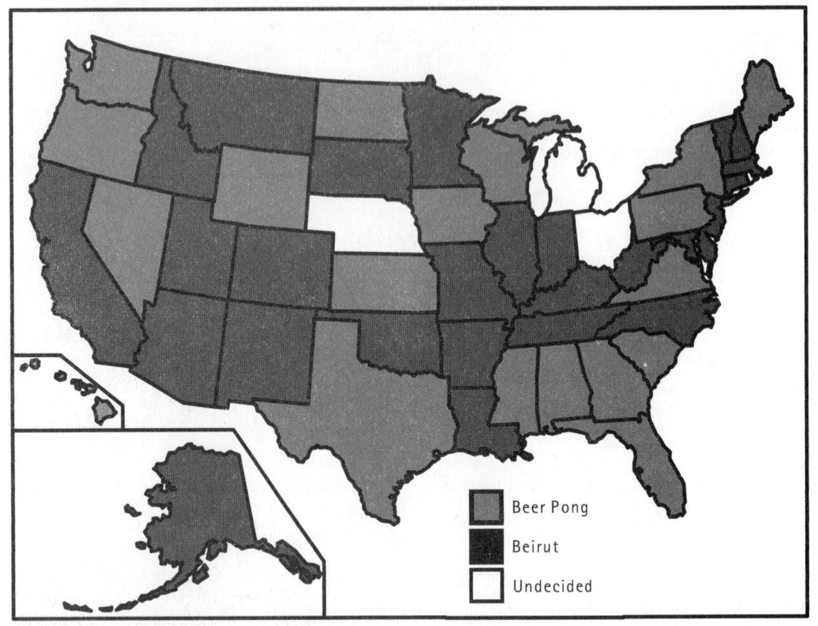

Kegstand Stopwatch

How long can you last?

How to Tap a Keg

Kegs are a great idea if you're hosting a big party or have a horrible drinking problem, but lots of students don't know the proper way to tap one. Unlike tapping an ass, tapping a keg is a delicate process.

WHAT YOU'LL NEED

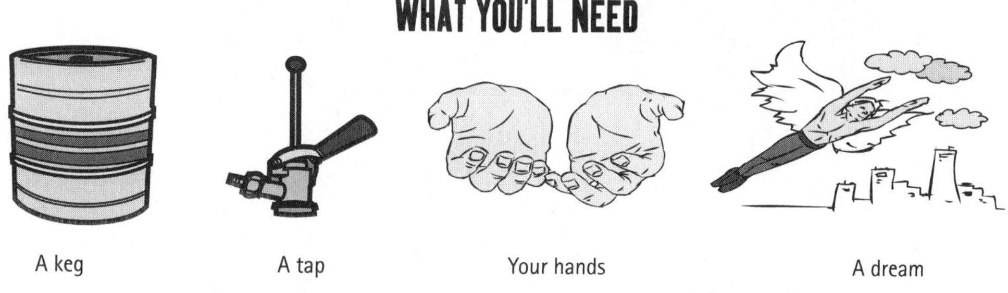

A keg A tap Your hands A dream

Step 1: Align and affix the bottom of the tap to the fixture on the top of the keg.

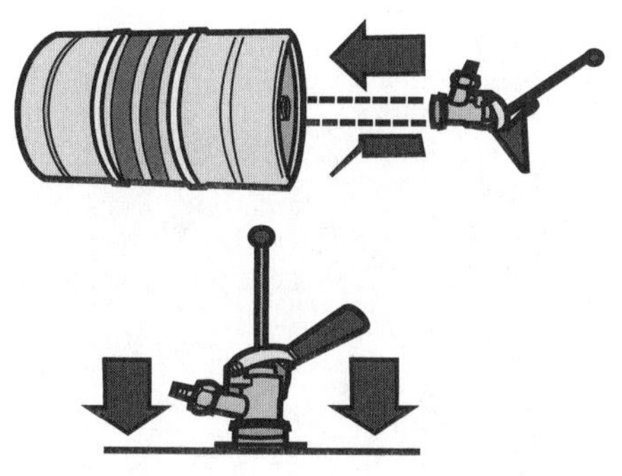

Step 2: Twist the tap counterclockwise until it threads with the fixture and can no longer be twisted anymore.

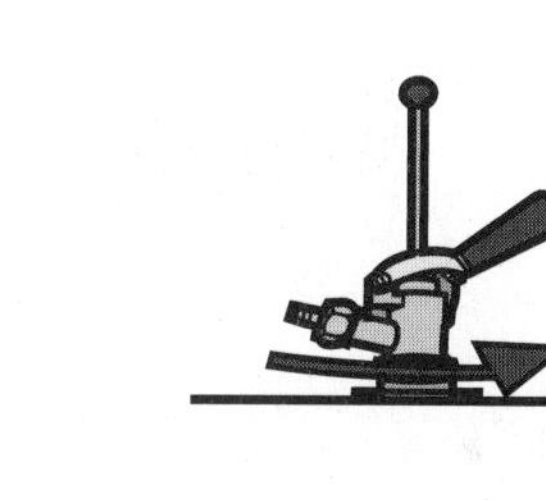

Step 3: Pull the lever on the tap out and push it down until it locks.

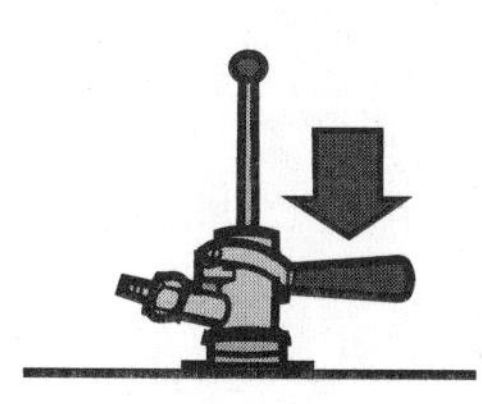

Step 4: Pump the keg twice and hold down the hose to let the foam out.

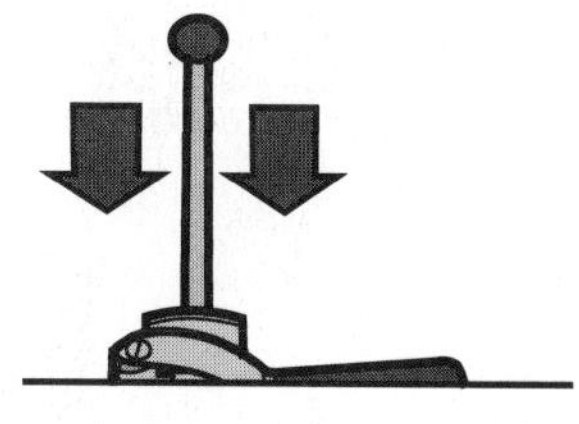

(cont'd)

Step 5:

Dude, Can You Hold My Feet?, by Blake

Dude, do me a solid and hold my feet while I do this kegstand. Word, bro, I'm gonna get shitty. Don't hold them for too long cuz I don't want to get a tan line. Nah, just kidding. Dude, watch out for my tat, it's new. What is it? It's this tribal my boy Beandog drew in a notebook. I saw it and was like, "Bro, I NEED that shit tattooed on my ankle." Bro, you sure you can handle holding my feet? My calves are pretty jacked up right now from all the toe raises I did before I left my dorm. Bitches go fucking nuts for tight calves. I could write out my workout plan for you if you want to pump up your calves. No? Suit yourself, chicken leg. Yo, bro, don't be looking down my shorts while you're holding my feet, aight? Okay, ready, dude? Lift!

How to Crush a Beer Can

Crushing a beer can on your head says to everyone at the party, "Please, please, be my friend . . . please?" Become the ultimate party animal by showing everyone that though it is a formidable task, you will conquer this flimsy piece of aluminum with your skull.

First, dent can on both sides so it will compact easier.

Next, crush can against forehead with one swift motion.

Then, look like a complete asshole meeting your girlfriend's parents.

According to *Friends That Go to Different Schools* magazine, this year there are seventy-two colleges on *Playboy*'s Top 10 Party Schools list.

Glassware Equivalents

College students have devised an ingenious way to consolidate literally a cabinetful of glassware into one simple vessel. Consult the chart to see the magic unfold.

All cameras are disposable cameras if you're rich enough.

Fake IDs

Just because you're out of high school doesn't mean you can legally buy beer, unless you planned it that way (suddenly getting held back three grades on purpose doesn't sound like such a bad idea, does it!?). Most students will have to survive two or three years of college without being able to legally purchase their first can of beer. So how does one purchase alcohol during their freshman and sophomore years? The answer is simple: fake IDs.

Fake IDs look exactly like real IDs except instead of being made at the DMV, they're usually made by an eccentric frat-based entrepreneur who has mastered the art of laminating.

Most people will tell you that the key to a great fake ID is choosing a state whose ID is easily replicated. The old 1854 Kansas ID was notorious for being faked because the actual 1854 Kansas IDs were made by handwriting the year you were born on a piece of scrap paper. However, bars and mini-marts stopped accepting those as legal forms of identification in 1888. So what now?

Your safest bet is an ID without a hologram, which means choosing IDs from states that don't know what holograms are: Alabama, Arkansas, and Mississippi. You can go for a state ID that nobody has ever seen before, that way the bartender/store clerk has no idea whether or not your ID is fake; Alaska and North Dakota are safe bets. If you're even more adventurous, make an ID for a state that doesn't exist. If anyone asks you where exactly Texlahoma is, just shrug and say, "Eh, the Midwest."

As for the age, most people will tell you that making yourself exactly twenty-one seems too shady. But don't get greedy. Nobody is going to believe you're forty-eight, and we don't care how real that fake mustache looks.

You will need to remember your address and fake name, so give yourself some pretty easy-to-remember fake information. Kate Smith is better than Farhadzabib Houshvandzedizadeh. And 33 Maple Lane is easier than 33 Farhadzabib Houshvandzedizadeh Avenue.

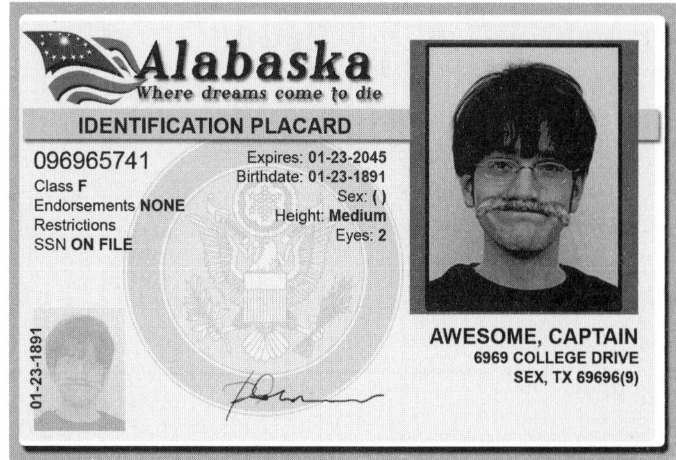

Different Bar Types

Although colleges are now in many different cities (what a time to be alive!), each college town has pretty much the same types of bars. Here's a handy guide for how to tell them apart.

YE OLDE IRISH FAUX PUB

Distinguishing characteristics: Lots of shitty prints of foxhunting scenes on the walls, lots of imports on tap, lots of Catholics on tap

House specialty: Pint of Guinness, bare-knuckle boxing (sometimes against a kangaroo)

Clientele: Upper-middle-class white college students, Irishmen, balding thirty-somethings who like to tell the other guys in the mail room how many college chicks they talk to, guys who know Golden Tee is great when you want to go to a bar and not talk to women

Unfortunately: To the Irish, the drink name "Irish Car Bomb" is about as clever as sucking down a "Your Mom Has Terminal Cancer" on the rocks.

DOWN 'N' DIRTY

Distinguishing characteristics: Cheap beer, cheap women, bad lighting, lots of menthol smoke, and denim

House specialty: Anything in a can, including tuna

Clientele: Blue-collar industrial workers college students look down at, college kids trying to get drunk cheaply before moving on to a better bar

Unfortunately: Pretty much anyone in the bar can kick your ass while remaining seated.

RICH MAN'S RENDEZVOUS

Distinguishing characteristics: For the price of a martini, you could buy several houses in Belize—not very nice houses, but they've got four walls and a roof. And they'll get you fucked up.

House specialty: Pretentious conversation, voting Republican

Clientele: People with name-brand undershirts that match their socks

Unfortunately: You're not rich, and trying to pay for those drinks with chocolate gold coins isn't fooling anyone.

CLÚB LE CLÜB

Distinguishing characteristics: Long line to get in, ridiculous cover, music by DJ Adjective-Letter-Verb

House specialty: Making you realize you're not a very good dancer

Clientele: Girls who don't like to wear much clothing, and the hair-gelled men who love them

Unfortunately: The floors get pretty slippery when ballers dump Cristal on them; dancing is only fun for the 3 percent of the population that's good at it.

SPORTY SPORTS SPORT

Distinguishing characteristics: Eat wings for just nickels; seven screens of explosive, fast-paced WNBA action!

House specialty: Pitchers of anything light, classmate waitresses that get increasingly attractive as the night progresses

Clientele: Boys heading out to watch the game, girls who feign interest in sports to curry boys' attention

Unfortunately: No matter where you go, you meet a Yankees fan.

True College Stories—Getting in Trouble, by Jake

Campus police are not your friends. They are your enemies. If they catch you breaking rules, they will do their best to put you through the school judicial system, which could land you on probation or even kicked out of school. If one of them catches you doing something, you have to switch your brain into a new mode: you must become a professional actor playing a character who is completely convinced that he did not break any rules. Sometimes this means telling a completely outlandish lie, but it doesn't matter—the second you start cooperating with your enemies, they have a huge advantage.

"No, sir, I wasn't just drinking a beer."
"I didn't TOUCH my smoke detector; it looked like that when I got here."
"I did not just stick a pipe in my pants, that's ridiculous. Please stop harassing me, I have to study."

It seems ridiculous, but you HAVE TO lie to them. Campus cops are not omniscient. They'll act like they know you broke a rule, but they can't search you (thanks, Fourth Amendment!). They will try all sorts of dirty tricks, like pretending to be your buddy who just wants you to tell the truth. Don't tell it to them! Emphatically, categorically deny everything. You'll be in much better hands, and for the love of everything that is holy, DO NOT SIGN ANYTHING! It's like those old movies where they tell a prisoner to "sign this confession, and we'll let you go," and the second he signs it, they execute him.

Of course, if you do end up at a judicial hearing, it's the same strategy: deny, deny, deny. Come up with the most plausible story that excludes you from any wrongdoing, convince yourself it's the truth, and argue it passionately. Do not give up, and don't let the awkwardness of the situation throw off your judgment. It's you against them. It's you against your enemies. And if you escape unscathed, in a few years you might run into the person who conducted the hearing, selling iPod skins at your hometown mall,* and you'll think to yourself, "I am so happy I lied to that fucker."

***ACTUALLY HAPPENED TO ME**

When people tell you that vodka "mixes well with anything," slide them a jar of mayonnaise. It's time for them to practice what they preach.

What Drunk People See

Puking

Unless you're the daughter of a particularly irresponsible mother, you've always been taught that throwing up is a bad thing.

There will be times in college when you drink way too much. These times will be called "weekends." The room will start to spin, and you'll start to wonder if doing shots of varnish and vodka is really called a "Russian Woodworker." This is when it's time to pull the trigger. You've got a stomach full of toxins, and you can expel all of them in under ten seconds.

A few quick pointers: first, find the bathroom. If you're discreet enough, there's still a chance you can take a girl home if you swish your mouth out with Busch Light first. Always carry around a Werther's Original butterscotch candy. Not only does it conceal the taste of vomit, but it reminds you of Grandpa, the oldest vomiter in town!

Next, don't throw up in your sleep while you're on your back. We know what you're saying: "But then I can be just like Hendrix!" Yeah, in case you hadn't noticed, Hendrix was good at guitar, too.

Finally, don't brag about how much you puked. People like to boast of their drinking feats, but saying, "Dude, I ralphed until my spleen was in the frat house driveway last night!" doesn't make you sound awesome. It makes you sound like an alcoholic . . . the HARDEST PARTYIN' ALCOHOLIC IN THIS WHOLE DAMN FRAT!

Shamings

Finally, something to do with those Sharpies besides sniffing them.

It's every college student's dream to draw pictures of genitalia on their friends' faces. This task is made much easier when said friend passes out due to drunkenness. However, much like casual sex and snorting study drugs, shaming must end when college does. Why, you ask? Here's why:

The number-one mistake college students make is not staying hydrated after drinking. Number-two mistake? "Your" means "belonging to you." "You're" means "you are."

Hangover Cures

A lot of people are going to tell you that the only way to cure a hangover is to not drink. These people are preachy losers who don't know the difference between "curing" and "avoiding." Besides, the truth is that hangovers are a lot like herpes or lisps; there's no cure, only treatments.

Treatment #1: The best idea is to drink a lot of water and take a multivitamin before you go to sleep. We've heard a shot of water for every beer you drink, but this unfortunately would require going up to the bar and ordering shots of water. What kind of tip do you leave on that? Instead, just chug a few glasses before falling asleep with your face on the bathroom floor. At this point, your body will be pretty full of liquids, so focus on not wetting the bed. If you do wet the bed, defensively yell, "Everybody does it sometime!" to no one in particular. Then pull your diaper up and finish the day strong.

Treatment #2: Some people will tell you that the best way to treat a hangover is to go "hair of the dog" and have a beer first thing in the morning. These people do poorly in school and generally have turbulent relationships with their parents. We don't really know if this will settle your stomach so much as it will immediately induce vomiting. You might be better off actually eating the hairs off your dog; at least that won't taste like Colt 45.

Treatment #3: Try the miraculous "hangover pills" you often see in reputable pharmaceutical retailers such as gas stations and strip clubs. If you read the fine print, most of these pills require you to take them with thirty-two ounces of water. After thirty-two ounces, your hangover is already as cured as it's going to be—you could follow it with a Pez and you'd still feel better (lemon is rich in antioxidants, purple has B-complex vitamins).

A Final Note on Alcohol

Like religion, alcohol is only safe in moderation. If you or somebody you know has been praying to escape reality, or going to church after work every day in order to "unwind," contact a health-service professional at your local university.

6 PARTIES

Introduction

People say college is one big party. We don't know what college they went to; a bar mitzvah is one big party. College is a lot of smaller parties that come together in a veritable Voltron of Awesomeness.

As the sun sets over college campuses throughout America, the question is not whether or not there is a party to attend, but rather which of the four to five parties are worth attending. You'll hear mutterings like, "Yeah, my friend is having a party, and I know there's this big party at some frat, and there's some bar party going on, but I think I'll probably hit up this other party first and see if it's any good."

All parties will generally be exactly the same, and usually what separates the "good parties" from the "bad parties" is how drunk you are. You'll notice the best parties will not be the ones you arrive at in the beginning of the night, but rather the ones you stumble into at the end.

These parties will be exactly the same: mix CD blazing the hottest hip-hop 'n' R&B, a keg of beer, a table with mostly empty bottles of hard alcohol and chasers, and girls and guys you recognize from class drinking as much as their red Solo Cups will hold. If you are sober, these will all be very annoying, but if you're drunk, oh man, what a fucking awesome party.

Every once in a while you'll get the stupid idea that you should throw your own party at your own apartment. Finally there will be a party tailor-made to fit your needs and wants. Unless your needs and wants are to run around worried as hell hoping nobody spills anything, breaks anything, tears anything, or steals anything, your party will not fulfill anything but your deepest desire to talk to the cops and explain to them that the man currently pissing on their leg didn't get drunk at your party. It's much better to keep the party-throwing to losers who enjoy sacrificing everything they hold dear, and keep the partygoing, spilling, breaking, tearing, and stealing to yourself.

If you do decide to throw your own party—and don't tell us we didn't warn you—your first priority should be choosing a great theme. Because nobody would attend a "Naked Girls and Horny Dudes"-themed gathering, you need to achieve the same results while remaining as discreet as possible. "Toilet Paper and Tin Foil" is a safe bet because girls are usually too lazy to construct full dresses out of Charmin. You can call it a "Heat Party" and steam girls out of their clothes by setting your thermostat to 115 degrees. Just make sure your thermostat is on Fahrenheit settings, because 115 degrees Celsius will burn people alive.

This chapter will go over everything you need to know about partying, from pregaming to post-vomiting, and everything in between. However, the most valuable learning tool is experience. So get out there and party hardy and hearty.

A good way to determine which of your friends is least drunk to drive is to play Mario Kart first, and the fastest time is usually the most sober. This works especially well if the party you're going to is on Rainbow Road.

Dear CollegeHumor,

I'm having a get-together and I don't know how much alcohol to buy. What is an acceptable amount?

Soberless in Seattle

Dear Soberless in Seattle,

This is a complex situation to which there are three schools of thought. One, take the party budget, subtract $2.39 for a bag of Baked Lays to serve as hors d'oeuvres, and spend the rest on kegs and whatever liquor comes in plastic handles for $11.

The other method involves more math. Take how many people you think will come to your party and double it to account for uninvited guests. Multiply this number by six beers per person. If there will be a funnel, double this number. This is how many beers you will need to buy for your party. A full-sized keg is roughly 150 beers, so plan accordingly. The equation looks like this:

Average number of beers consumed

Account for uninvited guests

If funnel is present

$$\frac{[(\text{Invited guests} \times 2) \times 6 \times 2]}{150} = \text{number of kegs}$$

Number of beers per keg

A third school of thought is: Buy 200 kegs of beer your first day of college. Keep them in a refrigerated warehouse and throw fifty keggers throughout your college career, each one better than the last. Congrats, grad; you've earned it.

Love,

CollegeHumor

What to Hide During a Party

College kids love stealing, and there's no better time for thievery than at a party. If you happen to be the unlucky soul throwing the party, you must take extreme care to hide your belongings. But what to hide?

You've got some cool stuff like your Super Nintendo and that sweet "Have a Day" poster; these things must be protected. To make sure all your valuables are still there when you wake up naked on the bathroom floor the next day, follow these simple instructions:

1. Hide all posters, CDs, DVDs, kitchen appliances, clothing, and electronics in your closet. Lock closet.
2. Put all sheets, pillows, and other furniture in bedroom. Lock that door as well.
3. Unscrew all lightbulbs and remove all carpeting. Bury in crawl space below the floorboards.
4. Dismantle all window treatments and place under bed. Cover window holes with plywood.
5. Throw actual party at neighbor's house. You can never be too careful.

If a party of all guys is called a sausage fest, would a party of all girls be called a clam bake?

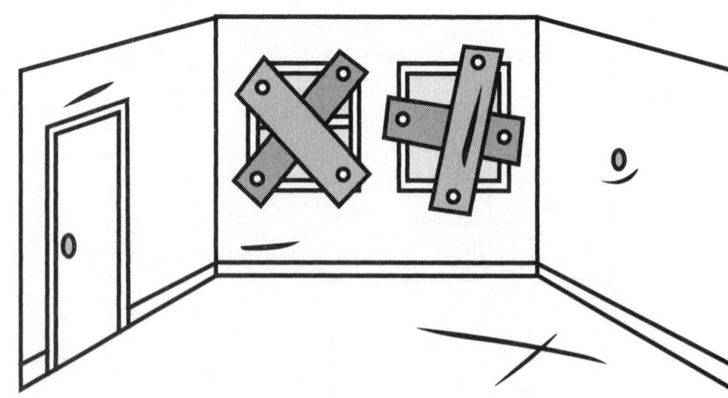

Partygoer Trading Cards

Favorite saying: "I could drink any one of you under the table. . . . Can you hold my beer? I gotta get to a bathroom."
Last seen: Stumbling around campus, puking in garbage cans
Party stats: One shot of tequila, half a cup of keg beer.
Where he'll spend the night: On steps of the Science Building, alone

The Dude

Favorite saying: "PAAAAARRRRRRTY!"
Last seen: Funneling a beer, touching your girlfriend's ass, doing push-ups in between drinks, and punching holes in the wall
Party stats: Six games of beer pong, ten cups of keg beer, three shots of Jägermeister, one glass of water (mistaken for vodka), four kegstands, and three lines of Ritalin
Where he'll spend the night: Wherever the hell he wants

Favorite saying: "My friend made me come here tonight."
Last seen: Shuffling awkwardly around the couch, deciding if he should talk to anyone
Party stats: Half a cup of keg beer, one shot of raspberry vodka (half spilled on shirt)
Where he'll spend the night: At home, alone

Favorite saying: "No way! I am sooooo Carrie . . . Ooh, he's a fine piece of meat."
Last seen: Hitting on richest-looking male partygoer while simultaneously complaining to host about lack of cosmo- and appletini-making ingredients
Party stats: Three cosmopolitans (mixed at home) drank out of keg cup, one funnel (while other bitchy girlfriends were in the bathroom)
Where she'll spend the night: Wrapped around the hairy thighs of the party host

Favorite saying: "Could you hold my legs while I do another kegstand?"
Last seen: Being generally awesome, winning on the beer pong table, being cute
Party stats: Four games of beer pong, two kegstands, three cups of keg beer, one hit from gravity bong
Where she'll spend the night: Hopefully with you

Favorite saying: "I'm not crying!"
Last seen: Crying about something and vehemently stating that it's NOT a guy
Party stats: Seven beers, two lemon drops, one half rum and Coke that was accidentaly knocked out of her hand and started the sobfest
Where she'll spend the night: Cockblocking her roommate

Uncoolest excuse to give your friends when leaving a bar early: "Yeah, guys, I'm gonna peace out. I've gotta hit up some TV DVDs and then catch up with the comments on my ex-girlfriend's Xanga blog."

Drinking Games

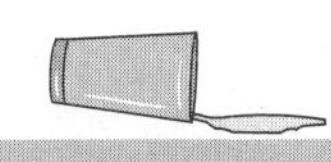

Name:	How to Play:	Worst Part:	Drunk Factor:
Flip Cup	Two teams line opposite sides of the table and race to finish their beers and flip their cups upside down in order.	Somebody peed in the beer. Fucking rival frat!!!!	
Edward Fortyhands	Tape two opened forties to your hands. You can't remove them until you've completely drunk them both, not even to pee!	Driving your buddy to the hospital for alcohol poisoning with bottles taped to your hands proves exceptionally difficult. But hey, rules are rules!	
Power Hour	Take a shot of beer every minute for one hour.	After 10 minutes you realized you'd rather drink without some dude yelling "SHOT" every minute.	
Drink	Players all have beers. The first player to finish his beer has to go to the fridge and get a fresh one.	You've accidentally played this game every day last week.	
Honey I Drunk the Kids	Watch any Rick Moranis movie and take a shot every time he looks nerdy.	Watching any Rick Moranis movie, dying from alcohol poisoning after six minutes.	

Guide:

Sober Tipsy Drunk Drurunk Ddddddddrnkku

How to Cut a Keg Line

Everybody knows that the best thing about kegs is the beer inside, and the worst thing about kegs is waiting in line to get the beer inside. But don't fear—we know a few ways to skip right to the front of the line, without the use of illegal back-cuts, just like all the popular kids in middle school used to do at lunch:

1. Yell "House cup!" and run to the front of the line. Everyone will think you live there and step aside while you fill your cup. If a real resident of the house calls you out, stick to your guns. Tell him that you don't recognize him either, but that you don't blame him because you spend most of the time in your room "doing your own shit."

2. Fill a pitcher. Every party's nerve center is the beer pong table. If that nerve center shuts down, the party will have a seizure and foam at the couch. Make sure the party doesn't swallow its tongue by repeatedly filling a pitcher for beer pong. If the party you are at doesn't have a beer pong table, just pretend that it does. Nobody wants to commit the ultimate party foul of not knowing that there is a beer pong table.

3. Start a small, controlled fire. People will smell the smoke and run out of the line and into the safety of the yard, leaving you alone with the keg. If your fire rages out of control, extinguish it with your ample supply of beer. Nothing douses a fire quite like gallons of alcohol!

4. If none of these work for you, get a tiger or something. That should work, too.

Grenade!

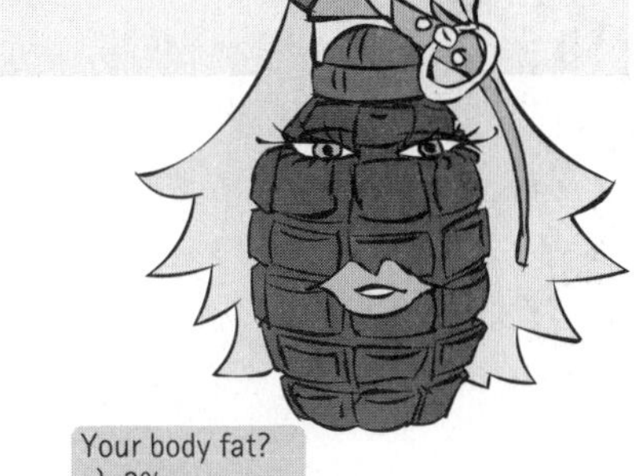

The grenade: that one unattractive girlfriend that a guy's buddy has to "jump on" to clear the way for the seduction of her hot friend. Everyone fears having to take the grenade, but ladies, how can you tell if you are the grenade? Take this simple quiz:

Your body fat?
a) 3%
b) 8%
c) 10%
d) Yes.

Which snack most accurately defines your body type?
a) Thin Mints
b) Average-Weight Cheerios
c) Slightly Fat Baked Lays
d) Morbidly Obese Baby Carrots

How do construction workers heckle you?
a) "Hey, baby, you lookin' for a good time?"
b) "I'd like to airhammer that!"
c) "You wanna see this piledriver in my pants?"
d) "Did one of the oxen get loose again?"

When dancing, what jiggles?
a) Nothing—my breasts are so perky, they barely move
b) My breasts and butt, but not in sync with each other
c) My entire body
d) The Earth

Fill in the blank: When I get stressed out, I _________.
a) Exercise!
b) Watch TV
c) Read
d) ME HUNGRY!!!

Who is your role model?
a) Martin Luther King, Jr.
b) George Washington
c) Your father
d) 15 cheeseburgers

What is your favorite pizza topping?
a) Broccoli
b) Olives
c) Artichoke hearts
d) Pizza bagels

CORRECT ANSWERS: d,d,d,d,d,d,d

Things to Do with an Empty Keg

Kegs cost money; every college kid knows that. However, what some of you may not know is that kegs are good for more than just the shitty beer that comes in them. There are countless things you can do with an empty keg, and here is just a handful of the best:

Keg-rolling:
See who can break both their legs first in this modern take on the classic barrel-rolling contests of yesterday. This game is especially amusing if it takes place immediately after finishing the aforementioned keg.

Keg-brity:
Dress the keg up like your favorite celebrity. Brag to all your friends that you "totally tapped Mischa Barton." Pat yourself on the back for being so clever.

Kegging:
Similar to the popular high school prank where you threw eggs at the house of your enemy, choose an unsuspecting victim and throw the empty keg at his house. If your aim is good enough, it will break through a window and kill him.

Unlike political parties, college parties are fun and don't nominate presidents.

Keg-leg:

Duct-tape the empty keg to your left leg. You may have some trouble getting around, but it'll be worth it when someone asks why you have a keg taped to your leg and you can answer, "Arrrr, they was out of pegs."

Keg-ata:

Fill the empty keg with candy and take turns hitting it with a baseball bat. Days and days and days of fun!

Keg Pyramid:

Instead of a flimsy, one-dimensional pyramid of beer cans, start a 3-D pyramid with empty kegs in your backyard. Try to complete the pyramid within two months. Then, when you die of liver disease, leave explicit demands for your body to be sealed inside with your *SNL: Best of Will Ferrell* DVD and a few cats.

If somebody asks you, "What's your sign?" say "Cancer." Then vomit due to excessive chemotherapy. Hang in there, champ.

The Circle

Just as some species of fish have false eyespots and chameleons can change their color, the average college girl has a pretty handy defense mechanism of her own to deter unwanted party predators. This mechanism is what we at CollegeHumor like to call "The Magic Circle."

"The Magic Circle" is that group of five to eight girls dancing in a tight-knit circular formation in the center of any given party. They seem completely content with just watching each other dance, oblivious to what is happening around them. That is, until an awkward guy decides one of the girls is cute and begins his terribly choreographed approach.

Here's where the magic comes in:

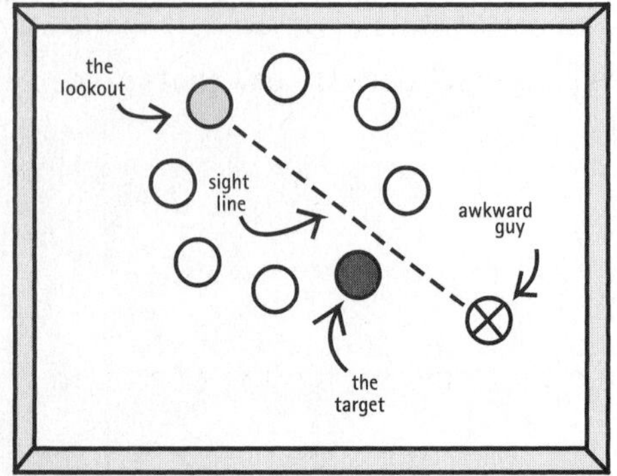

Awkward guy identifies his target and approaches from behind. Across the Circle, he is spotted by the lookout.

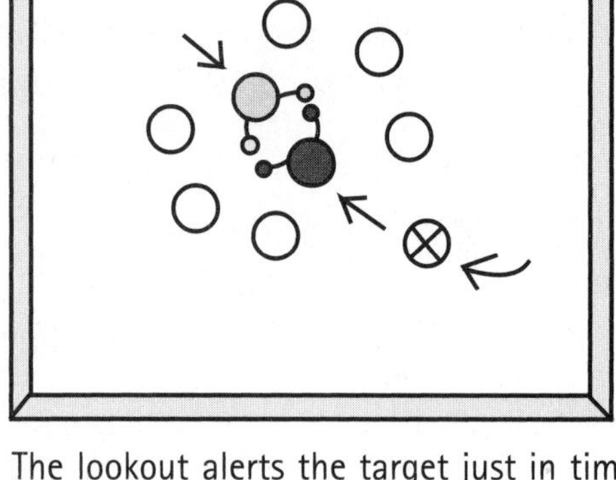

The lookout alerts the target just in time and draws her into the center of the Circle "to dance."

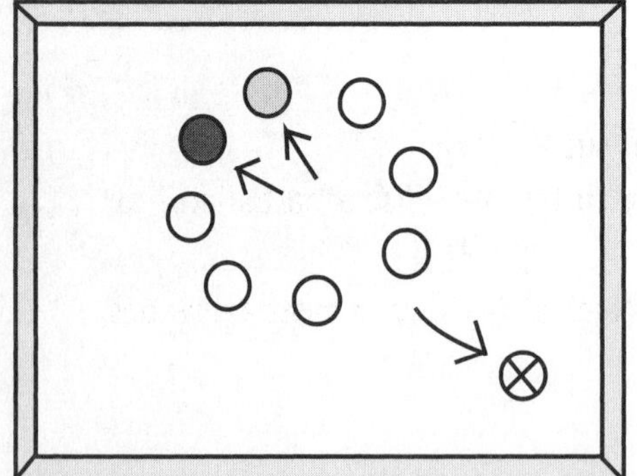

The target is quickly led back to the opposite side, where giggling commences. Awkward guy leaves, rejected.

It is for this reason that "The Magic Circle" is every guy's most revered and most dreaded formation. On the one hand, it's a large circle of girls grinding on each other. On the other, it is an impenetrable fortress of feminine wiles. Oh well, ain't nothing wrong with voyeurism.

Fiiiiiiiiiight!!

College kids have been fighting at parties since fighting was invented almost four hundred years ago. It seems that the mix of testosterone, alcohol, and douche bags creates a good environment for violence to breed. Although everybody loves hearing stories about getting into fights, you often find yourself at peaceful parties, but that doesn't mean you shouldn't lie to your friends! Just mix and match the elements of the story below, and you'll have yourself ultra-realistic fighting stories for weeks to come!

REASONS

"So this dude's slut of a girlfriend hooked up with some other dude and . . ."
"So this gay-ass member of the Delts kept spilling brew-dogs on our couch and . . ."
"This fucking tool was looking at me funny and . . ."

ALTERCATIONS

"I picked up a beer bottle, broke it on one of the dudes' faces and stabbed the other guy in the throat and . . ."
"I took my shirt off just by flexing and used the fabric to choke the shit out of the dude and . . ."
"I slapped my chest a lot to intimidate the fucker, and he just ran away and . . ."

RESULTS

"Doctors say he'll probably never walk again, but whatevs."
"His fucking parents called me the next day to tell me what a barbarian I am. I just barked like a dog and hung up on their ass."
"We have a study date on Tuesday. Isn't that such a silly way to meet a new best friend for life?"

When someone says, "Good times, good times," they mean 11:32 a.m. and 6:47 p.m., respectively.

True College Stories—The Hugging Game, by Amir

The average student will attend roughly fifteen hundred parties over the course of his college career. In order to maximize fun at these parties, I highly suggest playing the "hugging game." My friends and I created this game during our senior year, and it increased our good times by 50 percent. That's exactly half! If you are still a freshman or sophomore, then you are in luck. You have two to four years of hard-core hugging-game action to look foward to, a privilege I didn't have when I went to school.

The rules of the hugging game are quite simple. Each person takes turns having to hug a person that the other members in the group decide on. For example, if you are with a group of six of your friends, then they collaborate and choose somebody for you to hug. You then have to approach that person, regardless of who they are, and attempt to hug them. There are no passes and no vetoes. When you return to your group, they should already be cracking up, and you will receive a round of high fives. Then it is time for the group to choose a partygoer for the next person to hug. This process repeats until everyone has hugged and it is your turn again. You keep going until the party is over or one of you gets punched in the face for "acting like a fucking queer."

There are many techniques when it comes to choosing somebody for your friend to hug. If your friend is a guy, then your best bet is choosing a large frat-type guy or a really hot girl; the results are equal parts embarrassing and hilarious. If your friend is a girl, then your best bet is to choose an ugly guy in one of her classes. It may not be funny at the moment, but the stories you receive for the rest of your semester as he develops a crush on her are a worthwhile investment. The one tip that you will need to follow as the hugger is to get as drunk as possible. You need to make sure the rational part of your brain is completely shut off before you approach that large scary man and ask him to embrace you.

I was able to play the hugging game over a dozen times, but one time in particular really stands out. After a couple rounds of hugs, the clientele at the party seemed to be wearing thin. It was my turn, and I was feeling rather relieved that there was nobody really scary left to hug. Until he walked in. "He" was a six-foot-six, 250-pound behemoth of a man. If his given name wasn't "Ox," then surely his nickname was. Backwards hat, girlfriend in hand, this man walked into the house, but I was quite certain he could lift the whole house over his head if he chose to do so. My one hope was that nobody from my group had noticed. I was not so lucky.

In terms of its noise-to-level-of-intoxication ratio, a tambourine serves as a pretty good Breathalyzer substitute.

They pointed, so I had no option but to walk up to him and hug him. I felt the best approach would be to use the accidental hugging method in which I hug the other person without any warning, then tell them, "Oh, I'm sorry, wrong person." It's not as if I could mistake him for anyone I knew, but there was no way I could walk up to him and simply ask for a hug. I was full of fear, but I made my move.

I weaved through the normal-sized humans and finally got to him. He barely glanced at me as I went in for the kill. As my arms finally reached around his back and our chests were about to meet, I noticed we simply couldn't connect. Not spiritually—you see, he had pushed me onto the floor. "What the fuck was that, faggot!?"

Well, that hardly went according to plan. Okay, brain, act quick. Care to explain the game to him? Nah, somehow I don't think he'd understand.

"Sorry, dude, I thought you were somebody else."

"Who did you think I was, you fucking fag?"

Jeez, what's with the third degree? I couldn't see my entire group of friends cracking up, but I could feel them.

"Sorry about that," I said as I got up and walked back to my friends, who were practically in tears.

I flatly said, "Well, that sucked."

"What are you talking about!?" they replied. "That was by far the greatest thing that happened this month!"

I realized they were right. This could not have gone better for them. As far as the hugging game is concerned, this truly was the pinnacle.

I suppose the great thing about the hugging game is that it turns any routine party into a great event. Or you get pushed on the floor in some embarrassing fashion. Either way, you win.

A Final Note on Parties

When it comes to throwing parties, there are many variables: how many people to invite, how much alcohol to buy, which theme to have. However, there is one thing that everybody can agree on: Chex Mix and Baked Lays. If a party ends with several people dying in a horrible gas fire, but there were also Chex Mix and Baked Lays being served, nine students out of ten will agree that the party, as a whole, was "pretty good."

I wonder if there has ever been an infant smart enough to ironically make the joke, "I wasn't born yesterday."

7 GREEK LIFE

Introduction

If you believe movies, and we do, everything worth talking about, thinking about, or filming about in relation to college has happened in a fraternity house. From *Animal House* to *Old School,* the Greek system is the icon of the debauched, promiscuous mayhem that high schoolers and people over forty associate with college. This may sound like it overstates the importance of the Greek system, but if anything it's an understatement. Without the Greek system there would be no frat parties, no laughter, no college, and probably no polio vaccine. (Jonas Salk was a Phi Delt and could funnel faster than anyone else in the house.)

When you tell your parents that you're considering joining a Greek system, your dad will probably say, "Don't go rushin' into anything," and then he'll laugh and laugh. He doesn't actually know that fraternities and sororities select new members through a process called rush; he just loves making puns on the fact that you go to college in Moscow. In any event, during rush you should shop around and see what fraternity really fits you the best. A fraternity where you could really feel at home. A fraternity in which you can trust your brothers and your brothers can in turn trust you. Then you should just conclude that the best fit for you is the coolest frat that gives you a bid; you're really only doing this to get laid.

This is not to say that you must join a Greek organization, though. Just as the basketball team isn't for short people and the equestrian club isn't for horse murderers, the Greek system isn't for everyone. GDIs, otherwise known as "God Damn Independents," are those students who refuse to take part in the Greek system. Independents see Greeks as exclusive, self-important, and superficial. Greeks see independents as prone to using too many polysyllabic words. We're not going to say who's right here, but we do know one thing: the Greeks are right. If some GDI accuses you of "paying for friends," look him dead in the eye and say, "Well, I pay for clothes, too. What are you, some kind of shoplifter?" His head will probably explode.

If you go to a school without a Greek system, we're sorry, but you knew you would have to make trade-offs if you wanted to enroll at a university in which you could create your own major: History and Culture of Pottery.

If you go to a normal school and have decided to join the Greek system, then congratulations! This chapter should be a crash course in everything you wanted to know but were too afraid to ask for fear of being a "curious pledge," because "curious pledges" get "curious beat the fuck up, maggot!"

CollegeHumor's Guide to Hazing

So you've decided to let yourself be beaten with a paddle. Great choice! Now that you're pledging a fraternity, the hazing will begin before you know it. A lot of pledges fear this breaking-in process more than they should, so we've assembled this guide to hazing to allay some of your fears.

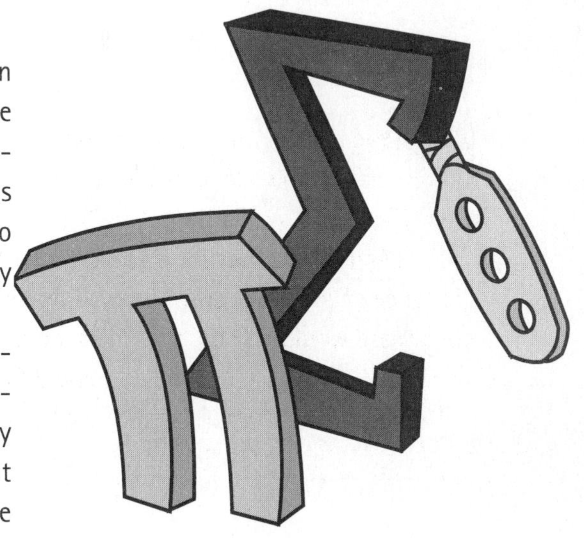

Hazing comes in five basic flavors: physically painful, completely disgusting, emotionally jarring, extremely inconvenient, and thinly veiled homoerotic. Here's a breakdown of what each type entails with some completely true examples we took from CollegeHumor readers:

PHYSICALLY PAINFUL

Bodily abuse is the granddaddy of all hazing, and it's the hazing type most people associate with the Greek system. Simply put, these activities are designed to inflict serious, but not permanent, harm on the pledges. Paddling is the great hallmark haze, but there are other commonly employed methods involving ridiculous amounts of exercising. Physically painful hazings are especially versatile and can be coupled with any other type of sadism to double the pledges' punishment.

Some examples:

"Eight of us were forced to split a handle of cheap vodka in under five minutes. Then the brothers took us all into a courtyard and made us do fifty push-ups. If any member of the pledge class stopped doing push-ups, everyone had to start over from zero. It kept going until we all collapsed."

—Mark, 24

"We would always be made to 'wall sit' by bending at the knees and leaning our backs against a wall. This doesn't sound so hard, does it? It's extremely difficult to do for an hour at a time, though; it feels like your hamstrings are about to pop."

—Scott, 23

COMPLETELY DISGUSTING

Another time-tested method is making the pledges ingest things that they ordinarily would not go near on a dare. Any disgusting hazing worth its weight in Greek letters has a single conclusion: everyone in the pledge class throwing up.

Some examples:

"We all got invited into the fraternity house for 'Chocolate Night.' We were all given a dish of chocolate foods—icing, candy bars, chocolate chips, etc.—that we had to eat in ten minutes without using our hands. As the pledges scarfed this super-sweet concoction, the brothers circled around, taunting us and asking if we needed a drink to wash it down. I stupidly said yes, and the brothers presented me with a nice tall glass of chocolate syrup. Then we had to go on a two-mile run; there was puke everywhere."

—Dave, 26

"Every pledge class invariably has a 'mouthy kid' who likes to talk a lot. We would take that kid and dress him in full Elizabethan garb and force him to stand on a stool inside a trash can. We'd give him a book of Shakespeare sonnets and tell him to start reading them aloud. At this point, his pledge brothers were all seated down around him and forced to drink big glasses of any gross concoction that we could make from the frat house fridge. Ideally, this mixture involved gin, mustard, the juice from a can of Spam, etc. The pledges would eventually have to vomit, but they were forced to puke in the can where their brother stood reading sonnets. No matter how much this kid got barf all over him, he had to keep reading sonnets aloud."

—Garrett, 22

EMOTIONALLY JARRING

After the previous examples, emotional torture may sound pretty enticing. This hazing, however, involves toying with the pledges' feelings and making them feel like they may be the biggest pussies to ever walk the earth. Imagine having not two verbally abusive parents, but a whole fraternity full of them.

Some examples:

"Every year, we'd tell the pledges that they were without a doubt 'the worst pledge class this frat has ever had.' In fact, they were so bad, they would have to continue pledging into the next year. They would think the torture was never going to end! This was always a lie; everyone who was already a brother had been at some point 'a disgrace to the brotherhood' when he was part of 'the worst pledge class ever.' "

—Eric, 23

"The guys in my pledge class all had to wear costumes for a week. I had to dress as the Hamburglar for a solid week. It was humiliating; it's hard to get professors or girls to take you seriously when you have to start each sentence with 'Robble Robble!' "

—Will, 24

EXTREMELY INCONVENIENT

This kind of hazing isn't going to make anyone embarrassed, injured, or sick, but it is going to waste colossal amounts of time. These activities are designed to build cooperation among pledge brothers and test commitment to the brotherhood. They usually involve waking up in the middle of the night or some similarly annoying element.

Some examples:

"We would all get lined up in a row in the fraternity house and be forced to answer questions regarding information we had memorized about the brotherhood (fraternity history, current brothers' hometowns and majors, etc.) while having beer or water splashed on us. This would go on for several hours at a time and require that each of us stand bolt upright and not look anywhere other than straight ahead no matter what happened. My legs got so tired, and I smelled like warm beer."

—Michael, 25

"My pledge class was given a large jar of ice-cream sprinkles and given an hour to separate it into piles of individual colors. If at the end of the hour any sprinkle was in the wrong-colored pile, they were remixed and we had to start over. It took us seven tries."

—Todd, 23

"Our pledges must 'guard' a bench on the college's campus for one week. During that week, at least one pledge must be sitting on the bench twenty-four hours a day, rain, shine, or hailstorms be damned. They get hot, drenched, or just plain fucking cold; it's a major hassle to be out on a bench doing nothing at 4 a.m. on a Tuesday."

—Greg, 26

THINLY VEILED HOMOEROTIC

Any fraternity member will tell you that the "gay fraternity" stereotypes are way off base. To prove this statement, they will then make pledges do things with each other's dicks. Some examples:

"They would force us to do an 'elephant walk' in which each pledge was stripped naked and forced to walk in a line while holding the genitals of the pledge behind him. A variant involves walking with your nose in the ass of the guy in front of you. Worst thing I could imagine."

—Richard, 25

"Pledges were taught that the old adage that things only come out of the anus is way off base by having a wide variety of things shoved in. Brooms, the curvy part of field hockey sticks—it was all fair game to go up the chute. I think this is still done only by particularly sadistic frats, i.e., all of them."

—Brett, 23

A Quick Note on Fraternity Hazing

If you choose to rush, you're going to hear, "Dude, we totally don't haze our pledges" at every fraternity. And you'll think, "Oh, man, fraternities have given up this barbaric relic of a bygone era." If you say this, you have a very nice vocabulary for a freshman. You've also made a serious mistake.

Due to the inherent legal liability of forcing beer cans up people's asses, frats have to say they don't haze. DON'T BELIEVE THEM. The second you start pledging a "non-hazing" frat, you'll have a syringe of antifreeze jammed in your arm just to test your commitment to the brotherhood. It doesn't sound so bad until they let the antifreeze-eating pigeons out. Then you're truly fucked.

Sorority Stereotypes

When joining a sorority, it is important to meet as many sisters as possible in order to get a true feel for the group. Then it is important to throw all that knowledge out the window and make your decision based purely on that sorority's nickname.

It may seem like a certain nickname doesn't fit the girls you know. "Chi HOmega? But most of the Chi O's I know are saving themselves for marriage!" Bottom line? Those virgins are lying. Everybody knows that Chi Omegas are sluts. If they weren't, where would that nickname have come from? We don't make this stuff up.

As a rule of thumb, it's generally a good idea to avoid any sorority whose nickname refers to weight issues. You think those girls at Phi Mu are cool? How about those girls from . . . Phi MOO? Yeah, that's right. You didn't think they were all fat, but they are, and if you join their ranks you'll become fat, too. Why don't you look at Slap-A Kappa instead? They seem . . . nice.

All sororities try to make themselves out to be the best. If it's not the best grades, it's the most members. If it's not the most members, it's the most members without syphilis. But the truth can only be found in the nickname. Psi Beta Phi claims to have the highest number of members? More like highest volume: Fry Burger Pie.

CATEGORY	ANCIENT GREEKS	FRAT GREEKS	EDGE
Muse	Calliope	That chick with the rack from Spanish class	Ancient Greeks
Party garment	To-GA, to-GA!	To-GA, to-GA!	Ancient Greeks (points for trendsetting)
Fuel	Wine in a calfskin	Light beer in a can	Frat Greeks
Extreme ritual	Virgin sacrifice	Formal weekend	Frat Greeks
Comedic genius	Aristophanes	Belushi	Frat Greeks
Supreme power	Zeus	Guy who does the hiring at Bank of America	Ancient Greeks
Ambition	Intellectual growth, valor in warfare	Successful run for state senate	Ancient Greeks
Brought down by	Ruthless overexpansion	Ruthless fun-hating dean	Frat Greeks
Middle Eastern foe	Persians	Engineering student	Everyone loses with racism

How to Host a Frat Party

It's Friday night, you're the social chair of your fraternity, and the time has come to host your first spring party. You have some big shoes to fill—rumor has it that the previous social chair had a spring kegger so insane that Kyle Bowman woke up spooning Clark Gibson's left arm. ONLY his left arm. But don't worry, just follow these simple steps and you'll be a legend in no time.

Step #1. Pick a good theme. The best themes require that girls dress provocatively while still allowing guys to yield some sort of weapon guaranteed to cause at least three serious injuries before the evening is over. Some classic themes include Golf Pros and Tennis Hoes or Pirates and Eye-Patch Bra Models.

Step #2. Make sure to decorate well. Pre-party, pour at least two cases of beer on the floor and litter the empty cans generously along the walls. Pee in a corner if you're feeling really crazy. Nothing says "this party rocks" quite like human waste.

Step #3. Carefully calculate how much beer you need, and then only get half as much. Girls get desperate when the flow of free alcohol is cut off, so you can use the coveted last case of beers to your bartering advantage.

Step #4. Utilize the pledges. Everybody likes a spectacle, so "strongly encourage" your pledges to do something completely dehumanizing at the peak of the party. Anything involving a blindfold, a fly swatter, and fire should do nicely.

There's a proper time to express your political views, but your "Tortured Souls of Aborted Fetuses" Halloween costume was really just a huge buzzkill. Where did you get that blood, though? It looked really good.

If every member of a frat knows what its Greek letters represent in the world of physics, it's a nerd frat.

Hierarchy of Being Served at a Frat Party

The ease with which you can get a beer at a frat party says a lot about you. Which one are you?

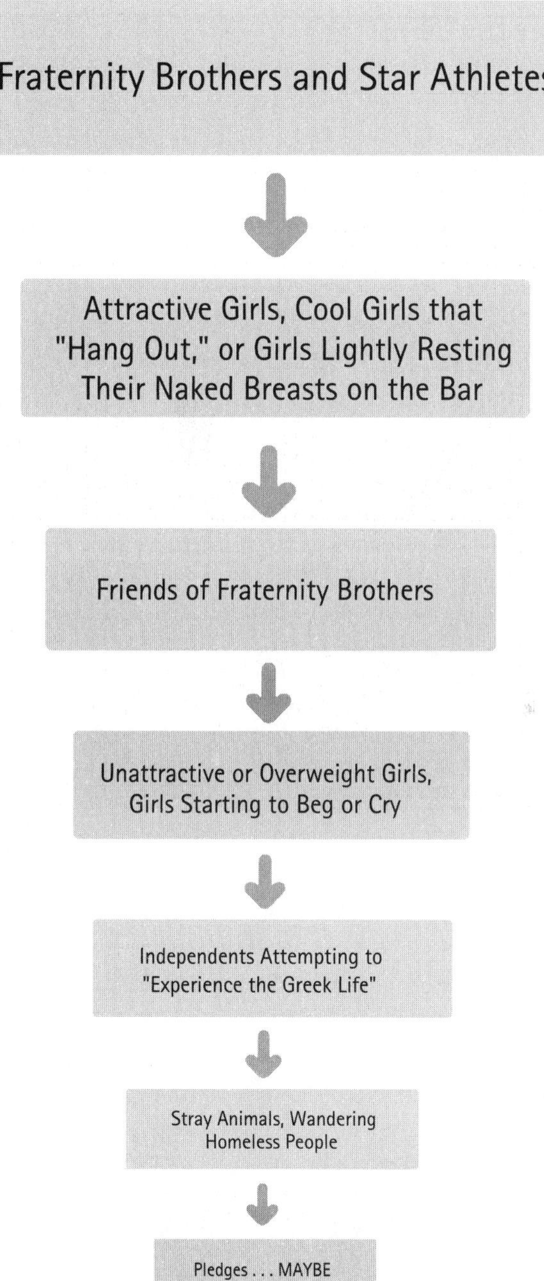

Fraternity Minutes

zeta

123 Zeta Lambda Street
Collegetown, USA 15068

ZETA LAMBDA BROTHERHOOD RULES!!!

8:02 p.m. High Zeta Henderson's call to order is met with a rousing round of "Calls to Boner." The minutes note that this makes no sense.

8:06 p.m. Laughter from the "Calls to Boner" subsides, then restarts. Final chortle at 8:09 p.m.

8:13 p.m. The ongoing struggle with the rigid policies of the Dean are discussed. It is resolved that if a peaceful solution cannot be found, the situation will be adapted into a screenplay. At this point, it is mathematically impossible for the fraternity to lose.

8:22 p.m. On the subject of this weekend's parties, it is decided that there should be beer at the party. Moreover, there is a strong motion that hot freshman poontang be available at the party. All in favor said aye, one opposed said "gay." More laughter.

8:35 p.m. As required by university policy, anti-hazing regulations are read aloud to the fraternity. Brothers enjoy a laugh, and even pledges are allowed to remove their ball gags to laugh along.

8:42 p.m. The topic of rival fraternity the Sigmas is brought to the floor. It is resolved that their snobbish preppery no longer be tolerated. The High Zeta suggests that their rivers be made to run wet with the liquid of a thousand water balloons.

8:47 p.m. The pledges are given instructions to design the greatest Homecoming Parade float of all time. The inter-fraternity trophy will come back to Zeta this year!

9:00 p.m. Dismissal.

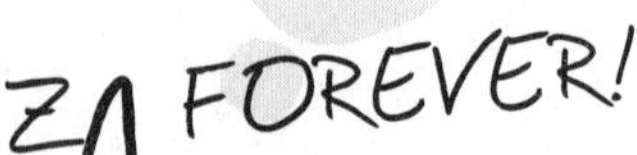

ZETA LAMBDA BROTHERHOOD

Where Your Greek Dues Go

As this diagram clearly shows, you're paying for more than just friends:

Frat Dues

Sorority Dues

How to Read Greek

The Five Stages of Frat Membership, by John Roy

I was a frat boy. Some of you may be, too. Some of you may live next door to them and have to see their genitals when they relieve their bladders of Keystone Light on your lawn. Some of you may date them and wonder why they like to put their arms around other men and sing songs like it's the wrap party for the cast of *Hairspray*, or why they yell chants full of 1920s nonsense like "Rah Rah Bon Ton!" or "Roo Rah Ree!" when rappers like Mike Jones have provided perfectly contemporary nonsense to chant instead. What's going on in their brains that makes them act this way? A long and arduous psychological process. Here are the five stages of the frat boy mind:

Stage One: "This is gay."

A guy has just come up to you at a party during your freshman orientation and talked to you the way guys talk to girls when they hit on them. He's also trying to get you drunk, which also doesn't make sense, because you aren't a girl. What's wrong with him? He wants you to go to a "rush" party. You wonder if he means that Canadian band with the mullets in that poster your pothead uncle had over his waterbed. It turns out to be something much worse: a party where that guys' friends will try to get you to sleep full-time in their house, oh, and do stuff for them. Four more kegstands later (sometimes with that rush party guy holding your legs with a big smile on his face, cheering you on to get even drunker even though you're still not a girl) you stagger back to the dorm and forget that you gave him your number.

Stage Two: "This is the greatest decision I've ever made in my entire life!"

The rush party turned out to not be gay at all! Or rather, it was gay, but its gayness was offset by the fact that you got laid! An equally confused female counterpart to yourself decided to comfort her own insecurities about starting college life by having a mindless hookup with you! For some reason you associate this event with the fraternity! Now it's clear: hang out with these guys and this kind of thing will happen all the time! It's like you joined Mötley Crüe, but without having to learn how to play music or go on grueling tours or do heroin! Hanging out with the ambiguously gay rush party guy is so small a price to pay for the secret to eternal groupies! "Roo Rah Ree!"

Stage Three: "Some of these motherfuckers are gonna have to die!"

When you saw *Old School*, pledging looked like so much fun. Now you suddenly remember that you were laughing at the pledges in *Old School*, not with them, and that they had rocks tied to their balls. Guess what? So do you! And an ex-fat kid with a Napoleon complex is shouting at you to eat an onion like an apple! Ha ha ha! Once this shit is over, he's gonna get to eat a gun barrel! Hey, rush party guy, how come you didn't mention the part where my pants are off and a closet case paddles me while telling me I don't know the true meaning of brotherhood?

Stage Four: "This is the greatest decision I've ever made in my entire life!"
After some amateurish brainwashing that would make a Scientologist laugh, you have miraculously forgotten how much you hate these people. When they told you you were a brother after making you think you had failed, you even cried actual tears, which you haven't done since *Saving Private Ryan.* And guess what, the hazing had a purpose, just like the Marines' hazing does! Of course, Marines have to go to war, and the most dangerous thing you'll be doing is throwing an empty keg through a window, but who cares, you're a brother! And guess what, it's not just drinking! You get to wear wizard robes and share a secret handshake. You have a vague philosophy that sounds like it might be the meaning of life if you've had a bong hit and a tall margarita. Your fraternity had impressive-sounding dudes in it like Nathaniel Mayflower III and John Waylon Winchell or some shit, and you already forgot what they did. There was even some president dude! There's rich dudes who might want to hire you 'cause they had to eat an onion, too! What this all has to do with living in a shithole that smells like Keystone and ass and waking up with hangovers is unclear, but who cares, that chick you hooked up with at the rush party is now in a sorority and she's bringing over more drunk freshman girls! "Rah Rah Bon Ton!"

Stage Five: "This is gay."
When the beers wear off, you remember something. Except for two actual friends you managed to make, you don't have anything in common with these people. Also, wouldn't it be cool if your house didn't smell and thirty guys didn't try out their Ultimate Fighting moves every night at four in the morning? And the girl you're dating now is twenty-one and likes to see bands instead of stand around a keg while men hold each other upside down. And when they told the new kids to eat the onion, you got mad and punched the ex-fat kid in the face for being a Nazi faggot. You weren't sure what this meant, but after the bong hit and tall margarita, it summed him up perfectly. Besides, your freshman roommate plays soccer and their parties are better anyway. You get your two friends together and find an apartment, sign a lease, and never go back except when you're broke and have no beer.

Hey, frat bros, maybe you wouldn't need those sunglasses if your hat wasn't on backwards.

If you have not hit Stage Five by your first semester of junior year, you are either

(A) Gay, and need to reevaluate your life, starting with a five-day trip to Miami in which you burst out of the closet like the Incredible Hulk;

(B) A wounded ex-nerd who cruelly hazes people to calm his inner demons, at which point it's best to voluntarily place yourself on an FBI watch list to prepare them for your future crimes; or

(C) Destined to work for the national fraternity organization your entire life, and can look forward to spending your twenties traversing the United States in a Hyundai, writing reprimands to teenagers for wearing their wizard robes wrong.

Fatty Sorority

Every campus has certain things. A library. A rec center. And at least one fatty sorority.

Even in predominantly fat colleges located in fat states, there reside fat sororities who seemingly push the envelope—push it into a vat of cheese and then eat it.

It's a fact that in any sorority, one girl emerges as "the hot one." In the fatty sorority, this girl is usually just ugly instead of ugly and fat like her sisters. Or she's more ugly but less fat. The math is fuzzy. What's clear-cut, though, is that we don't want some fatty or ugly skipping around like she's hot stuff. The last thing you want is for a fatty to gain any semblance of confidence. Next thing you know, she won't have an eating disorder because she thinks her weight is in the "normal range." Yeah, the normal range for SUVs!

Moreover, fatty sororities still have sorority events just like normal ones. That means that guys are going to get asked to be a fatty's date to fatty sorority functions. This just isn't fair. Guys have better things to do with their time than rejecting fatties—like banging skinny chicks.

Furthermore (or should we say "fat-thermore"?), it's confusing for freshmen when the first girl in sorority letters they see is a fatty. They could be soured on Greek life for the rest of college. And that would be a shame.

On the other hand, fat fraternities (or fat-ernities) are awesome. Those dudes are fucking party animals, bro! I once saw a dude eat forty Whoppers in one sitting! He was a god among men.

Menstruation is the grossest thing college girls do. Period.

Nerd Frat

The nerd fraternity is college's oldest oxymoron, predating jumbo shrimp by three years. Nerd frats, or, as nerds call them, "smart frats," are social anomalies. There is no reason for nerds to be drawn toward the fraternity lifestyle. Drinking, partying, and Ping-Pong are usually reserved for students who don't know that "modem" stands for "MOdulator-DEModulator."

So what are these nerds trying to prove, anyway? That they're cool? Cracking open some beers at the nerd frat after a tough engineering final doesn't make you any cooler; it just makes you a phony as well. It's clear that you'd rather celebrate by downloading anime porn, so just go ahead and do that; at least people will respect you for keeping it real.

You don't see normal frat guys infiltrating math clubs or starting their own local area video game network; they're at least being honest with themselves. Regular frat guys have to deal with nerds all day long in classes and will have to call them "boss" for the rest of their adult lives, so at least let them have their final safe haven among the kegs and discarded pizza boxes of fraternity row.

It may seem a little extreme to say that there should be no such thing as nerd frats, but if you give these nerds just one frat house, the next thing you know they'll be marrying a horse.

And to any nerds out there, you don't have to join a frat just to get back at all those meatheads who picked on you in high school. Living well is the best revenge of the nerds.

A Final Note on Greek Life

You wouldn't call your country a cunt, so don't call my fraternity a frat. It belittles the brotherhood. Same with "refrigerator" and "fridge."

Obituaries: Read 'em and weep.

8 DRUGS

Introduction

Welcome to the drug chapter! It would be really socially irresponsible for us to encourage the use of illegal drugs, so we're not going to do that.

By the same token, it would be pretty shortsighted of us to not point out that the following great Americans probably used drugs at some point: George Washington, Ulysses S. Grant, Henry Ford, Jonas Salk, and Charlie Sheen.

You're an adult; you can use this information to come to your own conclusions.

That being said, if you're looking to experiment in college, one of the first things you should do when you get to campus is find a drug dealer. Seriously, before you even start unpacking the minivan, start asking people if they're "holding." If they say, "Yeah, holding the Rubbermaid container I'm moving into my freshman dorm room," keep walking. You don't need to be friends with that well-organized wiseass. When you find a drug dealer who is "holding," ask to buy an "eighth" from him. Smoke whatever he gives you, even if he gives you one-quarter of a half of a pie. Drugs taste like cherries. And filling. And dough.

In college you'll hear the ramblings of many future politicians silently lobbying from their oddly comfortable, really old sofa: "Dude, they should legalize it. When our generation's in power, things are going to change." No, they're not going to change. When our generation is in power, we won't want our kids taking drugs that make them think leaning over the edge of a roof and standing up really fast is a good idea.

At your drug dealer's apartment, you will be bombarded with sayings that resemble "It's not addictive!" and "I totally pay attention in class better when I'm stoned" and "Alcohol is probably more dangerous, but it's a big industry so Congress won't hit it." Just smile, nod, and say, "Totally." The more that hippie likes you, the less he'll charge you for the goods. But don't get too close or he'll be using that one phone call to contact you for bail money. Drug dealers are your best friends until they get caught; then they become bad influences.

Finally, nothing says, "I guess marijuana is a gateway drug," quite like injecting something into your vein with a syringe. Congratulations, you've ruined your life.

CollegeHumor's Guide to Drugs

So now that we've established that you're probably going to try drugs at some point, you'll probably need some cursory information on each one.

Marijuana
aka: weed, grass, pot, herb, reefer, ganja, Shrek, cannabis, 'dro, turbo-heady, Shrek 2, superskunk, purple haze, rocket fuel, white widow, hash plant, ghetto blaster, Snuffleupagus, sticky icky, cheeba, da chronic, crippy, la-la, Mary Jane, nugs, trees, stuff, wacky tabacky
Administration: Smoked in a joint, blunt, bowl, bong, pipe; cooked into brownies, tea cookies, corn on the cob, spaghetti sauce, cake, government mind-control paste
Effects: Mild euphoria, making jam bands tolerable, relaxation, perceived improvement in everything, extreme chillness
Side Effects: Extreme hunger, memory loss, excessive laughing, eternal cotton mouth, paranoia, excessive blinking in a futile attempt to remoisturize eyes
Famous Users: All musicians. All the good ones, anyway.
Users Often Say: "Yeah, you hear the song, but I *feel* the song."

Drugs are just rugs without the "D," but that doesn't mean you should have bought that hemp carpet.

Cocaine

aka: coke, blow, nose candy, white lady, that drug from that movie with Johnny Depp, that drug from that documentary about Robert Downey, Jr.

Administration: Snort it through a rolled-up fifty (so people don't think you're poor), form crack rocks and smoke it, inject it directly into your veins

Effects: Elevated heart rate and mood, hyperactivity, euphoria

Side Effects: Nosebleeds, potential strokes or cerebral hemorrhages, up to seven times increased likelihood of eventual heart attack, blowing your career as a rising rock star, deeply involved conversations about how you're not addicted to it . . . you just like a little taste every now and then. Oh, and possible death.

Famous Users: All actors. The good ones, anyway.

Users Often Say: "What? It's not that late! Fuck it, we're going to Atlantic City!"

Heroin

aka: horse, H, Spanky, Hoboken, needle juice, Siberian twilight, Singaporridge

Administration: Boiled in a Snapple cap (REAL FACT #939: You're going to die soon.) and injected mainstream, snorted up nose

Effects: Confusion, drowsiness, euphoria

Side Effects: Nausea, drooling, being Corey Feldman, death from OD, death from AIDS, slowed respiratory processes, awful withdrawal process, losing all of your belts, comical itching

Famous Users: The guy who created ALF, the guy who created heroin

Users Often Say: "They call it heroin because it's like your mind is being rescued by a female hero. Isn't that right, Wonder Woman? Man, I'm gonna puke."

LSD

aka: acid, candy corn, blotter, the eye of Nosferatu, the inspiration behind the last six Beatles records

Administration: Tablet form, on blotter paper, on sugar cubes, flown directly into brain by omnipotent blue eagle

Effects: Vivid hallucinations and distorted perceptions

Side Effects: Bad decisions made while riding the flower boat through tulip land. And that magical elf looks angry.

Famous Users: The Moviefone Guy

Users Often Say: "Nobody warned me we would be visiting the rainbow factory! I should have worn my 4-D glasses!"

Adderall/Ritalin

aka: The Pink Lady, A-Dizzy

Administration: Pharmaceutical pill, crushed with school ID card and snorted

Effects: Enhanced focus and energy, extreme determination to excel at tasks, lack of appetite, rampant studying

Side Effects: Restlessness, addiction, repeated bowel movements, excessive sweating, thinking things are way more interesting than they actually are

Famous Users: Your cousin who gets D's in the third grade. Christ, it's just reading; what's so hard about that?

Users Often Say: "What's your favorite prime number? No, not seventeen; I mean one that you really, really love."

Inhalants

aka: huffing, Pam, paint, Whip-Its, airplane glue

Administration: Throw a bunch of aerosol in a paper bag. Inhale it.

Effects: Short giggly dizziness followed by a three-hour headache

Side Effects: Being a suburban middle schooler, depriving your brain of oxygen, inspiring awful public service announcements about how you're drowning your mind

Famous Users: Chef Boyardee

Users Often Say: "Hurry up and finish it before Mom gets home, dude. This is some really cool Whip."

Robitussin

aka: Robo-trippin', Robo, Tussin, The Substance

Administration: Drink a lot of cough syrup that contains dextromethorphan, preferably straight from the bottle rather than the little plastic cup they provide.

Effects: Euphoria, hallucinations, zero coughing, laughing, the urge to talk about feelings

Side Effects: Sexual dysfunction, trouble walking like anything other than a zombie, confusion, nausea, heatstroke

Famous Users: You when you were ten

Users Often Say: "(sound of vomiting)"

Ecstasy

aka: X, E, and sometimes Y

Administration: Pill form in the shape of some of your favorite Disney characters and some of your least favorite cereal characters

Effects: Euphoria, dancing with lots of arm movements
Side Effects: Drinkin' Hennessy, sucking on pacifiers, touching/sleeping with people you wouldn't ordinarily go near on a dare, elevated body temperature, sweating, death
Famous Users: Eminem, the Olsen twins . . . probably
Users Often Say: "This is the best senior trip ever! Can I lick your hair?"

Painkillers
aka: Vicodin, OxyContin, Lortab, Percocet, Hillbilly Heroin, the rich man's Flintstone Vitamin
Administration: Pills
Effects: Drowsiness, euphoria
Side Effects: Itching, nausea, the armed robbing of pharmacies, constipation
Famous Users: Your rich aunt. Or, failing that, your richer uncle.
Users Often Say: "The regular Tylenol's just not doing it for me anymore, Doc."

Peer Pressure

You may think you're not susceptible to it, but peer pressure can lead to some shocking compromises.

> "No thanks."
> *becomes*
> "Just one hit."
> *becomes*
> "Pass it to me again."
> *becomes*
> "Where'd you get this?"
> *becomes*
> "Hey, I need some more; are you still awake?"
> *becomes*
> "Eh, I never wanted to go to college anyway."
> *becomes*
> "Can you spare some change?"
> *becomes*
> "I know my rights. I ain't saying shit."
> *becomes*
> "I wish I were dead."

becomes

"The court ordered me to undergo a rehabilitation program."

becomes

"And remember, guys, I overcame my drug addiction and so can you. Thank you so much for coming to this assembly, Fairfield Middle School!"

An Open Letter to Hemp Wearers

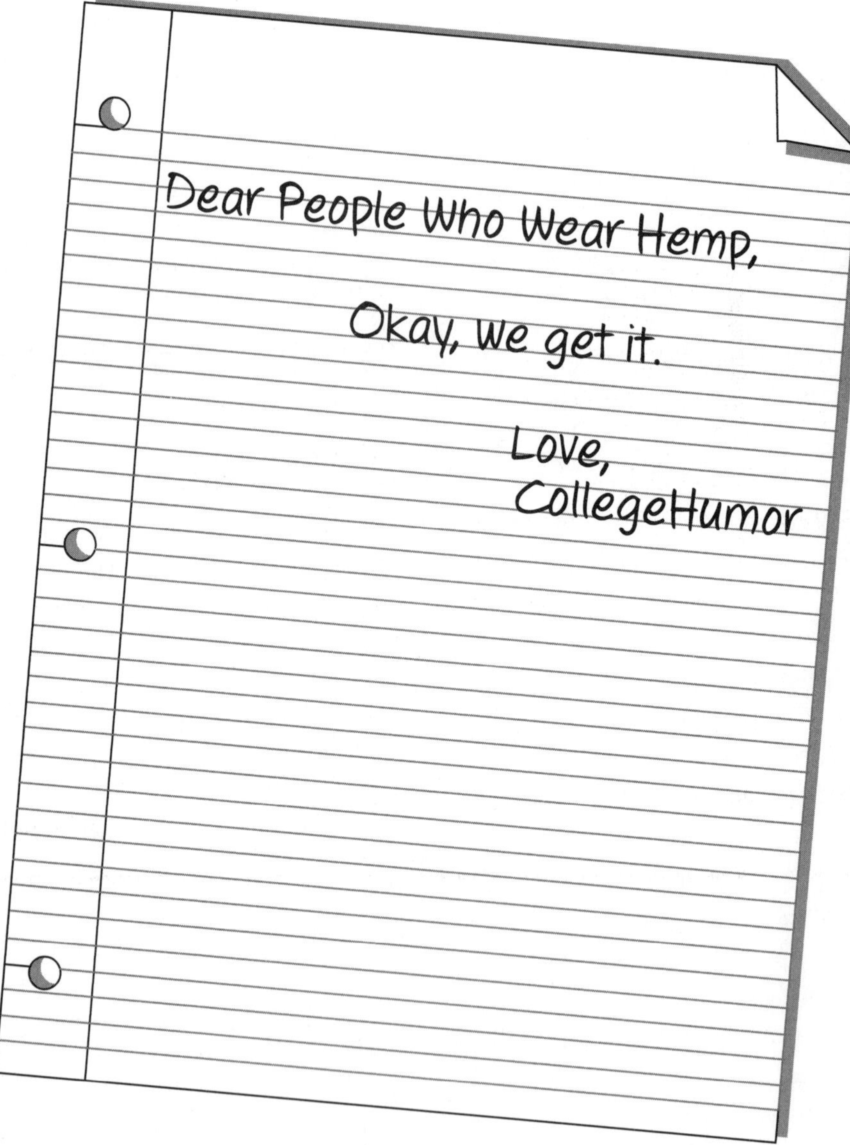
Dear People Who Wear Hemp,

Okay, we get it.

Love,
CollegeHumor

Tired of getting arrested for smoking weed in your dorm room? We can help! For years this product has only been available to fabulously wealthy students, but now Todd'sCoolProducts Inc. is bringing it to you! We proudly present . . .

The Dorm Stoner's Survival Kit

BUSTED AGAiN?!

Packaged conveniently in a suitcase, the Dorm Stoner's Survival Kit has everything you need to get high and NOT get caught. In the kit you'll find . . .

- Paper towel tube and dryer sheets to blow through
- 3 bags of heavy-butter microwave popcorn to cover the smell
- Rolled-up towel for dorm door. Keep smoke in, so you can keep smokin'
- Minifan for the window
- RA detector
- Inflatable escape chute
- A bobblehead of Jerry Garcia that repeats, "Dude, you're being paranoid, calm down," every thirty seconds or when you press a button

Send your cash to:

Dorm Stoner's Survival Kit
Todd'sCoolProducts Inc.
Todd's Garage
Weed, CA 96094

Nickname

Address

City State ZIP

Addresses without ZIP codes cannot be honored. Allow 6-10 weeks for delivery.

OFFER EXPIRES April 20, 1987.

Blowtube

"Shut up, dude, what if the RA smells us?" Nobody wants to get expelled, so if you're going to smoke in the dorms, you've got to disguise the scent somehow. Although popping some heavy-butter popcorn can cover the scent, as can incense, a popular option remains making a blowtube.

Want to make your own? Here's what you do:

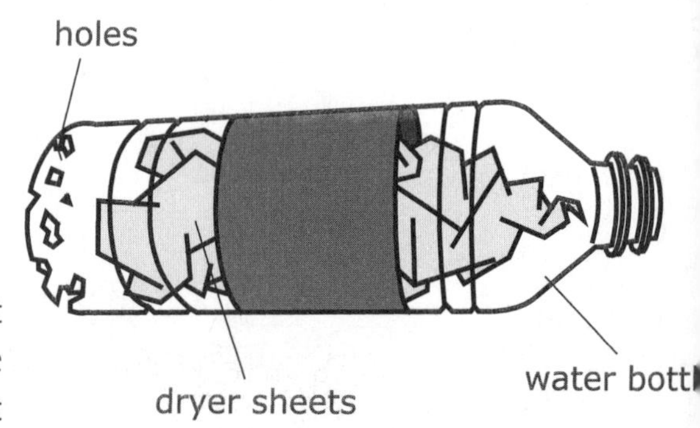

1. Get a plastic soda or water bottle.
2. Poke some holes in the bottom.
3. Fill the bottle with dryer sheets.
4. Blow smoke through the mouth of the bottle. It *should* come out the other end smelling like dryer sheets. Instead, it usually comes out smelling like pot that went through the laundry.
5. Fool no one.

The Perfect Bong

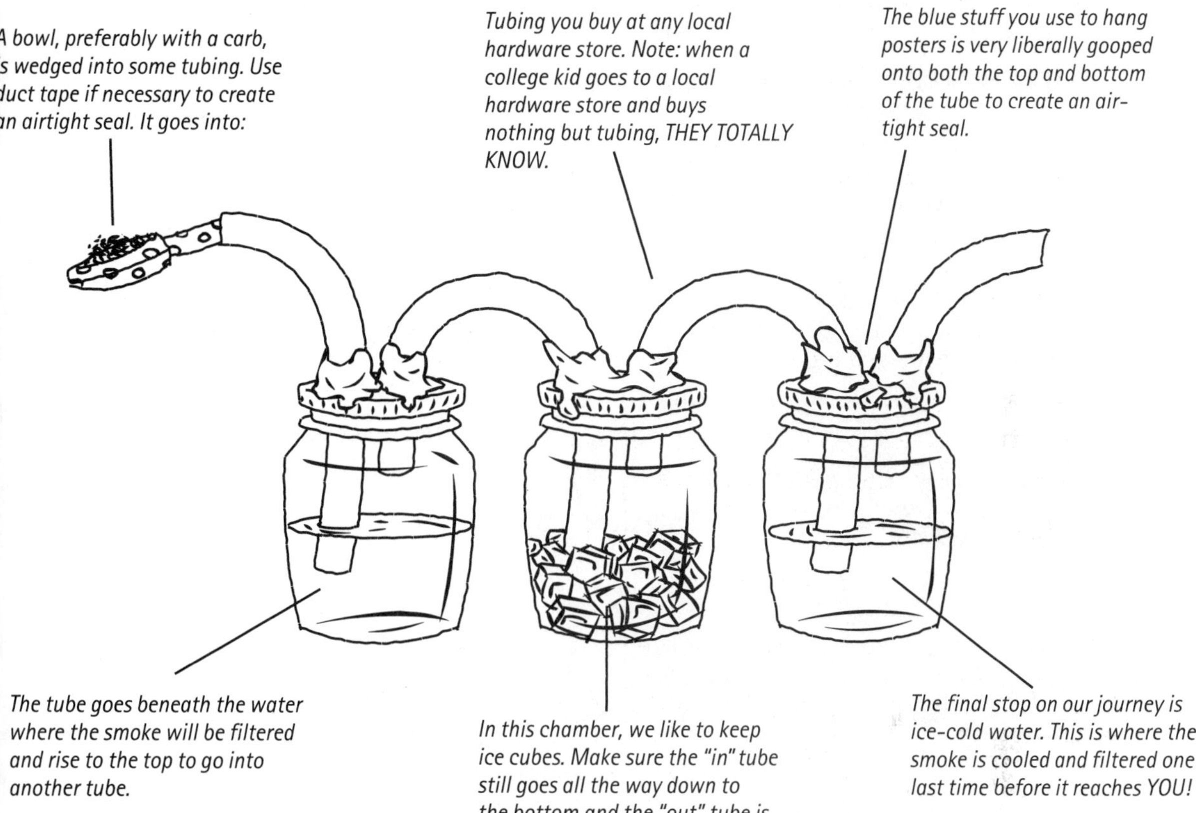

How to MacGyver a Pipe Out of Anything

Apple: Take a nice, firm apple. Grab the stem at the base and carefully rip it out. Using a skinny knife, dig out a nice little hole about halfway down. Clear the hole of gunk. Now make a similar hole, except this time horizontally.

A ballpoint pen: Remove the ink so all you have is a plastic cylinder. Wrap aluminum foil around one end and bend it up. Poke holes in aluminum foil to make a bowl. Use the other nine pens from the pack to write what you're thinking about.

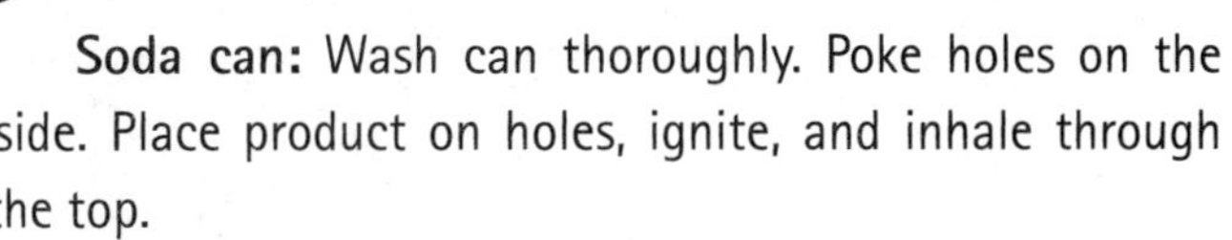

Soda can: Wash can thoroughly. Poke holes on the side. Place product on holes, ignite, and inhale through the top.

A roll of toilet paper: Dispose of toilet paper (possibly on the lawn of your sworn enemies). Poke a hole in the side, about three-quarters of the way down the tube. Put aluminum foil on top; poke some holes. Cover one end of the roll with anything. Smoke from the other.

Metal butter knives, an electric stove, and a plastic bottle: (Obvious warning: handling red-hot knives while inhaling drugs is dangerous.) Stick knives in coils of the electric stove. Heat until red hot. While you're waiting, take a tiny piece of finely ground product and put it in a tiny pocket of aluminum foil with holes poked in it. Now, when your knives are ready, squeeze the aluminum foil between the two pieces of metal you are wielding. Catch the vapor that rises with the top half of a milk bottle. When the bottle fills up, remove the cap and enjoy. Serves 2–3. Goes well with French fries.

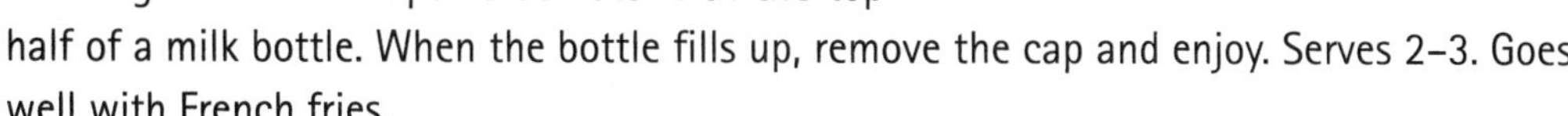

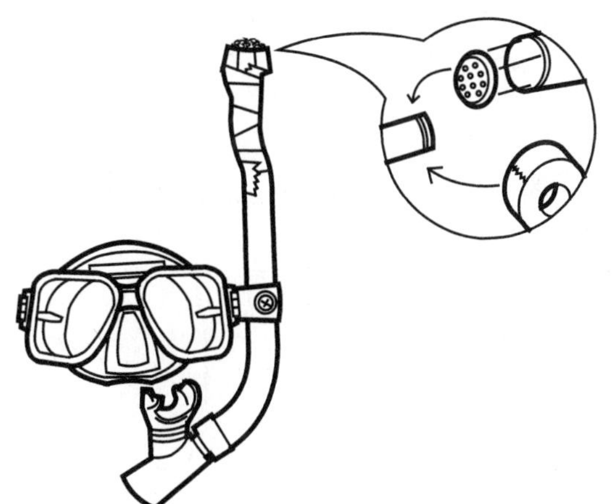

Snorkel: Take a saltshaker cap and turn it upside down. Put it in the top of the snorkel. Make the seal airtight with a liberal amount of duct tape. (Note: requires two people to operate, looks hilarious.)

An upside-down bong: Turn bong right side up. Proceed as usual.

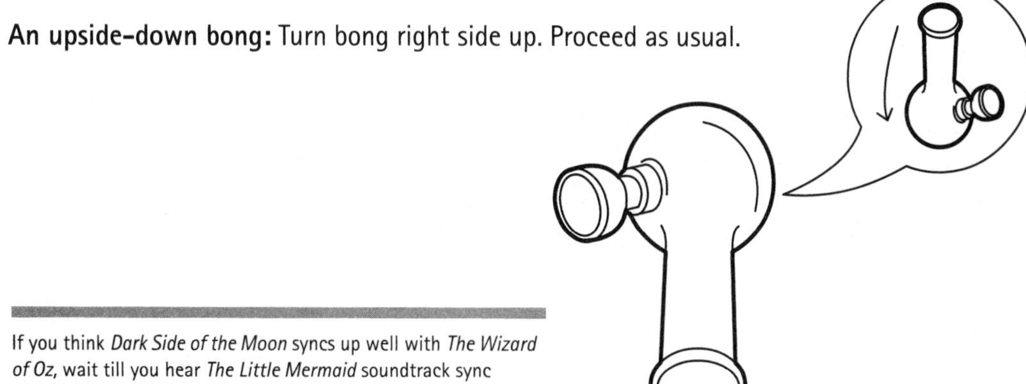

If you think *Dark Side of the Moon* syncs up well with *The Wizard of Oz,* wait till you hear *The Little Mermaid* soundtrack sync up with *The Little Mermaid.* Spot fucking on.

WANTED

JASON AKA "LET ME GET A HIT OF THAT"

DEAD OR ALIVE OR TIRED

Wanted for:
Inviting himself over
Mooching off your stash
Eating your Cheez-Its
Leaving as soon as he's baked

Description:
May claim to be "totally tapped for cash"
Pleasant demeanor so you won't get pissed
Laissez-faire attitude toward monetary policy

Reward:
A DVD my roommate burned of *Wizard of Oz* with the Pink Floyd album already dubbed over.

Pot Brownie Recipe

Pot brownies: they cause AND cure the munchies. A delicious paradox.

- 1 Boxed brownie mix—the most delicious you can find
- Whatever the little pictures on the back of the brownie box say you need
- ½ ounce of pot

Get a frying pan and heat the butter or the oil from the recipe to medium heat. Break up the pot, remove all stems, and place it into the simmering oil. Stir it around for five minutes. Let the oil/pot mixture cool, and filter out the pot through a strainer. Follow the brownie directions. Eat rapidly and wait for results. If your mouth gets a little dry, we recommend a tall glass of cocaine milk or heroin water.

Stoner Movie Guide

Unless you are a major, serious pussy, you are going to do drugs in college. We did. Lots of 'em. And when you're feeling the effects of psychotropic drugs, or "stoned," you're going to want to watch movies. We did. Lots of 'em. Allow us to recommend a few personal favorites for your viewing pleasure. Write these down, because you will probably forget them. And then write them down again because you're a stoner now and you'll probably forget where you wrote them down the first time.

<u>The Wall:</u> Pink Floyd, better known for their bloated, often pointless prog-rock, makes a bloated, often pointless animated movie about a totalitarian state.

Bongtacular: Great visuals, cartoons are neat, killer tunes. May instigate deep, hard-hitting conversations about why totalitarianism is sorta bad.
Buzzkill: Isn't actually, you know, good.

Half-Baked: Dave Chappelle and Jim Breuer combine comedic forces to chronicle the travails of a seamlessly interracial group of stoner friends.
Bongtacular: They're stoned, and so are you! Copying down their list of munchies word for word leads to delicious results.
Buzzkill: The impetus for drama is the painful and tragic death of a horse.

Cheech and Chong's Up in Smoke: The archetypal stoners your parents laughed at get stoned and, um, do some stuff. There are jokes.
Bongtacular: Cheech Marin's voice never gets any less funny. Feel a connection to the history of other stoners because, like, even right now is history to people in the future.
Buzzkill: There's an unconfirmed rumor that three Irishmen and five Chinese migrant workers died during the construction of the set for the railroad scene.

Spy Kids 3-D: The kids from *Spy Kids* attack an uncharted territory: THE THIRD DIMENSION.
Bongtacular: Watching a 3-D movie when you're stoned is like watching a 4-D movie when you're sober. So you can only imagine the power.
Buzzkill: Antonio Banderas is still in it. His three-dimensional hair and accent may just be too much.

Schindler's List: A noble gentile, Oskar Schindler, hires Jews to work in his factory during World War II.
Bongtacular: Let your mind fill in the color to this otherwise black-and-white movie!
Buzzkill: Over 6 million dead :(

Dealing with a Drug-Addict Roommate

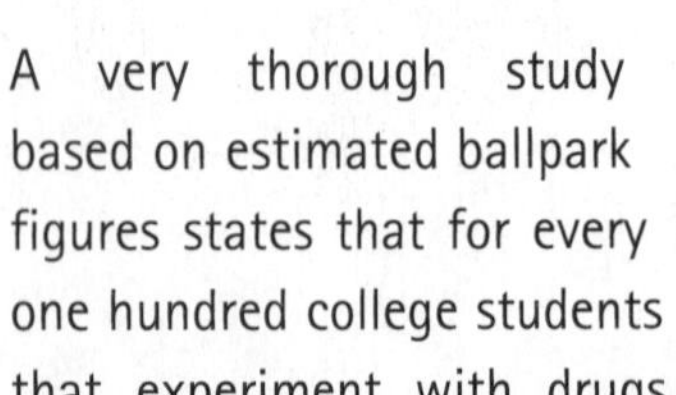
A very thorough study based on estimated ballpark figures states that for every one hundred college students that experiment with drugs, fifteen will become addicted.

Out of those fifteen, one will be seriously addicted. That one will be your roommate.

If your roommate is addicted to drugs, you basically have two options. You can either get him to seek professional guidance (boring!), or you can mess with him. Games such as Hide the Drugs and Watch Him Cry are usually a fun way to pass the time. You can send him fake e-mails from federal officials stating that a campus-wide raid is scheduled for "five minutes from now."

Other, more abrasive games, including Cut His Hair while He Sleeps and Blame It on the Tooth Fairy or even Replacing His Drugs with Grass and Sugar, are also humorous but can be quite dangerous.

Is this mean? Well, he should have thought about that before he bent up all of the spoons.

How to Spot Someone on Coke

Cocaine, once only available to your mom in the seventies, is now being used on college campuses across the country. Like crystal meth and cutting, cocaine is not an openly displayed hobby, so how will you know if your friend is a user and/or abuser?

Physical Signs

- "Jawing," or grinding of the teeth
- Excessive lip-licking, sweating, and running to the bathroom
- Rolled-up money stuffed in blood-caked nostril

Emotional Signs

- Ability to discuss the perils of U.S. military occupation in foreign lands . . . for six hours
- Deep, abiding love for fighting
- Deep, genuine desire to "get another bag"

So there you have it: if your friend displays any of these signs, you should contact someone immediately for another 8 ball before he freaks out and breaks a lamp.

Bagel Uses

Depending on what drug you're abusing, common objects can be used for many purposes. Take, for instance, a delicious poppy-seed bagel.

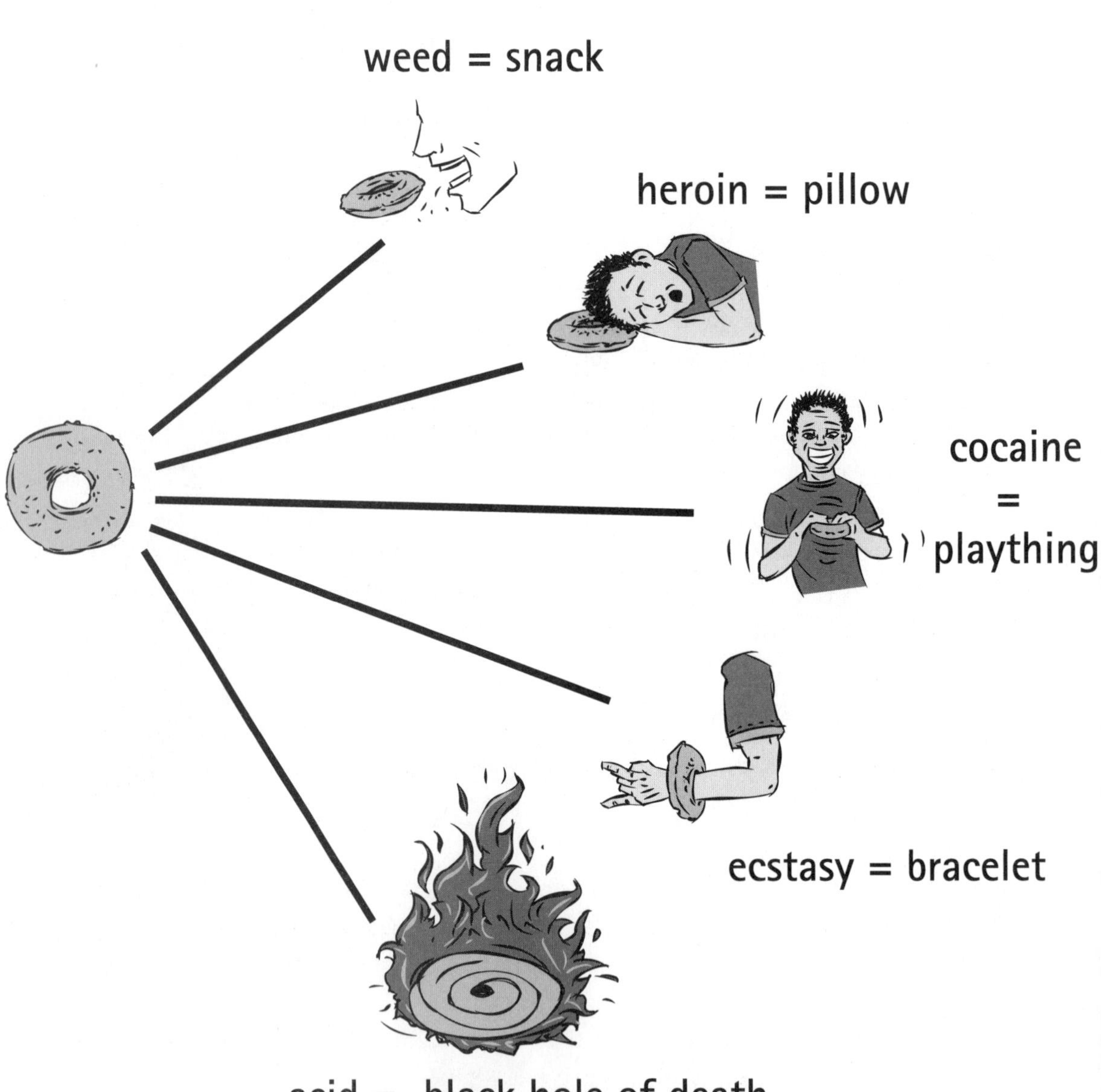

How to Beat a Drug Test

"Yo mama so stupid, she studied for a drug test!" Oh, yo mama, you just can't get a break.

But seriously, folks, you're going to have to take a drug test at some point. The whole point of these tests is that they catch you off guard and see if you have been using drugs. This practice may seem like it infringes upon your privacy, but there's probably no way that someone who smokes marijuana could be a contributing member of the Kinko's team. If you absolutely can't stop for a few days, it's time to make like your dad on a business trip and cheat!

The type of test you're taking dictates how you're going to cheat. Here's a quick run-through:

Hair Test: This test involves scanning your hair follicles for drugs. Unfortunately, your hair follicles have a much longer memory than you—up to six months. You might say, "Hey, I'll just shave my head," but they can use any hair on your body. Unless a full-body wax sounds good to you, you're kind of screwed. If a full-body wax does sound good to you, your fraternity brother's dad who got you this banking job can probably pull some strings in HR. There are also some shampoos on the market that claim to clean out your hair. However, the leading brand of this shampoo is offering a "200% satisfaction guarantee," so approach with caution.

Blood Test: Blood tests are generally only given for very serious or important positions. Try finding a friend who doesn't like drugs as much as you, and then replace all of your blood with his, only for a couple hours.

Urine Test: This one is the great scourge of adolescence, but it can be beaten like a disobedient redheaded wife who's also somebody's stepchild.

If you have a friend who's clean, just have him pee in an unlubricated condom. You have always wondered why they still make unlubricated condoms; it's not just because lots of guys can't come unless the woman's in serious physical pain. Tie it off at the end, slide it in your underwear, and let fly at the testing site. No one's going to watch you pee because they're afraid you'll think they're gay. Homophobia: the glue that holds America together!

If you know one of these tests is coming and can manage to tear yourself away from the cheeba for a week, there's a very good chance you can pass the test without having a friend pee in a condom. Make sure to drink lots of liquids to dilute your peepee. Every testing facility has a different threshold of what they consider a "drug user," so again, your mileage may vary.

If you don't have the slightest modicum of self-control, you can take your chances on a "urine cleaning kit" online or in a smoke shop. These kits can get expensive, and there's no guarantee that they work, but what else are you going to do? Stop smoking for a week? Yeah right, bro, you hit that herb twenty times a day.

H-Code

Here is a new drug making its way from Central America that will have colleges buzzing very soon. Invented in a small unnamed country, this drug combines the characteristics of marijuana, cocaine, heroin, and a Slurpee. The creator refers to it by a series of grunts, but America will soon embrace it as Herocodonkywanapee.

Herocodonkywanapee, or H-code for short, is a pill that is melted, then smoked, then the smoke is placed in a needle for you to inject into the bloodstream and, finally, drink.

Seems like a lot of effort? Well, so is murdering your dad for H-code money, but you're going to be doing that, too.

H-code is so extreme it should wear a cape. In fact, it does. The cape is purple. Early results showed that an H-code addict is able to eat a block of cocaine like cotton candy and feel no effects.

H-code is so strong it beat Sylvester Stallone circa 1984 in an arm-wrestling match. It didn't even need to go over the top. H-code is so addictive that just by reading this sentence, you are already addicted to H-code.

H-code is so powerful it is going to be three new elements on the periodic table very soon, all of which may very well replace hydrogen at number one. A mythological creature made entirely of kilos of heroin once tried H-code and said, "Damn. That's some strong shit." Then it exploded.

For students getting a little bored with "conventional drugs," help is finally on the way.

Note: H-code more than likely will kill you.

A Final Note on Drugs

Drugs, drugs, the musical fruit, the more you eat the more you may have a daily cough and phlegm, symptoms of chronic bronchitis, and frequent headaches. Damage to the brain caused by meth usage is similar to Alzheimer's disease, stroke, and epilepsy. Chronic meth use can cause violent behavior, anxiety, confusion, insomnia, auditory hallucinations, mood disturbances, delusions, and paranoia. Heroin use may cause collapsed veins, infection of the heart lining and valves, abscesses, liver disease, pulmonary complications, and various types of pneumonia. An overdose on heroin may cause slow and shallow breathing, convulsions, coma, and possibly death. There is growing evidence that chronic, heavy use of ecstasy is associated with sleep disorders; depressed mood; persistent elevation of anxiety, impulsiveness, and hostility; and selective impairment of episodic memory, working memory, and attention. Ecstasy users performed worse than control groups in complex tests of attention and memory, learning tasks, and tasks reflecting aspects of general intelligence. Marijuana may cause frequent respiratory infections, impaired memory and learning, increased heart rate, anxiety, panic attacks, greater and greater tolerance, and physical dependence.

So eat some drugs with every meal!

If you cough a lot when you smoke pot, say, "I've got more coughin' than a funeral home." This is especially ironic since you're going to die soon.

9 SEX AND DATING

Introduction

If you've ever seen a movie, read a book, or masturbated to a copy of *Ladies' Home Journal*, you're aware of how deeply sex permeates our society, and college is the pinnacle of sexual activity. In fact, you can't spell "college" without S-E-X, unless you want to spell "college" correctly.

College isn't all about sex, but it's at least 40 percent about sex. Remember, you're an adult now, so sex needs to be taken seriously and not thought of as something that's just done for fun or for making money on the Internet. You can't avoid sex in college, but you can control sex in college. Imagine you're Sonic the Hedgehog, and sex is like a ring. That's right, you need to collect as much sex as possible in order to defeat Dr. Robotnik. If you understand this analogy, you probably won't be having sex during college. That's a really nice Sega CD, though.

Never have sex on ecstasy. The pills are way too small to balance on.

In all seriousness, a lot of you may still be nervous about losing your v-cards. You remember the time you lost your pen and it wasn't a big deal? Losing your virginity is like that but more moist. There's no easy way to put this, but if you don't get laid in college, you are going to die one loveless son of a bitch. On the bright side, sitcoms are going to get so good in a few years, you won't even notice how lonely you are.

College sex comes in two varieties. The first is the kind that happens in loving relationships with people you're trying desperately to cheat on. The other, more important kind is the "hookup," which is slang for a brief sexual encounter that you really only do because you're lonely and want to impress your friends. That, and you love getting your dee-ock sucked.

The sexual imperative is clear: you should try to hook up with as many people as you possibly can while you're in college. If people tell you these hookups are emotionally vacuous and borderline nihilistic, tell them that ruining other people's fun isn't going to bring their puppy back to life. Don't feel bad when they cry; tears are the eyes ejaculating.

The more you hook up in college, the more fun you're going to have. The ideal hookup ends with one of two sentences: either the girl saying, "That was amazing," or the guy saying, "Hmmm . . . usually doesn't happen so fast. Weird. Sorry. Maybe we could try again next weekend?" Either way, somebody came, and that's all that's important. Mutually gratifying sex doesn't happen until after college.

When you're not just hooking up, you're probably dating someone. The most important part of dating is asking your friends, "You guys like her, right? You don't mind if I bring her along, do you?" Your friends will lie and say yeah, they like her, and yeah, you should bring her along. This is false. No guy has ever liked his buddy's girlfriend. If your friends could get away with it, they'd tie up your girlfriend and throw her on the next train to Zimbabwe. You should try to keep your girlfriend as far away from your buddies as possible. Your male friends will hate her, and your female friends will be jealous of that bitch.

But you . . . you're happy, right? I mean, yeah, you cheat on her every once in a while, but it doesn't really count, does it? Not if she doesn't know the girl, right? Well, if she knows the girl, but not very well? Well, if they were roommates, but they didn't get along very well? Yeah, this is really a gray area.

Finally, yes, buying condoms is embarrassing. However, you should probably use them. Saying, "We're in love; she won't get pregnant!" doesn't really count as a contraceptive; in fact, it's even less effective than not pulling out. We would say that if you're still embarrassed buying condoms, you're not mature enough to have sex. However, this would imply

---

If your girlfriend holds out on you, tell her that if you wanted to come every four years, you'd be in the Olympics. She'll remind you that they now have Olympics every two years. Then she'll dump you.

that no one is mature enough to have sex until they're too old and senile to realize how awkward this purchase is. Instead, just steal your roommate's—he took that enormous handful at freshman orientation and loudly said, "I'll put these to good use!" Turns out that good use was sitting in his sock drawer, untouched for six semesters. Nice work, stud.

Dorm Fire Drills

Dorm fire drills are a meat market. We've been saying this for years but have yet to see anybody actually take this advice to heart. The absolute best place in college to pick up girls isn't the bar or classroom; it's outside your dorm during a fire drill. Think about it this way: everybody (and every body) at a fire drill is usually cold. Their instincts are telling them they need to find warmth in some form. Why not have it be you? Keep an extra jacket handy in your room for late night fire drills, then a few minutes into it, find a cute girl, tell her that you thought she looked cold, and offer it to her.

Furthermore, at a fire drill, there's an instant conversation piece: you're both unhappy that you're standing outside in your pajamas. Pajamas? Even better—you're already dressed for bed. As the fire drill ends, you've just had a good conversation with her, she's wearing your jacket, and you're both walking in the general direction of your dorm. Now all you have to do is tell her you're going to make some ramen noodles and warm up and ask her if she wants to join you. The deal is done.

It's Just a Little Crush

By this point, you've probably chosen a crush. It could be a cute dude in your Spanish class or a hot sophomore in your dorm. The important thing now is making a plan to win his/her heart and his/her attentions.

If you have a mutual friend, just mention in passing no more than twice that you think your crush is pretty cool and you'd like to hang out. Only say it once or twice, though, so your mutual friend will just think you're kind of interested and not infatuated. The rest should pretty much take care of itself.

If you're going to have sex in a girl's parents' house, you need some cover noise. May we suggest a porno turned up really loud?

If you don't have a mutual friend, you're going to have to be more creative. This may sound like "stalking," but so does the word "stocking," and nobody complains about that. Some great ways to approach her include "accidentally" always sitting next to her in class (don't you dare get an erection). Make casual small talk before class; everyone always gets a good laugh out of the pre-class "So, you come here often?"

Progress to note passing. Girls love notes, be they F# or "Do you like me? Check yes or no." It is of paramount importance that the "Yes" box be noticeably larger and more inviting than the "No" box.

If you don't have class with your crush, find out where they live and literally bump into them each time they leave their room. As soon as your shoulders bump, always remember to say, "We have got to stop RUNNING into each other!" Laugh as loudly as you can. It might be a good idea to grab her ass and whisper "Is it fate?" before running away into oncoming traffic. Your odds of winning your crush's heart are now 7:2.

It's time to seal the deal. After some close encounters of the nerd kind, you're going to have to be cool in your crush's presence. Try talking on a really small cell phone in front of her, referring to "deals" that you look forward to "closing." End every fake conversation with, "Make it happen." Congratulations, you're now important enough to fuck.

True College Stories—The Magic of Dates, by Ethan

You're probably never going to make the NBA. You're probably never going to be an astronaut. You're probably never going to win a Skittles-eating contest at the state fair (those things have gotten so commercial anyway). However, with God as my witness, I am here to tell you that you can hook up with almost any girl you choose. You have a secret weapon in your arsenal, and you can use it to ensnare any young lady you'd like. What is this magic bullet, you ask?

Asking girls out on dates. Its success rate is so high that it's like legal, consensual rape.

I don't know why it works. I think it could have something to do with girls being impressed that you have the self-confidence/balls to approach them while potentially setting yourself up for rejection. Here's the thing, though: you won't get rejected. Unless a girl has a boyfriend, she will never, ever, ever say no. You've put yourself out there, and she's duly impressed. Even if she's a complete bitch, she will say yes 98 percent of the time. Any girl

Try as you might, there's nothing helpful about a morning-after condom.

who rejects you in this setting is obviously a black-hearted slut who doesn't warrant a second thought. Way to pick a shitty crush, dude. Your mom was right: you're a terrible judge of character.

Another reason why asking girls out on dates is so effective is that most girls have never been asked on a date. It sounds ridiculous, but pay attention. Every other guy at your school's preferred method of meeting girls is getting drunk at parties and hooking up with them. After six or seven bouts of nakedness and maybe one trip to Wendy's, he and his special girl are a couple without ever having gone on a date. Every girl wants to go on a date, though, and you look like some kind of knight dressed in white satin as you gallantly offer to buy her dinner.

She will say yes, and now you've just got to worry about the date itself. Honestly, you really have to try pretty hard to screw up this situation. Just tailor the date to your specific strengths. If you can't dance, steer clear of clubs or entering back-alley dance-offs. If you sweat a lot like I do, you should try your hand at a meat-locker date. Just lock the door, look her deeply in the eyes, and say, "Any of these sides of beef can be yours, angel." Furthermore, anything involving a chain restaurant will probably ensure that the only moist thing your fingers get into is the sour cream on your Chili's quesadilla. Movies are also a bad choice due to their lack of conversational opportunities and increasing reliance on Vin Diesel in leading roles.

Ideally, you should go to dinner somewhere quiet and quirky, and when you get there, the most important thing to remember is to never talk about yourself. No matter how egomaniacal you are, do not mention yourself, even in passing. If she says something like, "Isn't your hair on fire?" respond coolly with, "Eh, I don't really like to talk about myself. Say, what's your favorite book? You can do a top five if it's too hard to choose." Keep asking her questions about herself. Even when you don't care. I once spent an entire date listening to an impassioned monologue about the Powerpuff Girls. I got bored, but I also got a hand job. Sure, a hand job is no big prize, but you have to scale down your expectations when you ask out a ninth grader.

Not talking about yourself may be the most clutch part of the whole date-asking-out theory. You've proven that you're secure and self-confident by having the gumption to ask her out, but you've shown you're not self-obsessed and cocky by asking her lots of questions about herself. You've given her a reason to brag to her friends about going on a date. She will be off her guard because she's not used to this weird situation; you'll have drinks with

Guys, don't let her fool you that the vibrator is "just part of the fun." The other part of the fun is dumping you.

dinner, and then you'll retire to one of your places and make strange acquaintance love that usually involves someone saying, "I barely know you. . . . You're clean, right?"

Still don't believe me? In college, I had tragic sideburns and glasses that would fog up whenever I sweated. I didn't watch very much TV, so I had absolutely no pop-culture chitchat ready for these dates. I would just ask girls out in random places, like class or in line at Target, and they would invariably say yes. On the dates, I would mostly eat, make a huge mess out of my food because I'm a slob, and ask girls questions about their childhoods and their interests. Once you go out on two of these dates, you'll realize that the respective answers to those questions are, "My dad and I don't really get along" and, "I'm just really artsy." Then I'd end up naked in my bed saying, "No, I don't mind if you sleep here, but I get up really early. Yeah, maybe you're right. I'll get your coat."

There is only one context in which asking girls out on dates won't work. If you are a douche bag, you should just try to hook up with girls at parties and hope to stumble into a relationship that way. How can you tell if this douche bag is you? Do you have an armband tattoo? Did you wear flip-flops to the last funeral you attended because you "gotta keep it stylin' "? If so, don't ask girls out on dates. You can't get away with it. If, however, you're a normal guy who can listen and not use the word "fingerblast" on the date itself, you will definitely get to third base.

No Hugging Rule, by Jake

Boys meet girls at parties and try to hook up with the drunk ones. Men take girls out to dinner, one on one. It takes more effort, but the payoff is higher: you might be able to bang her dozens of times over the course of weeks, instead of just one sloppy, drunk time. But unless she's hornier than a rhino factory, it's unrealistic to expect her to spend the night on the first date. So instead, prepare yourself for The First Good-bye: the incredibly tense, often awkward end of the first date. This is the point where both your minds are racing, but externally you're "playing it cool." You probably have no idea what she's thinking, and as you clumsily wrap things up with small talk, two conclusions emerge: "Either she's going to hug me or she's going to kiss me." And here's our point: DO NOT ACCEPT A HUG.

Everyone knows why hugs from girls are fun: they thrust their breasts into you as if they

"How do you know YOU didn't give it to ME?" is not the best defense when your girlfriend asks if you got her pregnant.

don't even notice. In truth, they notice but don't care. It's so meaningless to them, and they know you love it, so it becomes a little consolation prize (noun: prize that makes a loser feel as though he has "won" by giving him something of insignificant value). By making you accept this consolation prize, she is exerting control over you and literally making you her bitch.

Grow some nuts. If she opens her arms and leans in for a hug, hold out your hand for a shake. This is your way of saying, "Oh no you don't." She's not getting out of this that easily. "If you're not going to kiss me, I'd rather just shake your hand." BOOM! You now have either preserved your dignity (handshake) or made serious progress toward getting your boner mopped (kiss).

If a girl didn't like you, she didn't like you. Do you think she's somehow planning to kiss you on the second date? Be honest with yourself. At that rate you would be having sex in the year three thousand. You would get laid faster dating a married Mormon.

True College Story—Dating Advice, by Streeter

When I was in college, I had tons of hot girls that wanted a relationship with me. It was so hard to pick just one that I had to call my dad for advice. "Dad," I said, "what should I do? There are so many of them."

"Don't worry," my dad said. "Here's a trick that's been in our family for centuries. It's called the blow-out test. All these girls are hot right now, but what about later? Have you thought of that?" I hadn't. "Listen, boy, all you need to do is look at the girl's mother and whoever has the hottest one, she's your girl. It's as easy as that." My dad is a genius, which is probably why he just got a promotion to ASSISTANT MANAGER at Walgreens.

Types of College Relationships

Whether you want to admit it or not, the truth is that at some point in your college career you are going to wake up and realize that you have entered some sort of relationship arrangement. If you're like most college kids, chances are your relationship will fit into one of these broadly generalized categories:

The Denial

Dating Stats: Hooking up since move-in day freshman year

How to tell if this is you: You go home with the same person every other night, but when your friends ask what's up with you two, you're "just fucking." "Just fucking dating" is more like it!

The Dominant and Submissive

Dating Stats: Six months, but it feels like 6 million

How to tell if this is you: When your girlfriend tells you to jump, you build a trampoline . . . out of your own skin.

The Distant Lovers

Dating Stats: Decided to "give this a try" right before leaving for college

How to tell if this is you: You have a five-figure phone bill and swear you "love her to death," despite the occasional blow job from that girl in your Econ class—supply and da' man!

The Exhibitionists

Dating Stats: One month, but you've been having sex for almost a year now

How to tell if this is you: You've either (a) gotten a hand job in class or (b) been asked to "please put your underwear back on" by someone in the library, over the loudspeaker

The Old Souls

Dating Stats: Been dating since the fifth-grade museum field trip when you sat in the back of the bus together

How to tell if this is you: If you are celebrating your ten-year anniversary in college

The Dreamer

Dating Stats: She met you on the Internet last week and it was love at first (web)site.

How to tell if this is you: If you doodle her screenname with your last name after it

---

Even though I never wear condoms, my doctor says I'm still safe from STDs because I also never have sex.

How to Act in a Relationship

Gallant's actions make his girlfriend proud.

Goofus's actions make his girlfriend want to kill herself.

"Let me help you with your coat."

"I can't believe you forgot your fucking coat!"

Gallant celebrates his anniversary in style.

Goofus celebrates his anniversary . . . barely.

"I'm sorry, honey, I'm just so drunk!"

"I'm sorry, honey, I'm just so drunk!"

Ribbed for her pleasure? Be a man and turn it inside out for your pleasure.

Relationship Myths

"On a break"

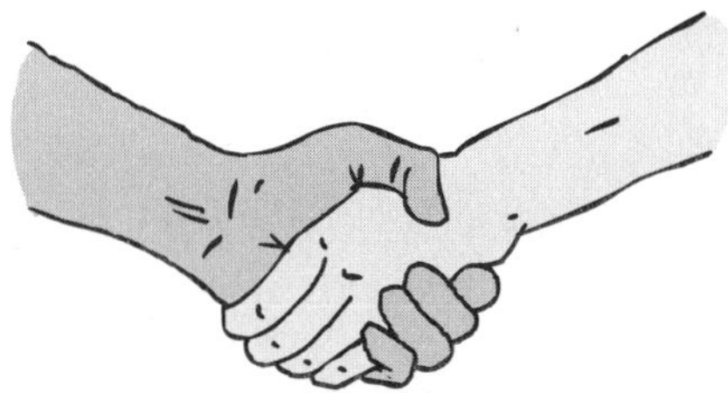

What you think will happen: You and your girlfriend will take a pleasant, temporary hiatus from your relationship, preferably over an opportune week such as Thanksgiving or Spring Break. Upon your return, no questions will be asked, things will go back to normal, and your relationship can continue as planned.

What actually will happen: You'll go on Spring Break with your buddies, have sex with a couple hot locals, no big deal. When you come home, you'll hear that your girlfriend drunkenly made out with some dude. "It was a mistake!" she'll plea. Yell back, "The only mistake was trusting a SLUT like you!"

"Open relationship"

What you think will happen: You'll be in a relationship but also be able to hook up with anyone else you want at the same time.

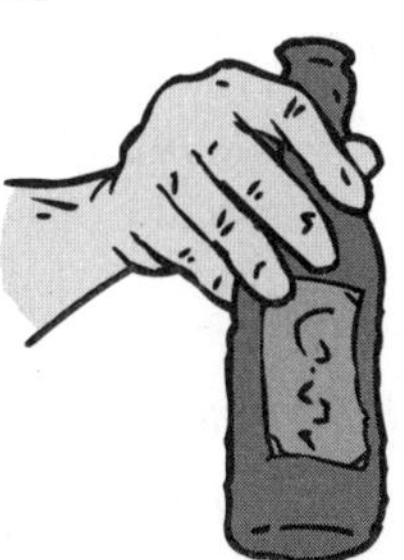

What actually will happen: Apparently the term "anyone" excludes all of your girlfriend's sorority sisters, hallmates, old roommates, freshman-year friends, and anyone she's ever had a class with or is planning on having a class with in the future. Which basically leaves a few random fat chicks and that girl who brags about having herpes. Meanwhile, she's banging your RA.

"Committed relationship"

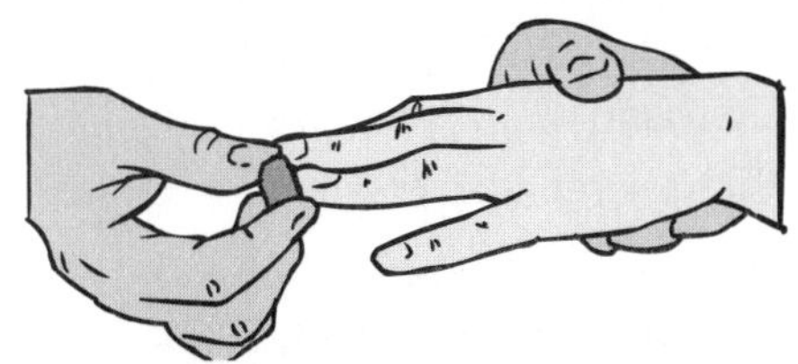

What you think will happen: You've found that one person who really makes you happy, and you're going to stay faithful to them as long as they'll have you.

What actually will happen: Except that hot chick is totally hitting on you. It would be adulterous NOT to go for it!

If your RA asks you what that blowtorch is for, tell her it's a DVD burner. The great thing is, you're not even lying!

The Process

There are two ways to get with a girl. The first involves drugs purchased at a Mexican pharmacy, and the other is "The Process." It's not illegal yet, but it should be. It's that good. It's like a really good pyramid scheme that ends with your hands smelling like a fisherman's.

To make this happen, you need to be more or less alone with the girl, and she needs to not have a problem with you. So don't try The Process on a girl who's already rejected you for being too much of an asshole, because you're just going to make me look bad.

1. Ask her if she wants a backscratch. After you ask, immediately say, "Is that a word?" and laugh at how cute you are.
2. Start lightly scratching. It's almost impossible to do it too lightly. If she starts getting red marks, you're doing it too hard. If there are all these bits of pus and dried-out skin accumulating under your nails, grab a girl who's alive instead.
3. Start accentuating the fact that wearing a shirt doesn't do the scratching justice. This can be accomplished by scratching extra poorly where her skin is covered and amazingly well where it's exposed.
4. Inch the shirt up a bit, hopefully to the point where it's all bunched up by her breasts. She shouldn't feel too naked at this point, but she might feel slightly uneasy if you're moving fast. Distract her by scratching her arms.
5. After some patience-trying, get her shirt off. A line like "Let's get this out of the way" would help, but I'm not about to put words in your mouth. Emphasizing the importance of scratching under the still-covered area will help you get the job done.
6. Undo the bra, pussy.
7. Coast for a little while, making nice chatter about what makes you happy. Don't get into your theories on a more efficient capitalism that embodies a significant number of moderate socialist principles. Just be like, "I know. Lying out on a blanket at the beach is nice." When the time is right, say something that has the effect of, "When you're ready, you can turn over." This is probably the most crucial part of The Process—saying this line just right. Make it sound as close to the opposite of urgent as possible.

We think a funny thing to do when you have an obvious boner showing through your pants is to walk into a room full of people, shuffle some things around for a few minutes, and then, with a frustrated look on your face, exclaim, "Hey, has anybody seen a boner around here?"

8. Don't squeeze the breasts. Continue scratching lightly, focusing especially on the one crucial area between and above her boobs. Don't dwell on any one area, though. Keep going into unexpected places, like her neck and face, her arms, her sides, and her femur. BONE JOKE!

9. Now she's obviously comfortable with being a little naked around you, but there's still the matter of the triangle of hair. Begin casually scratching the area that's directly underneath the elastic on her underwear. This ring has been pressing in on her hips from all sides since she got dressed, and could probably use some fingernailing. Do it lightly, as you have been the whole time.

10. If you've gotten into her panties, even a little, there's no stopping. Your hand is in her underwear, which is the only thing she's wearing, and you've been treating her like a goddess for the better half of an hour. And it all started with a backscratch.

Congratulations, you're on the road to loneliness through an unending string of emotionally vacant but moderately validating hookups! Now go meet a nice girl, get married, then divorce right when things start looking good and permanent, and repeat the process!
To summarize:

1. Offer a backscratch.
2. Make it so good she has to take off her shirt, then bra.
3. Let her know she can turn over when she's ready.
4. Make her feel good about her breasts.
5. Relieve the stress caused by overly tight panties.
6. Finger her / get a beej / go down on her / have sex / etc.
7. Get her pregnant.
8. "It can't be mine . . . you can't be pregnant."
9. Ask your mom if she'll take care of it.
10. Repeat steps 1–9 until too old to maintain erections or consciousness.

Ladies, if your shorts have something written on the ass, it should be either "Slut" or "Give me attention." You'd need a big ass for that second one.

Condom Advice

Dear CollegeHumor,

My boyfriend and I have started having sex. We are each other's first, so it's definitely been a learning experience for us both. We think it's time to start using birth control because we saw something on TV or some shit.

What do you do?

Responsible in Rochester

Responsible,

Condoms are definitely the best choice for preventing unwanted babies. When you finish having sex, be sure to have your boyfriend turn the condom inside out, and use the clean side next time. Pulling out can be effective, but keep in mind that it's only effective when performed within the first minute after ejaculation. After that point, as any doctor will tell you, it's only about 80 percent effective. Although that sounds like pretty good odds, it means that for every five times you have sex, one baby will be born. And with the average couple having sex three to four times a week, you can expect around thirty-six babies in the first year alone. Even though that's only a small fraction of the earth's population, it can still amount to several hours of responsibility each day. Even tending to twelve or thirteen babies can start to seem less like a hobby and more like a chore if your heart isn't in it. Try starting with just two.

Love,

CollegeHumor

Do, Dump, or Marry is a real easy game when your three choices are: a supermodel, a pile of garbage, and your spouse.

SEXILE ROOMMATE CONTRACT

This sexiling contract becomes effective on move-in day and is between______ and______.

Both parties have come to college ostensibly to learn, but furthermore to get laid. THEREFORE, it is agreed that the undersigned agree to be considerate with respect to privacy when sex is a possibility.

1. TERMS

1. Each of the undersigned may request privacy in the shared living quarters (hereafter "dorm room") a maximum of ten (10) times per 10-week semester with a maximum of two times per week. Heretofore, this shall known as "sexiling." Any overnight sexiling shall count twice against the semester total. Furthermore, it is agreed:

2. THE SEXILER'S OBLIGATIONS:

A. To give a clear signal; be it by sock on the doorknob, Post-it, text message, or predetermined whiteboard code.
B. To refrain from causing permanent damage to the room, particularly with regard to the sexilee's bed.
C. Thoroughly cleaning any stray fluids.
D. To reward the sexiled party for his trouble. For females this can include the promise of laundry, presents, quality time, or other favors. For males this can include such perks as not insulting the sexiled party's girlfriend's teeth.

3. SEXILED PARTY'S RIGHTS

A. The sexiled party shall receive one "veto" per semester, hereafter known as the "dude, are you blind?" clause.
B. A clear time for the guest's departure will be negotiated and agreed upon before sexilation begins.
C. If one party is consistently sexiled, but never a sexiler, he shall receive no compensation for his trouble. The onus shall be upon him to not be a pussy.

4. LIMITATIONS

A. There is to be no sexiling during the periods known as "finals," "midterms," or when an important paper is due.
B. No party may be awoken from slumber to be sexiled. The sexiler may proceed with the sex, but if the potential sexiled party is awoken, he shall be given full watching and whistling privileges.

5. OTHER

A. If one party exceeds their sexile quota, some sort of reimbursement, such as alcohol or chicken wings, can be negotiated beforehand.
B. If the sexiler brings home two "guests," all previous rules are off. Any decent roommate should be happy to make whatever sacrifice is necessary to facilitate this scenario, but he or she shall be reimbursed with graphic details.
C. If both parties request sexilation on the same night, the party with the hotter partner gets first dibs. If the hotter guest cannot be decided, the roommate with the top bunk gets preference. If there are no bunk beds, a simple coin toss shall decide which of the undersigned will receive sexiling privileges and which will be complaining for years to come.

Roommate Signature________________________ **Date:** ____________

Roommate Signature________________________ **Date:** ____________

How to Make Breakfast for a Hookup

Throw her out, you pussy. Add parsley for garnish. Serves 2.

The Walk of Shame

As the sun rises over college campuses across the nation and sheds light on last night's moral discrepancies, there is one pseudo-athletic event that permeates the morning dew and provides entertainment for the male onlookers: the Walk of Shame. As sunlight seemingly smokes these ladies out of their holes (male dorm rooms), they are seen scampering about, carrying the sins of a raucous drunken night on their shoulders and a bundle of party clothes in their arms. They keep their eyes on the floor because they can't bear to look at others noticing their modern-day scarlet letters.

But that doesn't mean you shouldn't go outside and play the Walk of Shame scavenger hunt game! Spot these ten items first and win a waffle!

- A girl with smeared or running eye makeup
- A girl stumbling in her high heels
- A senior girl coming out of a freshman dorm
- A girl crying
- A girl trying to avoid someone she knows
- A girl wearing any theme-related clothing (French maid, nurse, etc.)
- A girl with her head down, walking quickly past a tour group of prospective students
- A girl missing a piece of clothing (shoe, bra, sock, etc.)
- Two Walk o' Shamers passing in opposite directions, giving each other the "Nod of Shame"
- A guy in his boxers, walking tall and proud, waving to random passersby and smiling

---

You know that girl your buddy says was a real freak in bed? She didn't like rough sex; she just glowed in the dark.

CollegeHumor's Guide to the Bases

Elementary School

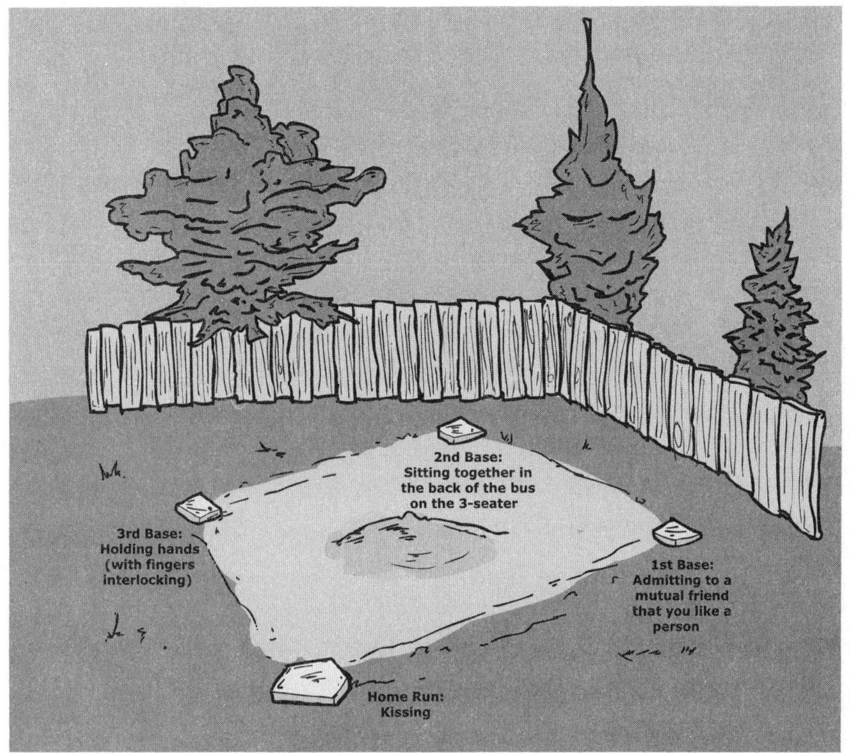

Worst English-Class Pickup Line: "I'd like to get my Dickens her."

High School

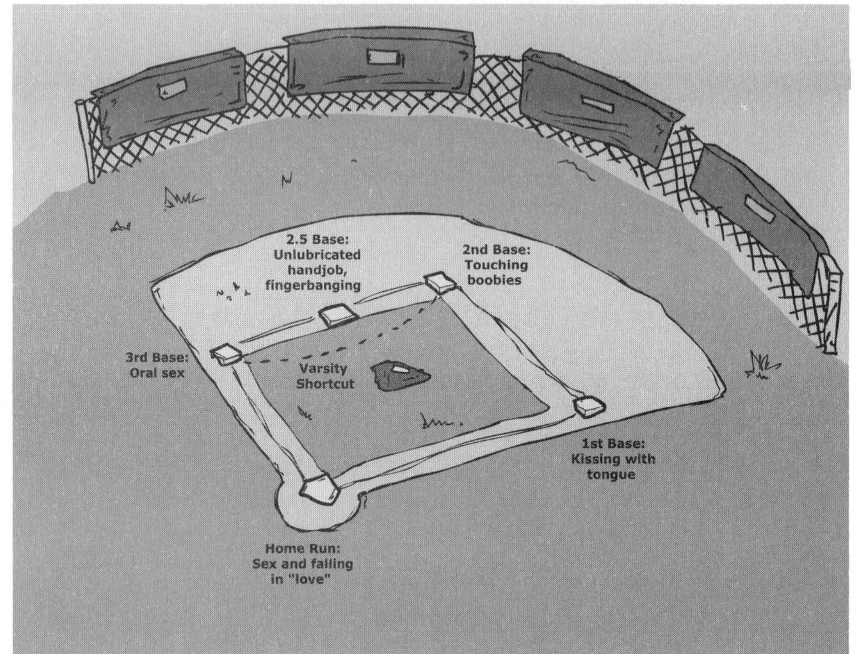

College

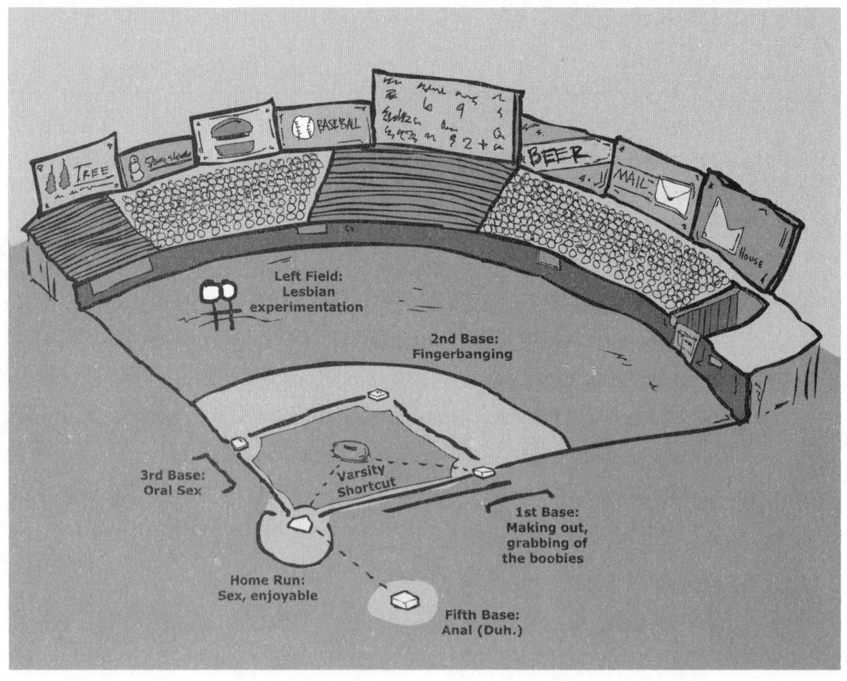

How to Give a Great Hand Job

1. Use your mouth.

How to Find the Clitoris

Avoiding Flatulence During Mating

Every relationship involves a little farting. You're going to let one go in front of a partner eventually; it's just a matter of time. Still, you are definitely going to want to catch her before she catches you. That way you'll have something on them. "No, honey, I never fart. You're gross. But I'll stay with you anyway." Point—you.

The road to not farting begins with preparation. If you were a boxer, would you eat a one-pound taco before you got in the ring? Of course

---

Sign #432 you're not going to get laid: She says, "We should probably watch the deleted scenes now."

not, so why would you eat greasy foods before hanging out with your girl? Certain foods, known as "magical fruits," are notorious for causing gas. If you can avoid them for twelve hours before you're ready to actually take off your pants with someone, you can save yourself a lot of trouble. The general rule of thumb is to avoid carbohydrate-heavy foods such as pasta or potatoes. Other troublesome foods include asparagus, milk, carrots, onions, and any snack that ends with an "itos." It also wouldn't hurt to chew thoroughly for once.

If it's too late or your intimate session with that special someone has come up unexpectedly, your first line of defense is the clinch. If you're lucky and don't give your gas anywhere to go, after a time it will simply recede into your body, where it will travel up your bloodstream to be later released as bad words. Problem solved, motherfucker.

What if it's not going anywhere? You can try to bide your time until it passes, but this is often a losing battle. Try to avoid bringing your legs any closer than ninety degrees to your stomach. Remember Rachel Bergen and the sit-up test blowout in high school?

Once you are in physical pain, you'll need to reconsider your options. If you let it build up, you may be doing yourself more harm than good. What you're going to want to do is let it creep out like a gentleman. It won't cover up a smell, but you may still have a chance to blame it on someone else. Use controlled bursts and hope that your companion will adhere to such a strict "Whoever smelt it dealt it" precedent that she may start to consider the possibility that she did indeed deal it.

If it's just you and your friends for a night, reverse all the above advice for hilarious results.

SO YOU'VE DECIDED TO Suck Your Own Dick

"Stupid dick! I wish I could just suck you myself!" Well, now you can.

What you need: Your dick, practice, a "#1 Playa' " hat

What you do: You're going to need to surgically remove a few ribs to make this even scientifically possible, but that shouldn't stop you. Rib removal is easy and often fun. After your rib cage has been reduced to a fraction of its old self, it's time to break your neck and spine. Don't let the pain stop you; this is totally worth it. After nearly breaking yourself in three rather important locations, obtain an erection, bend yourself toward your genitals, and begin sucking on your own dick. All done? Put on that "#1 Playa' " hat. You've earned it, stud.

Dorm Sex Acrobatics: Use That Crossbar!

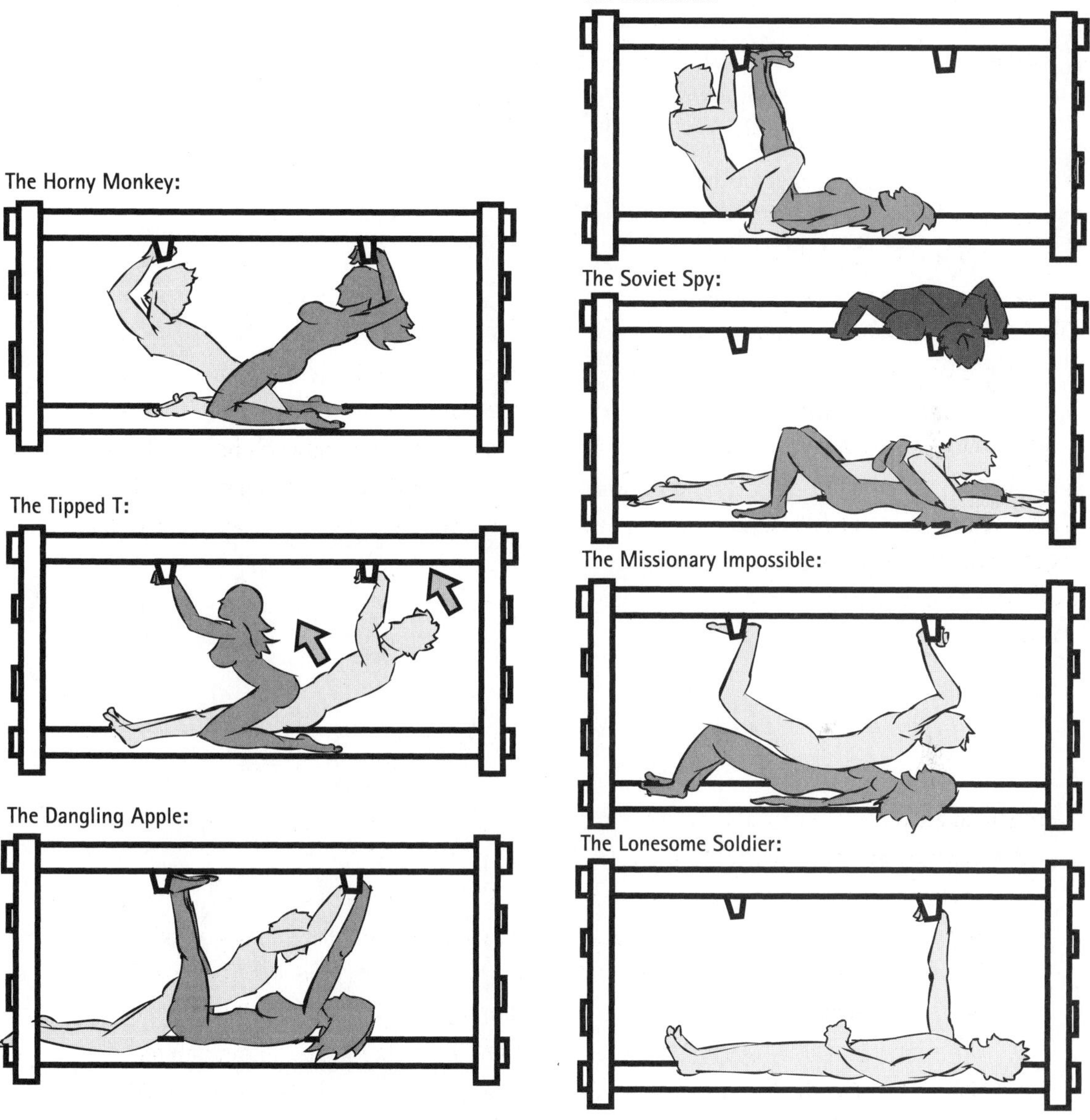

We had this great pickup line to use in the campus post office: "Hey, baby, wanna get some campus male?" In retrospect, it's only funny when it's written down.

If Your Dorm Bed Could Talk

I've been a bed all over this crazy world. I've been in the work camps of Siberia, barracks in 'Nam, and for the last twenty-five years, a dorm bed at this college. And let me tell you, you are the biggest pussy I've ever seen.

In Hanoi, men would wet their pants just to feel again. You do it for seemingly no reason at all.

You think you've made girls come, but you haven't. I've been around long enough to hear the difference between sympathy moaning and real moaning. You're getting sympathy moaning. But hey, nice egg crate, college boy.

Some years, I get a real stud in here, but you spend all night jerking off and talking dirty to yourself. I'm rocking so hard I can barely breathe at night. I try to pretend that I'm on a boat, but the waves in the real ocean don't say "Fuck my ass" as they break. Yeah, I seen some shit.

If you're not a fan of second dates, we recommend a strict policy of offering to arm wrestle for the check. Also we recommend kicking ass at it.

Your College Newspaper Takes on Sex

Every single college in America (and four in Europe) has a crappy newspaper run by wannabe Woodwards and Bernsteins. And every crappy college newspaper has a sex column written by an overtly slutty idiot trying her best to sound like Carrie Bradshaw.

Sex Column: Sluttin' It Up

By Jane Green

Something really weird happened the other night. I was naked in bed with this hottie and we were rubbing on each other. All of a sudden I feel it, like, slip in, kinda. So I go, "Are you in?" and he goes, "Yeah, is that cool?" I think about it for a minute – the dude looked a little dirty – and I go, "No, take it out." Then I blew him. But later I'm thinking, "Did I have sex or not? I've decided that, no, I didn't have sex, I had what I like to call a "stick-in." It's an easy way to talk yourself out of feeling like a slut. This has been Jane Green and I'll see you at the clinic!

STD Guide

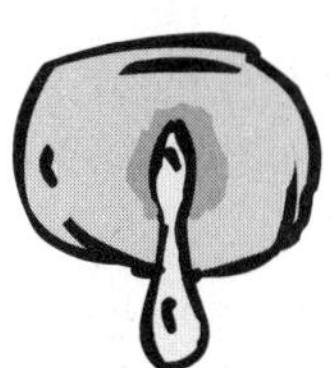

Chlamydia

Also Known As: Chlams Casino

Symptoms: Inflammation of the urethra (peehole), puslike discharge

Treatment: Short course of antibiotics

Lighter Side: Completely treatable. Most common STD, so it will help you fit in with friends.

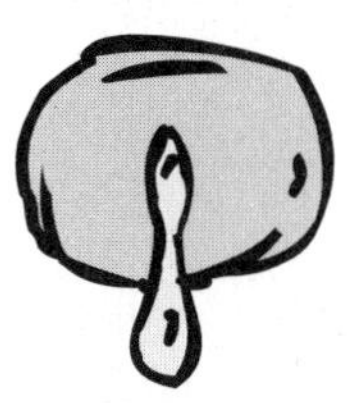

Gonorrhea

Also Known As: The Clap, the Drip, the Glete

Symptoms: Discharge, burning, bad conscience

Treatment: Antibiotics

Lighter Side: Look at all those hilarious nicknames! Plus, your father probably had it at some point.

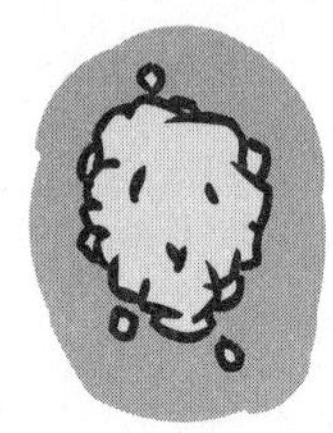

Syphilis
Also Known As: The Pox, Worst Birthday Present Ever
Symptoms: Painless lesion on penis; dementia if left untreated
Treatment: Antibiotics, denial
Lighter Side: It turns you yellow like you're on *The Simpsons.* "D'oh! It burns when I pee!"

Genital Warts
Also Known As: Mom's Little Secret
Symptoms: Having warts on your genitals. Duh. Can get "giant genital warts" called Buschke-Lowenstein tumors
Treatment: Burn/cut off/acid solutions
Lighter Side: Your urologist may be hot!

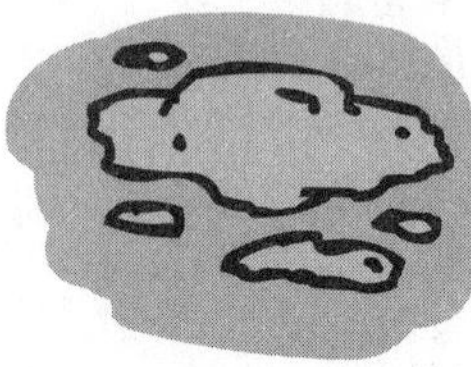

Genital Herpes
Also Known As: Your new best friend for life, more permanent than marriage
Symptoms: Painful sores on the mouth, vagina, and anus
Treatment: Thanks to Paxidil, I've got my outbreaks under control and I'm taking back my life. Remember, Paxidil is not a cure for genital herpes and it may be possible to spread herpes to others while taking Paxidil. Do not take if you are nursing, pregnant, or have tested positive for the AIDS virus. Paxidil is not for everyone, so consult your doctor.
Lighter Side: The Anal Sores would be a great name for a hard-core band.

Single-Parent College Experience

Wow, you've really ruined your life. Just kidding! You've only sort of ruined your life. College is already tough, and having a baby doesn't make it any easier. Here are some handy tips for surviving college while being a good parent:

- A standard backpack will hold a one- to three-month-old infant. You might want to leave it slightly unzipped at the top to let air and light in, but this step is completely optional.
- If you're a guy, people will throw the word "deadbeat" around if you consider leaving

your child. Eh, you can just change your name when you get to the pure, cleansing snows of Norway.

- Baby food on a college budget? Don't think so. Instead, get dining hall food and put it in a blender. Ninety percent of baby geniuses start their day with a buffalo wing smoothie and Salisbury steak bits. They have more nutrients than breast milk.
- Baby likes shiny things, so you might want to keep wearing that sequined belt.
- If your classes are graded on a curve, take baby to exams with you. Classmates will assume baby is some sort of precocious super-genius and copy off of his tests, even if it's all scribbles and drool. You'll get an A, and baby will get, at worst, a B–.
- If baby cries a lot in the dorm, say that he's just "really emo" and give him black plastic glasses and wing tips. Other residents will assume they don't understand his pain and envy his hip iPod library, which consists of four gigs of Raffi and three Radiohead B-sides.
- You would think baby would be deadweight on an intramural basketball team, but at six to seven months an infant is developed enough to dunk a basketball when held on his parent's shoulders.
- It's important not to let baby smoke. Except socially or when she's drinking.
- If baby wants to get her ears pierced, baby should get her ears pierced. It's important to be supportive; she's an adult now.

You can save $10 by giving yourself a haircut. You'll then save an additional $250 by not going on dates.

Calendar of Reasons Not to Break Up with Your Significant Other

August 28: Arrival day. You are single and looking to mingle.
September 9: Hook up at party, but you're not dating or anything.
September 25: You are officially dating.
October: Oh no, a tragedy in their family. You can't dump her now.
November 15: Well, at this point you might as well finish out the semester. Just go until break.
December 10: Christmas is coming up, and you have probably been dropping a lot of hints; let's see what you get.
December 27: Need to kiss somebody at New Year's.
January 14: Don't want to be alone for Valentine's Day, and you're not sure you can find someone else in under a month.
February 1: Are they seriously making birthday plans a month ahead of time? Ugh, looks like you're stuck now.
March 23: FORMAL!
April 10: Arbor Day.
May 5: You are going to need it for finals.
May 20: We'll take a break for the summer.
September 9: Hook up at a party, but you're not dating or anything.
September 25: You're officially dating . . . again.

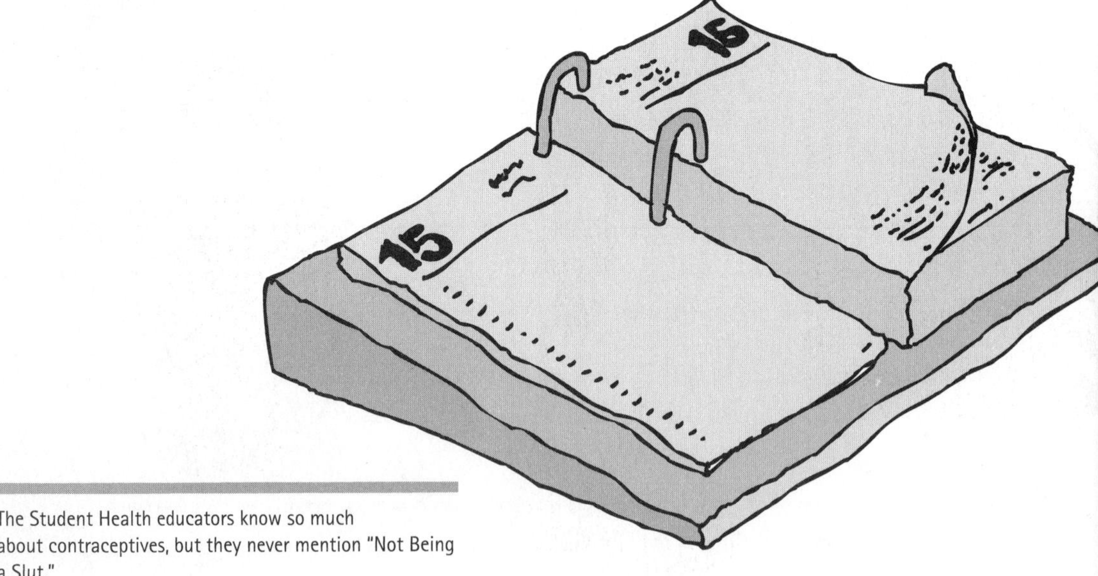

The Student Health educators know so much about contraceptives, but they never mention "Not Being a Slut."

Romantic Breakups

All good things must come to an end. If they didn't, you'd be orgasming nonstop, day in, day out. Relationships, while not as fun or tiring as orgasms, must end as well. The problem with this is that if you break up on bad terms, your significant other will spread the word about what a dick you are. Instead of slapping her mom in the face, lighting her car on fire, or publishing those naked pictures of her on the Internet, try one of these romantic breakups:

E-mail Dumping

It's hard to break up with somebody in person, which is why you should always do it over e-mail. You'll hear some opposition from feminists about vague rules that if a relationship lasts for a couple of years, it's common decency to break up in person, but that is simply not the case. Old men divorce their wives over e-mail all the time; it's practically as common as spam mail. If you're unsure about how to broach this subject, feel free to use this example e-mail to guide you:

To: Timbo245@hotmail.com

Cc:

Bcc:

Subject: Guess what

Tim,

Remember that night in Vegas when I was sick and you stayed in with me, even though it was your birthday and all your friends were outside partying? You said we should play Monopoly to pass the time, and we did, and I got a "Get Out of Jail Free" card? Well, I'm using it now.

Becky

PS—YOU are the jail.

Send | Save Draft | Attach | | Tools | Cancel

A Final Note on Sex and Dating

Holding her hand while she gets an abortion is not a good second date. Instead, how about renting a DVD?

What do you call a fat girl? We're sorry, we meant, "Why?"

10 ACADEMICS

Introduction

A Five-Paragraph Essay by the Writers of CollegeHumor

INTRO PARAGRAPH: Academics. Learning. Enlightenment. The "point" of college. At a private school, you could find yourself spending up to a third of your waking hours in class or studying. At a state school, you could waste valuable minutes having to walk around academic buildings to get to a raging kegger. THESIS STATEMENT: Either way, we have some jokes and valuable information about collegiate academics in this chapter, which we will present in diagrams and pictures because we dislike typing whole sentences.

FIRST POINT: College has been around for ages. In fact, "college" is Latin for "Mom, everyone gets a C in that class; the professor is so unfair." Bonus classical languages fact: when the ancient Greeks invented college, they would have toga parties, but they just

It takes community colleges two years to teach what regular colleges do in four. Now who's smarter, fuckface?

called them "parties." It's been said that college is the "best four years of your life," but if you perform poorly in the academic arena, you can stretch college into the "best eight years of your life and you'll go back and finish eventually, it's just that you're not really 'feeling' school anymore." Take that, conventional wisdom!

SECOND POINT: Class is boring, but grades are important. They determine what kind of job you'll get, what your income level will be, how much money you'll earn, and what the bottom line on your bank statements will read. The ideal college would give you good grades without making you deal with going to class. Something that great could never exist, right? Well, now it does! With the University of Phoenix Online, you can earn your associate's degree in just two weeks! And if you want an MBA? That's only another two weeks. Act quickly—you start with four lives and two continues; each continue after that costs two tokens.

THIRD POINT: The first notes were taken thousands of years ago by Moses on some stone tablets. At one point, he did ask of God, "Will this be on the exam?" And God did reply, "Yes, but it will be a take-home." And Moses did quitteth paying attention until December.

Similarly, homework was first invented in 1632. Dogs were invented the very next day for the purpose of eating said homework. The next week, it was referred to as "homo-work because it's so freakin' gay!" for the first time. Procrastination came later, but amateur crastination leagues had been enjoying widespread popularity for several centuries at that point. They'd just been putting off organizing until their dorm rooms were really, really clean and their DVDs were re-alphabetized.

CLOSING PARAGRAPH: So in conclusion, you should always start your closing paragraph with "So in conclusion." Class is a necessary part of college, and if you play your cards right, you can enjoy it. Playing your cards right in this situation requires a check-raise on the turn; remember that if you steal the blinds, you play for free. Cheating should generally only be done on boyfriends or girlfriends, and remember that it's not plagiarism if your school's library doesn't have the book you're copying out of. Then it's called getting an A+.

GRADE: C+/B-

COMMENTS: Not enough jokes about beer and pussy. You can do better. I expect to see you at office hours. :(

In your Shakespeare class, stare at the girls' breasts and call yourself "King Leer." It's not harassment if it's in pun form.

Let's Be Serious for a Second: Registering for Classes

Registering for classes is more important than taking final exams. While final exams could determine your grade in a class, what classes you take could determine when you wake up and how much fun you'll be having for the next six months. While it may seem like a nerdy thing to worry about, registering for classes as soon as possible could mean the difference between an 8 a.m. "History of Statistics: 1850–1900" and a 3 p.m. "Seminar on Getting to Second Base."

Class Names Can Be Deceiving

According to your school, every class is interesting, intensive, and "designed to inspire participation and conversation." Thank God we're here to tell you what college classes are REALLY like.

Real Class Descriptions 2

Physics 1: Sounds like an easy class because of the number next to the course, but Physics, regardless of the level, is way too hard to even attempt. This class should be called "Physics 1—You 0."

Art History 101: We know what you're thinking, −1 times −1 is +1, so two boring subjects fused together must be interesting. That logic is correct until you realize that two wrongs don't make a right. Instead, you find yourself in a class that's boring for TWO reasons. Time is Monet, so drop out immediately!

Military Affairs: Remember when General Schwarzkopf had sex with his intern!? The infamous Robert E. Lee–Ulysses S. Grant makeout session? Well, this class has nothing to do with either of those, and not because we just made them up, but because "affairs" in this instance means "conflict," not "adultery." Just a heads-up.

Women's Studies Seminar: You think this would be a great place to meet women, right? So did the other twenty-nine guys who registered for this thirty-person class. Oh, and the one girl in the class won't be impressed when you say the plight of women throughout history is "like, totally unfair, man." You meant "like, totally unfair, PERSON."

Asian Studies: Not just a needless newspaper headline, this class really doesn't have anything to do with all those Korean kids who fill up the library on weekends. It's actually a study of Chinese history, and you can't laugh about the Wu and Tang dynasties.

Urban Studies: Sounds like it would be about hip-hop and wearing your caps backwards. It's actually about where to put buildings in a city. If we wanted to do that, we'd play Monopoly. And we played Monopoly, so we already know the answer: Marvin Gardens.

Romance Languages: Turns out these are languages with Latin roots, not "Girl, you know I'm sweatin' you all the time, and I just thought . . . you want to slip into something more comfortable? Yeah, that's nice. Keep doing that. No, girl, slow down. Slow down or I'll . . . Oh, sorry, baby. I'll get you a towel."

Professor Personalities

The Golden Oldie

He's been teaching at your school since women were considered too fragile to work and indentured servants groomed the rose garden in front of the dean's office. He was offered tenure right after World War I and hasn't updated his syllabus since. Some of his required texts are now considered too racist to even own, and his idea of a lecture is a thirty-minute drool-filled rant with many, many long pauses. Your grades don't get posted for five months after the semester has ended, and once they do, they won't make any sense. Only take a class from this guy if you want a J+ on your transcript.

The Young Gun

He just got out of grad school and he is ready to change some lives. He's excitable and tries to stimulate your mind through fun, original teaching methods. His pedagogical techniques will be questioned by older members of the faculty. "It may look like we're having fun in there, but, by God, we're learning, okay!?" He'll make everyone stand up and say "vagina" or "penis" because that is supposed to "make us all comfortable with each other." You still giggle like a fucking schoolgirl, though, because those words will never stop being hilarious.

The She-Stomper

She got dumped once in college and hasn't forgiven the male population of the world for it yet. When you tell her it isn't fair that men have to take the harder version of the exam, she'll tell you, "Well, it wasn't fair of him to wait until our wedding day to break up with me! I had family coming in from out of town and do you know how pricey those appetizers were!?" You guess $13.99 a plate and people laugh, but you just failed her course, wiseass.

The Satellite Citizen

No, not the cool kind from space, the weird kind from Eastern Europe's former Soviet empire. He's probably a math or science teacher, since the Reds wouldn't allow him to learn anything fun when he was little. His accent is thicker than his mother's world-famous goulash, and his wardrobe looks curiously like it was purchased at Goodwill, while in reality everyone from his country wears blue slacks and a stained green blazer. He's not familiar with our customs, so it is easy to convince him that Friday is a half day, finals are just a formality, and grades are actually based on how cool your frat is.

Mark

He'll start the semester with, "Don't call me Professor ____, just call me Mark, okay?" He's the coolest professor on campus and is known for taking his classes to the bar after the midterm. He cancels class for nice weather and has his stand-up comic buddy come in for a guest lecture. He's ultra-nice until finals roll around and he realizes that he doesn't have grades for anyone in the class. He'll say something like, "Okay, no more Mr. Nice Guy!" and the next thing you know you have two term papers, three quizzes, and your final all due in the same week. "I thought you were cool, Mark. But turns out you're just like every other old professor at this damn school." Ouch, way to hit him where it hurts.

College of Humanities

Dr. Eric Yenco
Faculty Hall, Rm. 112
Office Hours: Mon 11–11:08
Wed 1:09–1:10, 1:13 ? 2:15
E-mail: DungeonSlayer2000@yahoo.net

Introduction to Philosophy:
Wanna Talk about Some Stuff?

Overview

The purpose of this course is to introduce students to some of the fundamental principles of philosophy and philosophical thought—and to fulfill the philosophy requirement for graduation. I know why you're all here. What makes philosophy so fascinating is its effort to address mankind's big questions through the human capacity to reason and analyze. These concepts have been explored by our greatest thinkers for centuries, but you should be able to get a pretty solid grasp of them after paying attention to some fifty-minute lectures in the three days immediately preceding the major exams. We're in the business of finding answers, people. Failing that, hopefully you realize how easily "Emmanuel Kant" becomes "A Manual Cunt." Same with "Descartes" and "Day Fart."

Course Format and Requirements

Class Attendance: Simply showing up for class will not improve your grade, because I'm boring and you can't really pay attention to me anyway. When and if I show up for class, I expect to see you there unless you have a written excuse from a school official and/or your roommate. I will give five random attendance checks during the semester; for every check you miss, your final grade will be penalized 3 percent of your grade. I'm not great at math, though, so don't worry too much.

Participation: I expect every student to participate each and every class period. At the end of the semester I will make a wild guess about your participation when deciding your final grade. The notes I'm scribbling after each student participates are actually part of a tic-tac-toe game I'm playing by mail with a professor in Finland. This may sound harsh, but the only way I can get people to show up is through fear of a low participation grade. Finally, please disguise your bullshit comments with the veil of an articulate, thorough response.

Papers and Quizzes: At some point I will administer a quiz that I will collect at the end of class. I will then lose said quizzes in my filthy Prius and give you a grade based on how attractive you are. Your final exam will be based solely on opinions, but you should back up your stance with at least one generalized sentence about something somewhat pertaining to something we supposedly studied at some point. If your mind goes blank, here's a tip: I can never read too many essays about dinosaurs fighting.

Texts I Will Assign/Texts You Will Leave on Your Bookshelf So People Think You're Smart

Descartes, René. Discourse on Method and Meditations on First Philosophy. Hackett, 1999.
Hume, David. An Enquiry Concerning Human Understanding. Oxford University Press, 1999.
Zwindle, Rany. Socrates: The Man, The Myth, The Mind. Doubledunk, 2003.

Texts I Will Actually Use

Ben Folds Five. Philosophy, *Ben Folds Five.* Passenger Records, 1995.
"God: Still Around?" Life Section, *USA Today,* September 2, 1994.
"Smarten Up to Get Laid," *Stuff Magazine,* November 2004.
Various. *The Big Bathroom Reader: Great People and Ideas in History.* Hanson Press, 2001.

Schedule

September: Talk about stuff.

October: Talk about other stuff.

November: PIZZA PARTY!

December: Final, winter break.

You can turn a D– into a D+ pretty easily, but people will still think you're retarded.

Office Hours

Some facts about office hours:

Fact: Every professor signs a contract with his/her university to begin any office hours session with the words "So, what's up?"

Fact: Although old male professors often fantasize about young, hot female students coming into their office hours and seducing them, their academic integrity does not let their fantasy get past third base.

Fact: After several weeks of nobody visiting his office hours, your professor will change them to "By Appointment Only," but in actuality he's "not fooling anybody."

Bookstore Scams

Deep in the heart of every college campus lies a corrupt and greedy organization trying to rob its students. They are known as "reverse Robin Hoods" because they steal from the poor and give to the rich, mainly themselves. They are campus bookstores, and if you aren't careful you may just find yourself on the wrong end of one of their multifaceted scams!

The first scam is by far the most prevalent. At the end of each semester, you'll find yourself with a surplus of books that you never care to see again. You'll think, "Gee, I wish I could get rid of these books, but who would buy them?" That's where your benevolent college bookstore jumps in to the rescue.

Let's say you have a Psych book that you paid $234 for three months ago. Your bookstore, nice guys that they are, will give you seven whole American dollars for it. In cash! Then, since they're nice guys, they'll stick a bright orange "USED" sticker on the side and resell it to your classmates for $52 in the fall. Everybody wins!

The second great bookstore scam is the donation box. It shows up every year in your dorm, and it promises to take your old run-down textbooks to starving African children. What's a starving boy going to do with your Computer Science textbook? Unless the pages are made of hepatitis vaccine, not much. Seriously, you can't use an Applied Economics textbook when you don't have an economy to apply things to. The bookstore's slapping a "USED" sticker on there and laughing all the way to the bank.

The edition switch is the final great bookstore scam. The changes are usually subtle, but the markup is not:

You don't have to raise your hand if you want to use the bathroom, but you should leave the room.

Edition 1 (1993): The 1960s were a time of radical change in American society. (Cover price: $54)
Edition 2 (2007): The 1960s were a time of radical change in American society BEFORE THE INTERNET EXISTED. (Cover price: $98)
Edition 3 (2011): The 1960s were a time of radical change in American society WAY BEFORE THE INTERNET EXISTED. (Cover price: $2,573)

So how do you beat the bookstore at its own game? Simple: you don't buy your books there. Under no circumstances should you ever buy your books at the bookstore before the semester begins. Professors often throw a couple of hundred bucks' worth of books on the syllabus even if they have no intention of using them. Wait until the second week of classes to figure out what books you'll really use in each course, then buy them on eBay or somewhere else online. You'll save hundreds of dollars a semester. Know what you can spend that money on? No, not textbooks for next semester! Were you even paying attention, nerd?

And Now a Word on Dressing for Class

Don't wear pajama pants on the first day of class.

Do wear pajama pants on the second through last days of class.

A funny thing to do is sign up for no courses one semester. Then say, "Hey, guys, I've got NO class!" while farting during a funeral.

Skipping Classes, a Lesson

It's okay if you skip class because the professor just reads out of the textbook anyway.

Who cares if she covers something not in the textbook because she puts all her notes online.

And so what if she doesn't actually put all her notes online, and you're actually thinking of your other class? Your cousin took this class last year.

What's the difference if it was another professor? The class is probably the same stuff. How much can "History of Landscape Architecture" change?

And even if it's not, you can buy the notes from that service on campus.

Those guys don't do every class, and sometimes they aren't too good. But whatever, you can borrow the notes from your buddy Marty.

Marty's dead? Oh no, man, what happened?

All right, everything's okay. We need to get the hell out of the state, right now.

So what if the car ain't starting, man, we don't got time for this! Just take what you can grab; we'll take the train to Louisiana. My cousin lives there.

THE MORAL IS, GO TO CLASS OR GO TO JAIL FOR MURDER.

Excuses for Tardiness

Here's a familiar situation: You wake up in a panic, glance over at your clock, and realize that you're already five minutes late for class. By the time you throw on some clothes, brush your teeth, and make your way to class, you'll be fifteen minutes late. There is nothing more embarrassing than having to knock on a locked classroom door, interrupt your professor's lecture, and take your seat while everyone stares at you. Here are some handy excuses for when that fifteen minutes of tardiness is unavoidable:

Excuse #1: Right before you enter your classroom, set your left arm on fire. Run into the classroom screaming, put out the fire with your right arm, shake your head, and say, "You do NOT want to know." Then quietly take your seat.

Excuse #2: Come into the classroom and walk straight up to the clock. Turn the minute hand back fifteen minutes. Clap your hands together and say, "Well, that settles that; who's ready to start class?" Your professor will start again from the beginning.

Excuse #3: Run in wielding a handgun. Tell everybody to "stay in their fucking seat or I'll blow the professor's head right off!" Then tell them you were kidding. They'll be so relieved you didn't kill anybody that they'll completely forgive your now seemingly-insignificant-in-the-grand-scheme-of-things tardiness.

Excuse #4: Walk in backwards. Take your seat upside down. Explain your tardiness in reverse. The professor will be convinced it's Opposite Day and that you've shown fifteen minutes early! F for Effort!

Excuse #5: Show up with a potato sack filled with your professor's favorite candy, and as you walk in, empty the contents onto his desk. He'll watch in amazement as his favorite treat overflows onto the floor, and he'll more than likely cancel class like a kid in a candy store. Note: this won't work if your professor's favorite candy is "Chicken Noodle Soup."

True College Stories—The Best Excuse Ever, by Ricky

I had a friend who slept through an important exam one morning. That evening, he sent the professor the following e-mail:

> Dr. Graham,
>
> I was unable to take this morning's exam because of a family emergency which required me to be out of town. Would it be possible to reschedule for tomorrow or later this week?
>
> Thanks,
> Mark

Clearly recognizing this excuse as high-grade bullshit, Dr. Graham replied with the following e-mail:

> Mark,
>
> I am truly sorry to hear about your family emergency. Please provide me with documentation of the emergency, and I will be happy to reschedule your exam.
>
> —Dr. Graham

At this point Mark was pissing his pants, and rightly so. This test was worth 30 percent of his grade for the semester, but he obviously lacked any documentation for his imaginary family emergency.

Mark came to me with nowhere else to turn. Holding his hand (proverbially, dude), I sat him down and began dictating what could arguably be the greatest excuse in the history of academia:

> Dr. Graham,
>
> I really don't know what I could give you for proof because they don't make any documentation for this sort of thing. The best I can do is try to explain, although I really am not comfortable with this and I would ask you not to speak to anyone about it.
>
> My younger brother lives at home and goes to community college in Pittsburgh. He just came out and told my parents that he is

a homosexual. It's a big deal in my family because we're Catholic. My dad still holds pretty tight to his conservative Irish upbringing, so he's devastated by this news.

I really felt that I had to go home and support my brother and help him deal with my parents. Family is the number one thing in my life, and I don't regret my decision. I hope that this is a good enough excuse, and I also hope I can take the test at a later date. If not, I will still continue to give your class all my attention, like I did before this family crisis.

Thanks,
Mark

There you have it, folks, the "dog ate my homework" of our generation. No professor wants to mess with any situation involving a gay family member. Within an hour, Mark had an e-mail sitting in his inbox from a presumably flustered Dr. Graham.

Dear Mark,

Don't worry, I will keep this issue completely confidential. There's no handbook for dealing with these things, so the only advice I can offer is to keep your head up and soldier on. Please don't worry about missing the exam; the important thing is that you take care of your family issue. You can make up the exam whenever it's convenient.

Best,
Dr. Graham

And that was it. Mark took the test a few days later and did pretty well. Dr. Graham never suspected anything and treated Mark with a kindness professors normally save for their best students. Mark passed the class, graduated, and got a great job, all thanks to this excuse. Use it wisely.

A good way to get a laugh is to show up for class wearing four shirts, two jackets, and seven pairs of pants. Then say, "God, I feel so overdressed."

Deaths in the Family

Nothing simplifies getting an extension quite like a dead relative. If your relatives are all healthy, there's no reason you can't make some up . . .

I'm sick of always thinking with my dick. Turns out, my dick doesn't know a damn thing about the novels of Hemingway. Another day, another F.

Michelle, 22. "A few weeks ago I was a mess . . . I mean, I was all over the place. But now, it's like, ya know, it's like I'm a focused beam of, um, light . . . Like a laser . . . a sweaty laser. And, and I'm just so, like, passionate or, like, blinded by clarity or whatever. GOD, I need some air . . . ok, ok, ok . . . what if we go to Chili's? You want to do that?"

Aderine

The latest technology in study drugs

Possible side effects include: dry mouth; repeatedly saying "No, really"; touching your face a lot; touching other people's faces a lot; heightened sense of your own intelligence, particularly regarding Impressionist painting; moderate bouts of incontinence; lack of appetite, even for pizza; the rampant making of plans; testicular contraction; eyesweats.

Before taking Aderine, always consult your doctor or some kid in your hall who had a prescription in high school.

Aderine is not for everyone. People who aren't cool, for instance.

Using literary references will only get you laid if you allude to a book that everyone didn't read in high school. Nice try, Dorian Gray.

All-Nighters

Ten-page paper due tomorrow morning and you haven't started? If you are going to endure an all-nighter, you are going have to use the following sayings from our all-nighter quote bank. Choose one or speak all ten!

"Ten pages, ten hours. Should be no big deal."
"I'm debating whether or not to go to sleep now and wake up really early tomorrow."
"It's only worth 35 percent of my grade, so . . ."
"I work better at night anyway. I'm a night person."
"Well, I basically have it all outlined. So now it's just a matter of writing the sentences."
"I'm gonna take a quick powernap and recharge the batteries."
"Technically, it's an eight-to-ten-pager, so I can make it like . . . seven point five."
"I'm going to the library to finish it up. I work better when I switch places."
"What's the difference between a bibliography and a works cited anyway?"
"After this is done, I'm going to get demolished."
"I'm gonna work for a few hours, head over to Jim's party, then come back and finish it up right before dawn."
"Next time I'm gonna write a page a day for ten days so I don't have to stress out."

A Fucking Fantastic Study Tip

Do you have a hard time forcing yourself to sit down and study for an extended period of time? Here's a little trick we figured out that will keep your ass in that seat and your eyes on that book:

Go to the library and sit down at a table with your textbooks and water bottle like normal. However, this time take the water bottle and empty about half of it all over your lap. You're not going to leave the seat for at least the forty-five minutes it takes all that water to dry because attractive people are always in the library. You don't want to look like a complete idiot who just pissed himself in front of attractive people, do you? We used it twice a semester in college, and it worked every time.

Library

Every once in a while you will hear somebody say, "We have a library?"

He knows we have a library; he's just trying to be as cool as possible.

See also: "I got drunk before my SATs" and, "I started my essay at four a.m. this morning."

Dick.

James Joyce wrote *Finnegans Wake* in a week. You've been trying to beat Mario Baseball for seventeen days. Just trying to put things in perspective.

Procrastination

Anybody can be productive, but it takes a real man to be lazy. So sit back, relax, and listen to that devil on your shoulder as he whispers great ideas into that nonproductive brain of yours.

No, don't turn off the TV! Sure, at first it may look like nothing's on, but try going through the channels one more time. Maybe there was an episode of *COPS*, but it was at commercial so you missed it. Besides, it's 2:20. If you go around the horn one more time, it will be 2:24, and then we're only a few minutes away from all the fresh programming a new half hour brings!

Hey, remember that kid in your Econ class bragging about how he could beat Mario 1 in less than ten minutes? I bet you could do that! You might as well try, right?

You've been wearing used socks for a week. Instead of T-shirts. People talk about that kind of stuff. C'mon, by doing laundry, you are being productive and unproductive at the same time!

Quick! That kid from your Intro to Spanish class has changed his away message. Hmmmm . . . Now he's at work and apparently he isn't looking forward to closing the Quiznos tonight. Didn't he used to have an "I ❤ Lisa" in his profile for like, a year? I guess they broke up or something.

Cheating

Cheating is a time-honored institution, but over the centuries, professors have gotten wise to maneuvers like the "cheat sheet," the "copy off your neighbor," and the "ether rag the proctor." However, it can still be done; here are some fun new ways to cheat:

The Bait-and-Switch: Don't study for your exam. When the test starts, get a quick feel for the format of the exam. If it's four essays, just bang out four essays about anything marginally related to the course, but make absolutely certain they do not address the question asked. Your poor assistant professor, eating canned soup in his unheated apartment, will surely think that he gave you the wrong exam, and will probably panic and give you an A so he can go to White Castle faster. He's finally going to talk to the cute cashier he's been telling his mom he's dating.

The Nonattend: Make like your deadbeat father and never show up. If the class is large enough, you won't be missed, and then when you get a zero on the exam, point out that your professor obviously lost it. You'll probably end up having to take the exam, but you'll buy yourself valuable study/mistake-sex-with-high-school-girlfriend time over winter break.

The Giveaway: Write the name of the class on the inside of your palm. When the professor hands you your copy of the exam, feign cheating by conspicuously looking at the word written in your palm. You and your professor will share a good chuckle at your dry, academic wit. He'll never even think to check for the rest of the cheat sheets hidden on your body (try the inside of your eyelids); he'll think you're just that committed to the joke. Yes, professors are smart, but they also think they look good in tweed. They can be fooled.

The Memorizer: Your human brain has the capability of memorizing an infinite amount of facts and pieces of information. Before the exam begins, take a few good weeks reviewing course materials and reading textbooks. When the test begins, use the information stored in your short-term memory bank to answer the questions. It's like putting lots of marbles in your mouth at a weigh-in. When the test is over, you can forget whatever it is that you learned—it's drinking time!

Dude, Can I Copy Off Your Test?, by Blake

Pssst, dude, can I copy off your test? I haven't even been to this class all semester. I don't even know what any of these questions mean. I've been so busy chilling with my crew and going to the gym that I barely even make it to any classes. Bro, move your arm, I can't see your test. That's better. Dude, it's not even funny how bad I'm doing in this class. I totally slept through the midterm, but the prof said I could still pass if I totally own this test. It's weird cuz I did mad good on my SATs. I'm definitely one of the smartest kids at this school, but I just totally forgot to study or go to class. Yo, lean back a little so I can see over your shoulder. Nice. Is that a b or a d? d? Cool. Yo, I don't know what I'd do without you, you want me to buy you a brew after class? You don't drink in the morning? Pussy. Bro, stop leaning forward, I can't see. Can you flip back? I didn't get all the answers from page four. So what if it's an essay test, didn't I just say I didn't have time to study?

Multiple Choice Probabilities

Chances of the answer being the same letter three times in a row: 1:64
Chances of the answer being the same letter four times in a row: 1:256
Chances of the answer being the same letter five times in a row: IT'S NEVER HAPPENED

Plagiarism

There comes a time when every college student has to choose between drunken sex with a declining Southern belle or writing a paper. The smart college student knows that he doesn't have to choose.

A word of warning: if you download a paper from the Web, you will get caught. You will have paid thirty bucks for a shitty paper about pandas that a quick Google search will expose. You have to subtly cover your tracks. For example, let's say you had to turn in a short story for a creative writing class. LAME ALERT!!! So just borrow a little from a proven source like *Moby Dick*:

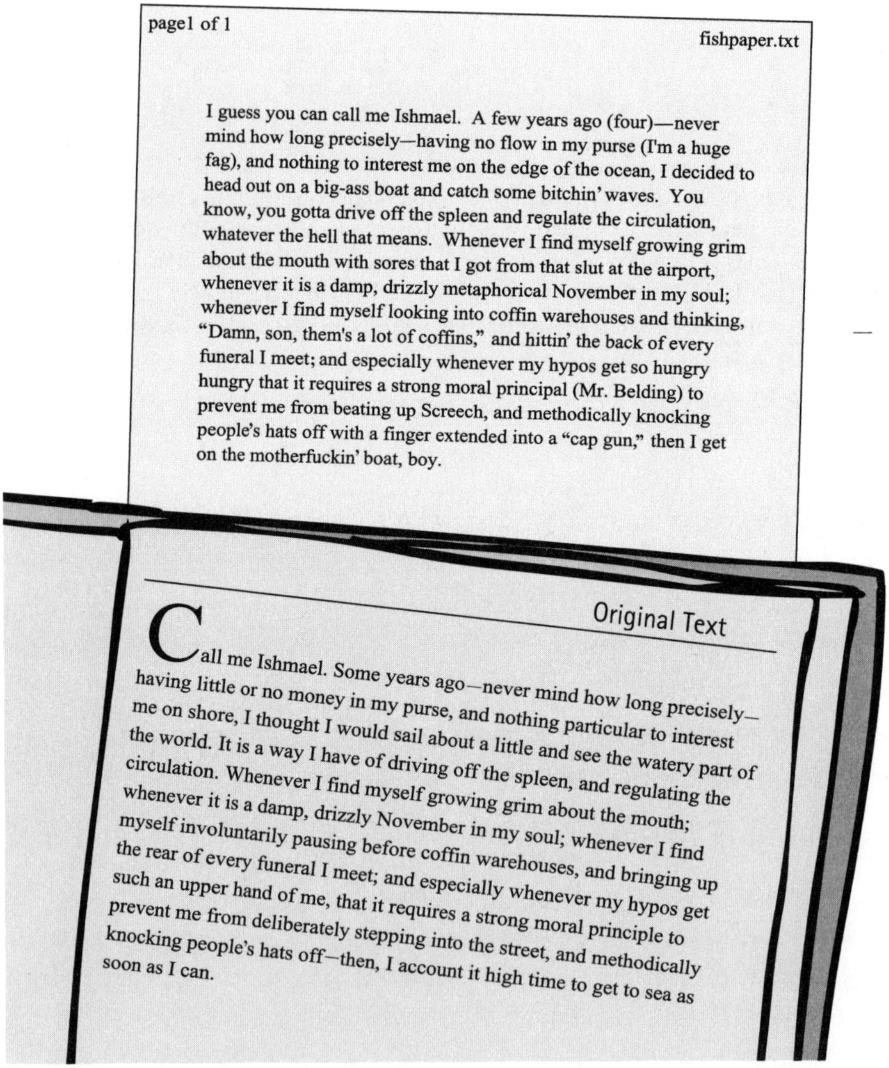

page1 of 1

fishpaper.txt

I guess you can call me Ishmael. A few years ago (four)—never mind how long precisely—having no flow in my purse (I'm a huge fag), and nothing to interest me on the edge of the ocean, I decided to head out on a big-ass boat and catch some bitchin' waves. You know, you gotta drive off the spleen and regulate the circulation, whatever the hell that means. Whenever I find myself growing grim about the mouth with sores that I got from that slut at the airport, whenever it is a damp, drizzly metaphorical November in my soul; whenever I find myself looking into coffin warehouses and thinking, "Damn, son, them's a lot of coffins," and hittin' the back of every funeral I meet; and especially whenever my hypos get so hungry hungry that it requires a strong moral principal (Mr. Belding) to prevent me from beating up Screech, and methodically knocking people's hats off with a finger extended into a "cap gun," then I get on the motherfuckin' boat, boy.

Original Text

Call me Ishmael. Some years ago—never mind how long precisely—having little or no money in my purse, and nothing particular to interest me on shore, I thought I would sail about a little and see the watery part of the world. It is a way I have of driving off the spleen, and regulating the circulation. Whenever I find myself growing grim about the mouth; whenever it is a damp, drizzly November in my soul; whenever I find myself involuntarily pausing before coffin warehouses, and bringing up the rear of every funeral I meet; and especially whenever my hypos get such an upper hand of me, that it requires a strong moral principle to prevent me from deliberately stepping into the street, and methodically knocking people's hats off—then, I account it high time to get to sea as soon as I can.

Margin-ally Funny

Eventually you'll have to write a paper that's more than four pages long. Unfortunately, papers stop being fun and start being a chore after three pages, so you'll need to use the built-in loopholes of Microsoft Word. If you're using WordPerfect instead of Microsoft Word, see page 217 for advice on how to burn your laptop.

Now, every writer has some options when deciding how to write his or her paper for a class.

Start with a title that wastes as much space as possible. If the information is even vaguely related to the class, it should go on your first page.

TITLE!!
(space!)
Class
Teacher
Class Section/Time
Due Date
(space!)

You just saved half a page!

Another popular option for such a situation is to use entirely too many words for any given situation and taking advantage of sentence and paragraph breaks to add spaces to your paper, like so: the use of pronouns should also strictly be avoided unless the person or object to which the purported pronoun would apply has fewer letters than the pronoun itself. In the event of a tie, the choice of pronoun or proper noun shall be left to the discretion of the writer of the relevant paper and a quorum of no less than five friendly parties.

See? That was easy. Now let's talk line spacing. Single spacing is good, double spacing is better, but 2.25 spacing is almost indistinguishable to the naked eye while saving you up to four lines per page. It doesn't sound like much, but it saves you half a page on a five-page paper.

Moreover, changing font size from 12 to 12.5 is almost impossible to notice, but it gets subtly bigger.

Character spacing or character size give your paper a certain character. A character of being done sooner!!!

Expanding your margins makes fewer words fit on each line and reflects the marginal effort you put into the paper.

Finally, make sure you end each paper with

THE END

There, you did it! Don't think these tactics will work? We just put this book one page closer to our publisher's minimum page count, and we got away with it.

SO YOU'VE DECIDED TO

Shit Your Pants During an Exam

"Stupid Exam! I wish I could just shit my pants while I take you!" Well, now you can.

What you need: Irritable bowel syndrome, 44 tacos

What you do: Eat 42 tacos right before taking the exam. As you sit down in your seat, feel the rumblings within your abdomen. That's what success feels like. Stare at the lady seated next to you with a glazed look and a smile that connotes, "That's right." As the professor says, "You may begin," interrupt him with the sounds of more exploding excrement than a populated Porta Potti. Your expression should be that of complete awe and love. Congratulations, you're definitely getting at least an A–. Now, about those last two tacos . . .

If you name the book *Great Expectations,* you're just setting people up for a colossal disappointment.

Spot the Group Member

Group work is designed to teach you how to work with other people. Instead, it teaches you that other people are all idiots. But what kind of idiots are they? Consult this guide:

THE GIRL WHO DOES EVERYTHING

How to Spot Her: She's constantly getting stuff done. When other group members start talking about what happened on TV last night, she throws her hot coffee in their eyes and yells, "Let's focus, people! We've all got families to get home to. And you. Go get me some more coffee; this cup isn't going to refill itself." If left alone, she will do the entire project by herself and passive-aggressively complain about it.

THE GUY WHO ALWAYS SHOWS UP LATE

How to Spot Him: "Hey, guys, sorry I'm late, I had a thing." This guy shows up late for every meeting, usually because he had a thing. He should not be trusted with anything more than assembling the project's bibliography. What he lacks in punctuality, he more than makes up for in his deft mastery of MLA citations. One book, two authors; two books, one author. Yup, he knows it all.

THE HOT ONE

How to Spot Him/Her: In any group, it is a mathematical certainty that there will be at least one person you want to have sex with. This person should be relatively easy to spot. Survey the group and say, "Who do I want to bang?" Best not to think this question out loud.

THE GIRL WHO DOESN'T KNOW SHE'S STUPID

How to Spot Her: This girl is full of ideas. Terrible, unreasonable ideas. However, she'll think she's ahead of her time and that your group is just too stupid to understand. She will want to give your group a name like "Team Puppy" because she thinks it will help the group dynamic. What will really help the group dynamic is complaining to each other about how much you hate this girl.

THE GUY WITH THE OTHER GROUP PROJECT

How to Spot Him: He's always running into meetings out of breath, with notes from other classes. "Sorry, I have this other group project also due tomorrow, so . . ." He is always confusing your class with his other class. Either that or he genuinely thinks that performing a scene from a Shakespeare play in Spanish is a good idea for your marketing brief.

THE GUY WHO'S ALWAYS EATING PASTA

How to Spot Him: Penne, bowtie, macaroni—this guy eats them all. He usually has spaghetti (or is that fettuccine?) hanging from his mouth. When it comes time to hand in his part of the group project, he reaches into his pocket and puts a handful of uncooked rigatoni on the table.

Labs

Your college science classes will require labs. The labs themselves will be full of warning signs about safety, but there's one warning they always forget to give you:

You think anybody's ever audited a Tax Law class?

Make Your Own Sociology Class

Philosophy of	behavioral tendencies	and the theories of	the Internet
Advanced	sociopolitical climates	as it applies to	society
Suppliers of	public relations	as a vehicle for	ethics
Disposable	basket weaving	. . . 's effect on	clients
Verisimilative	gender	of	the mole people
An overview of	technology	as a celebration of	family
Analysis of	social psychology	. . . 's legal impact on	the female anatomy
Interpreting	ethnic relations	. . . 's regulation by	consumers
The legality of	Big Tobacco	through the eye of	monsters
Perspectives of	culture	from the viewpoint of	mushroom technology
Notable women of	urban ecology	&	*Survivor*
The theory of	social ethics	. . . 's relationship with	the public
American	juvenile delinquency	with a focus on	Napoleonic history
Cultural aspects of	population issues	. . . 's role in	the judicial system
Emerging problems of	community building	according to	the political economy

You're not going to save yourself reading by taking a short story class; they just assign a lot of them.

The Old Classmate

"Hey, do you know Thelonius? He's an old classmate of mine."

"You mean, like, you guys go way back?"

"Oh no, I mean he's fifty-four years old."

They stick out like a sore thumb. Their white knuckle hair can be seen from upward of three rows away. They make no sense and pretend everything is just fine and dandy. They are old students, and they just don't give a damn.

As if their fuzzy ears don't say it all, these oldies always seem to open their mouths and remove all doubt that they were born in the 1800s.

"During the Depression, you needed a ration stamp to go to college. You could get one gallon of petroleum or two units of course credit."

"You think the Garfield the cat is horribly unfunny? You should have met President Garfield. That guy told the same knock-knock joke over and over, and it was the one about bananas. And no, I was never glad he didn't say 'banana!' I liked bananas!"

"Actually, the woolly mammoth didn't primarily eat leaves, I once fed it . . . ," and on, and on, and on, and on.

Even worse than old students are old dorm residents. These near-mummified sons of bitches are always lingering around the dorm, and they can't even chew their own food. Living on campus as a forty-something? Well, that's just worse than World War I. And you would know, you served in World War I, didn't you, oldie!? Yeah, served lunch. Pussy.

If somebody in your class is pregnant, tell her that her grade doesn't matter, because she's already failed the most important class of all: Life.

GPAs

Your grade point average will determine the course of the rest of your life. We cannot overstate its importance. If your GPA is poor, your life is pretty much over, but don't believe us.

Believe these facts:

- The average GPA of the 57 million people who died in World War II was 2.38. The average GPA of the survivors was 3.1.
- Famed aviatrix Amelia Earhart disappeared. Her GPA? A cool 1.94.
- John Belushi's character Bluto had a GPA of 0.00. John Belushi himself had a GPA of 0.7. And he died.
- John F. Kennedy had the lowest GPA of any American president. 2.00. That's two grade points for every time he was assassinated.
- The *Titanic* had a 1.64 GPA. The iceberg: a whopping 4.81.

So when you get a D+ and say, "My life is over!" you just might be right.

Grade Guidelines

Grades are like women: they come in five different shapes—A, B, C, D, and F. If you wanna collect all five you'll need to know what type of effort to give.

To Receive an A: You will have to know information. There is no way around that. However, whether that information is learned or inherently known is completely up in the air. The more you already know about a class, the less you'll have to study. If you need an A, choose a subject you feel fairly comfortable with. And no, "Hangin' Out" is not a class.

To Receive a B: If you are willing to get a B in a class, you're in fairly good shape. B's are for kids who know the material, but not very well. When studying, if you're not exactly sure how something works, just skip it! Let the A students figure it out; you've got more important things to do. Please note: you don't actually have more important things to do.

To Receive a C: If you want a C in a class and are interested in taking a three-week break from school, then you're in luck! C's are for students who simply forget about their classes for weeks at a time. If you're into taking personal spring breaks during February, or just forgot where one of your classes is being held and are way too cool to recheck, then getting a C is right up your alley. You will, however, have to show up for tests and at least pass the exams. If that sounds like too much effort, you may wanna know how . . .

To Receive a D: Receiving a D is like ordering tomato soup at a restaurant, but instead of enjoying it, it's cold and you spill it all over your shirt. If you really want a D, we suggest going to one class, and writing one paper, but not about the topic at hand. That should pretty much ensure at least a D–.

To Receive an F: You're going to need a lot of drugs and a complete lack of understanding of the course at hand to even think about receiving an F. Receiving an F is for students who have died during the semester, are planning on dropping out of school anyway "cuz it fucking sucks, man," or have enrolled in Engineering 506 on a dare to see if they would pass. If you ever receive an F in a class, you should print out your report card and put it up on a refrigerator that nobody uses, because this truly is an un-achievement!

Billy the Bigot

"Why do Korean kids study so hard? They know they're going to do well."

YOU accusing ME of overusing words I just learned in Psych 101? That's projecting.

How to Hide Grades from Your Parents

1) Receive transcript in mail.

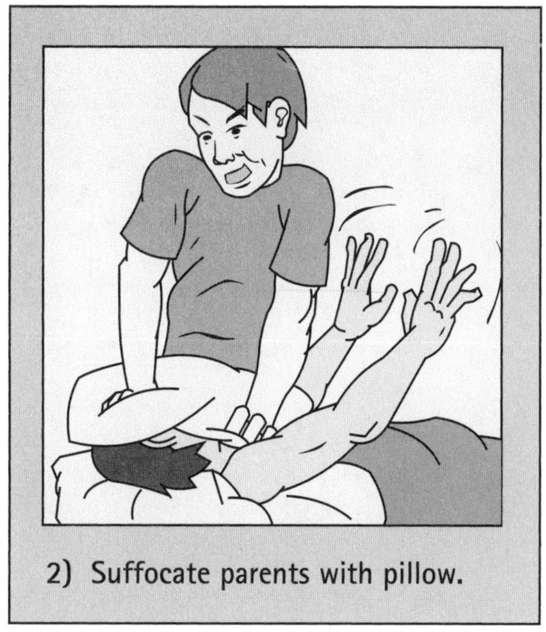

2) Suffocate parents with pillow.

3) Impress friends by using "patricide" in a sentence.

Dear TA

Dear Math 104 TA,

I'm a freshman with a serious problem. I just can't figure out how to take a derivative. Can you help me out?

Confusedly,
Un-Integrate My Heart

Un-Integrate My Heart,

Oh, I see how this is going to be. You make fun of me all semester and now you want help. It's hilarious that I wear my hair in one very long braid on one side of my head, and it's also just a hoot that I sometimes spill my decaf hazelnut on my screenprinted cat sweatshirt. I know you laugh at my sweatshirts, but we can't all afford fancy sweatshirts with no screenprinting. But when it comes time to take a derivative, which is basically the easiest thing in calculus, I'm the first one whose in-box gets full.

And another thing: I have to grade your exams, so if you don't know how to do a problem, don't waste my time. You can't fake your way through a fifteen-step math problem, and no matter how many sentences you write trying to explain yourself, I'm not going to give you partial credit. Speaking of which, I hope you realize that writing "Sir Isaac Newton, 1643-1727" on the back of your test isn't going to convince me that there was an extra-credit question, even though I did give you twenty bonus points for getting the years right.

Anyway, to answer your question, multiply by the exponent, then subtract one from the exponent. Dumbass.

Sincerely,
Math 104 TA

Understanding Your Professor's Comments

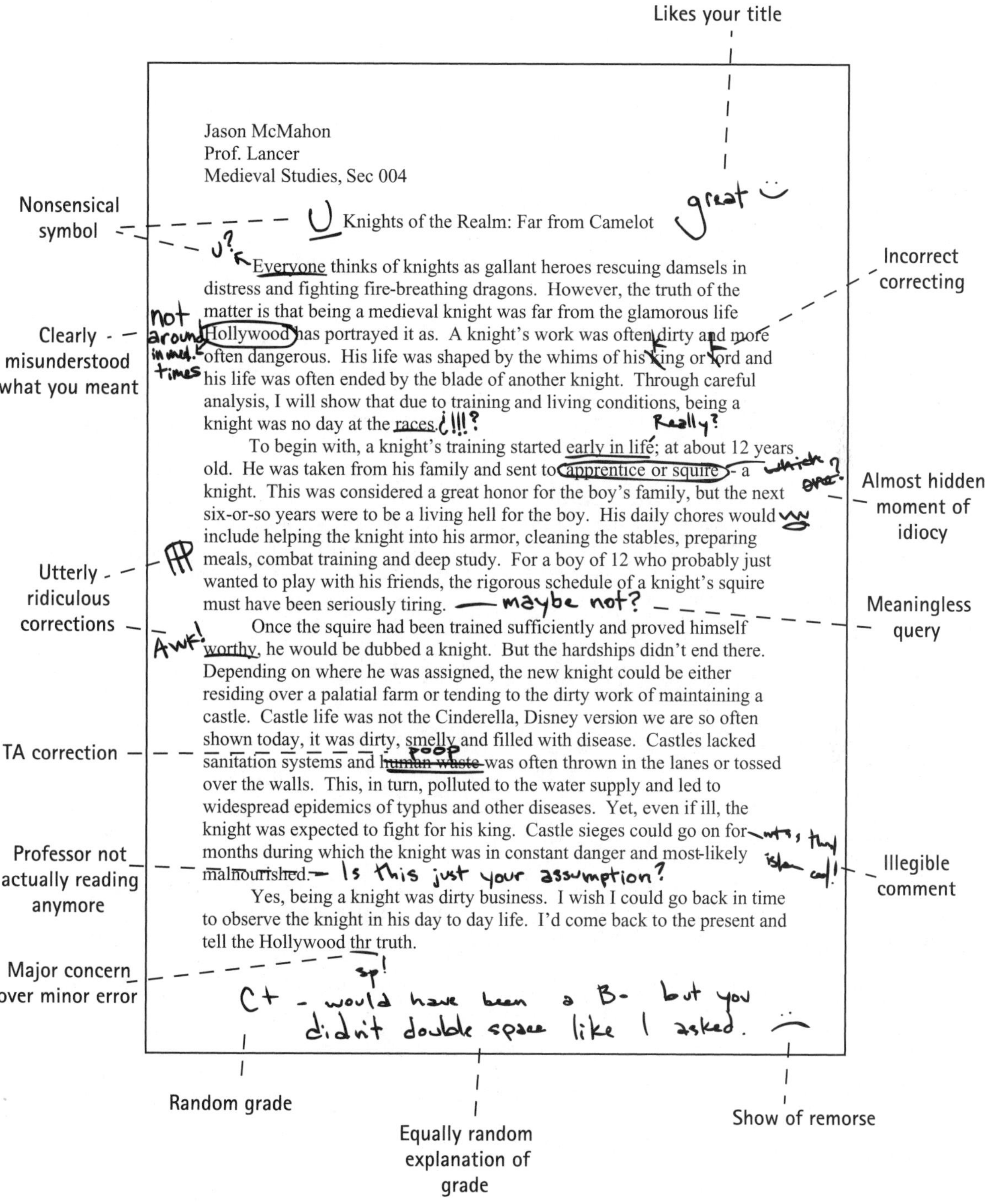
Jason McMahon
Prof. Lancer
Medieval Studies, Sec 004

Knights of the Realm: Far from Camelot

Everyone thinks of knights as gallant heroes rescuing damsels in distress and fighting fire-breathing dragons. However, the truth of the matter is that being a medieval knight was far from the glamorous life Hollywood has portrayed it as. A knight's work was often dirty and more often dangerous. His life was shaped by the whims of his king or lord and his life was often ended by the blade of another knight. Through careful analysis, I will show that due to training and living conditions, being a knight was no day at the races.

To begin with, a knight's training started early in life; at about 12 years old. He was taken from his family and sent to apprentice or squire - a knight. This was considered a great honor for the boy's family, but the next six-or-so years were to be a living hell for the boy. His daily chores would include helping the knight into his armor, cleaning the stables, preparing meals, combat training and deep study. For a boy of 12 who probably just wanted to play with his friends, the rigorous schedule of a knight's squire must have been seriously tiring.

Once the squire had been trained sufficiently and proved himself worthy, he would be dubbed a knight. But the hardships didn't end there. Depending on where he was assigned, the new knight could be either residing over a palatial farm or tending to the dirty work of maintaining a castle. Castle life was not the Cinderella, Disney version we are so often shown today, it was dirty, smelly and filled with disease. Castles lacked sanitation systems and human waste was often thrown in the lanes or tossed over the walls. This, in turn, polluted to the water supply and led to widespread epidemics of typhus and other diseases. Yet, even if ill, the knight was expected to fight for his king. Castle sieges could go on for months during which the knight was in constant danger and most-likely malnourished.

Yes, being a knight was dirty business. I wish I could go back in time to observe the knight in his day to day life. I'd come back to the present and tell the Hollywood thr truth.

Finals Countdown

Most universities schedule dead time between the end of instruction and finals week to allow the students adequate opportunity to study for their exams. However, most students will not make the most efficient use of this dead week. Remember, procastination is like masturbation: you shouldn't do either in the library.

7 Days to Finals:	Drink a fifth, hit things with golf club, but adhere to Finals Week quiet hours. If you're going to use a gun, please apply a silencer; it's just common courtesy.
6 Days to Finals:	Tell yourself that five hundred pages of reading is no big deal. That is just a hundred pages a day for the next five days. Consider yourself prepared for your Math 1C: The Arithmetic of Justifying Laziness.
5 Days to Finals:	Get out notebooks for classes. Skim over your notes and tell your roommate, "You can't REALLY study for this stuff; you either know it or you don't." Also, make sure to complain to your parents about how much "serious cramming" you've been doing.
4 Days to Finals:	Gradually come to the realization that you shouldn't have already sold your textbooks back to the bookstore, no matter how badly you needed money for that mint-condition Nintendo PowerPad.
3 Days to Finals:	Walk to your school's library. When you get there, take a long time setting up your workspace, then put your head down to rest for a couple minutes. Wake up five hours later and walk home. If anybody asks you what you did, tell them you "were at the library all day." That sounds productive enough.

2 Days to Finals:	Thumb through borrowed textbook, undermine confidence of other students by talking about how easy the exam is going to be. Streak whatever's cool to streak on your campus. We suggest your local quadrangle.
1 Day to Finals:	Frantically try to learn a semester's worth of material in an hour. Snort forty milligrams of crushed Adderall. Snort additional five crushed Sweet Tarts to take the edge off. Become fascinated with Gregorian chant, download three gigs of it. Realize that tests "don't really get to your understanding of the material, just what you've memorized."
30 minutes to Finals:	Forge obituary for father's death from tragic shampoo mishap. Receive one-week extension on final. Lather, Rinse, Reprieve!
7 Days to Finals:	Drink a fifth, hit things with golf club, but adhere to Finals Week quiet hours.

A Final Note on Academics

You keep asking for a take-home exam, but do you ever stop to think how that must make the homeless people in your class feel? Testing is a right, not a privilege.

I think Business majors should be offered a class called "Leaning Back in Your Chair and Crossing Your Arms in an Intimidating Manner."

11 COMPUTERS

Introduction

If you started college as recently as 1974, you probably didn't even have a computer. Those select few rich students who were lucky to have one had their entire dorm room filled up by the enormous processor and couldn't sleep due to the thunderous whirring of cooling fans. These seem like large sacrifices to make for a computer that could only play "Oregon Trail," especially since no matter how many you shot, you could only carry one hundred pounds of computer back to your dorm room.

Today, computers are much smaller, and will only fill up your entire room if your entire room is the size of your lap. It will not be long before college students will be able to download full movies faster than you can say "They made a *Rocky IX*?!" Instant messages will become even more instant, e-mail will be known as snail mail, and regular mail will be known as the Pony Express. Mailmen everywhere will be known as unemployed.

But you needn't look into the future to comprehend the importance of computers in college. College life has already been greatly influenced by computers as well as the Internet. Grades are received in e-mail form, entire university course catalogs are found online, and some professors even conduct classes and office hours on their Web site. However, regardless of how convenient and easy the Internet has become, you will always have one professor who is stubbornly sticking to doing everything by hand. "No, no, register for this class using a punch card! I don't trust these newfangled technology boxes! And if you need to get in contact with me, write down this telegram frequency!"

Computers have also helped college students score with the opposite sex. Getting a lady's screenname is almost more important than getting her phone number. You can now stalk your special lover by finding out their interests and course load online before even meeting them. That way you can walk narrowly close to them on campus, yelling on the phone to nobody in particular how much you love *Catcher in the Rye*, Stanley Kubrick movies, and shoe shopping. What's that, random hot stranger? You do, too? This must be fate! Let's make love!

Of course, there are some downsides to all these conveniences. College laptop thefts are at an all-time high, and there is only one way to avoid this larceny: buy a desktop. Furthermore, you will eventually have to deal with your school's tech support staff, who delight in nothing more than making you squirm before screaming streams of unintelligible computer jargon into the phone. "I don't know why I haven't committed my computer serial number to memory! I guess I'm too busy having sex with girls! Hello? Hello?"

Despite these scattered difficulties, computers will greatly enhance your quality of life while you're in college. Either that, or they'll become a vacuous black hole so dense that not even the most diligent students can escape, eating away your precious studying time as you check one more round of away messages or update your blog. Okay, we get it, you're on page zero of ten of your paper. Unless your class is at a state school, you're not gonna get away with printing that blog and calling it an essay on Faulkner's early works. So get back to work.

I'm so good at Adobe Photoshop I make Mother Teresa look like Joseph Stalin.

Warning Signs

Having a ton of Facebook friends is all well and good, but very few of them will show up for your funeral. And the ones who do will only be there to poke you.

IMing

Instant messaging (or IMing) has allowed for unbelievable advances in the world of gossiping, stalking, plan-making, and flirting. It's nearly impossible to imagine a world without instant messaging. We dusted off our secret selection of history books and we were able to piece together images of college life back before instant messaging was popular. So hop into the CollegeHumor time machine with us, as we travel back in time—all the way to 1995!

GOSSIPING

Gossiping over IM is really easy. All you have to do is copy and paste juicy tidbits of information over to your different friends! If you are having a really interesting conversation with somebody, you don't need to remember any details, you can just copy the entire conversation and instant-message the entire thing verbatim! In 1995, things were much harder:

"So, Stan, tell me more about what happened last night. And speak into my microphone-shaped brooch, please. Hey, where are you going!? Drats!"

STALKING

With IM, stalking is a cinch! Just add your infatuation to your buddy list and keep an eye on his away message. You can track each and every movement of his without the hassles of rummaging through garbage. In 1995, stalking somebody proved very difficult and rather creepy:

"Why am I in this Dumpster?! Because I can ascertain exactly what she had for dinner last night! This isn't a banana peel on my face, it's a clue! Now if you'll excuse me, I have to narrow this puree down to five fruits."

PLAN-MAKING

Instant Messaging allows for fast and efficient event planning. You can speak to several friends at a single time and decide on a specific activity within seconds. Everything is arranged and organized and you didn't even need to pick up a phone. In 1995, organizing your friends was harder than getting tickets to a Boyz II Men concert:

Steinem and dine 'em. It's the only way to win a feminist's heart.

"Yeah, I dunno. Let me conference call him. What's that? He's already ON conference call!? Well, I can barely hear him. Tell him to speak up! I don't care if he's at a funeral being held in a library, tell him to talk louder or we'll never make it to the matinee of *The English Patient*!

FLIRTING

Since the inception of IM into mainstream college technology, the amount of flirting across universities has increased by over 500 percent. All these online Casanovas need is a screen-name and a catchy joke, and they're as good as laid. Online flirting removes all the annoying awkward silences and nervous banter that exist in real-life flirting. It's amazing anybody was able to sweet-talk a girl way back in 1995:

"Hey, baby, lookin' fat. I mean PHAT fat. Not, fat fat. Hahaha. Sorry, oh God, I didn't just call you fat fat. No, I'm not looking at your breasts, I don't care about your breasts. I mean, they're fine, I just . . . Listen, let me start over. Hi. You're ugly. FUCK!"

Away Messages

You're away from the computer right now. At this point, the key is to choose an appropriate away message. A good away message has a healthy balance of reason and comedy. Anybody can write a funny joke in their away message, but if it doesn't explain where you are, there is no point. Likewise, anybody can write "out to lunch," but that won't make your buddies laugh.

An easy approach to coming up with a great away message is to narrow your reason down to one word, and then come up with a delicious movie title pun. For example, if you are going out to dinner, you can use "Eat the Parents" or "Food Will Hunting." If you are at class, you can use "Mississippi Learning" or "School Hand Luke."

Another way to make your away message fun and effective is to write the setup to a normal joke, and change your punch line to the reason you are away. Nothing says LOL quite like "What do you get when you cross an elephant and a rhino? I'm asleep." Or "A frog is looking for a loan, so he goes into a bank. He sits down at a desk and the nameplate says 'Patty Whack.' He talks to Patty about the loan and she asks him what he has for collateral. The frog replies, 'Well, I have this vase.' He pulls the vase out of a bag to show her.

My parents are terrible with technology; they can't even program the clock on their Betamax.

Patty says, 'Well, that's just a cheap knickknack.' Then the owner notices the vase and says to himself, 'Gee, that's from the seventeenth century; it's worth tons of money.' So he walks over to Patty and says, 'Dinner. BRB.' "

One last method of achieving a humorous and useful away message is to add the word "bacon" to the end of all your otherwise normal away messages. Watch as your friends instant-message you in confusion after reading, "Sleeping bacon," "Reading Bacon," and our favorite, "At a friend's funeral bacon." You've stuck to your guns even in these emotional and difficult times, and that is the most important lesson of all.

Getting a Grown-up Screenname

Growing up doesn't mean you have to stop using instant messaging devices; it just means that you have to get a new screenname. It's just that there aren't many adults with the screenname "CaliGirl14" or "Bongzilla420." You have to get a screenname that acts your age. Which means no more "NYDude1989" or "PlayaPimp6969."

Representing yourself as a mature adult is oftentimes more important than your actual maturity level. So no "FagBuzter4," "CandyLuvr88," "BugEater12," or "FrancisFordCoppafeel." And definitely no more "TitSquisherX," "BuggFuggler," or "TeabaggerVance."

An adult screenname could also help you score some points when hitting on ladies online. They don't want to see a "NipSuckle7" or a "PU55Y4CKER" on the other end, and they certainly don't want to chat with "CLYTBuster," "RapeMonkey," "TenYearDildo," "SpankadoodleDee," "CockTastic," "CaulkTastic," "CockPlastic," or "BabyMoLester."

Instead, choose a screenname with class, like "Lance."

Male/Female Profile Templates

Whether you like it or not, we are the first generation to be born into the age of instant messaging, e-mail, and high-speed Internet. For this reason, it is utterly important to portray a positive Internet persona of yourself NOW, while you still can! And the easiest way to do this is to create a truthful, stirring, and entirely unique IM profile. To help you out, we have provided a simple profile template for both men and women to use:

Computers can be a great help in college, but they can also be a great hindrance. If you or somebody you know has been molested by a computerized robot, don't stand idly by. Make a stance. Silence is what they want. Tell somebody.

(a complete list of everything you are going to do today, as if anyone cares)

(memorable quote from a song that seems like it was written for you)

(inside joke from the night before)

(where you live)

(countdowns)

(unnecessary amount of space)

(lame acronym that your boyfriend and ONLY your boyfriend understands, even though everyone knows who it's for and what it means)

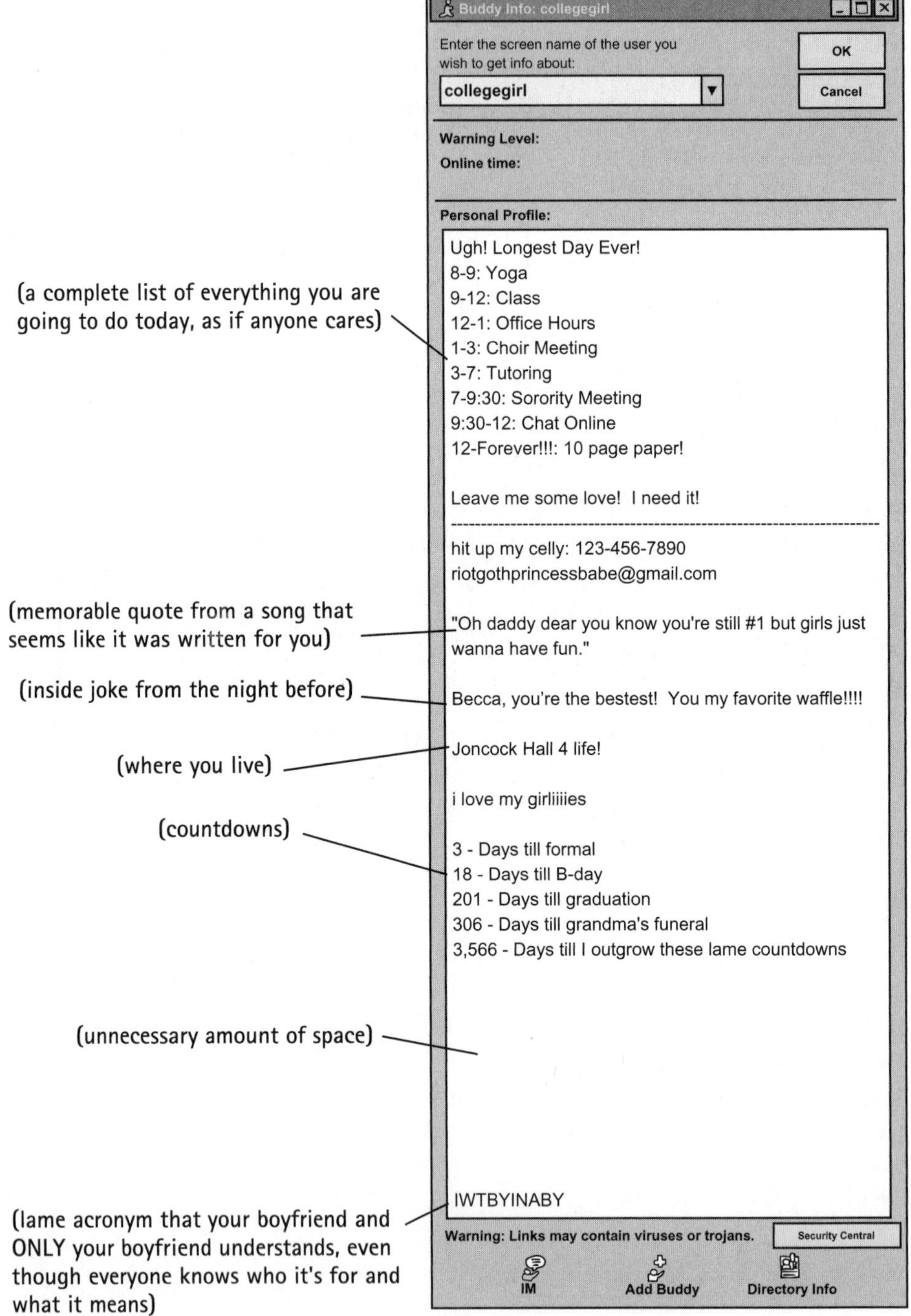

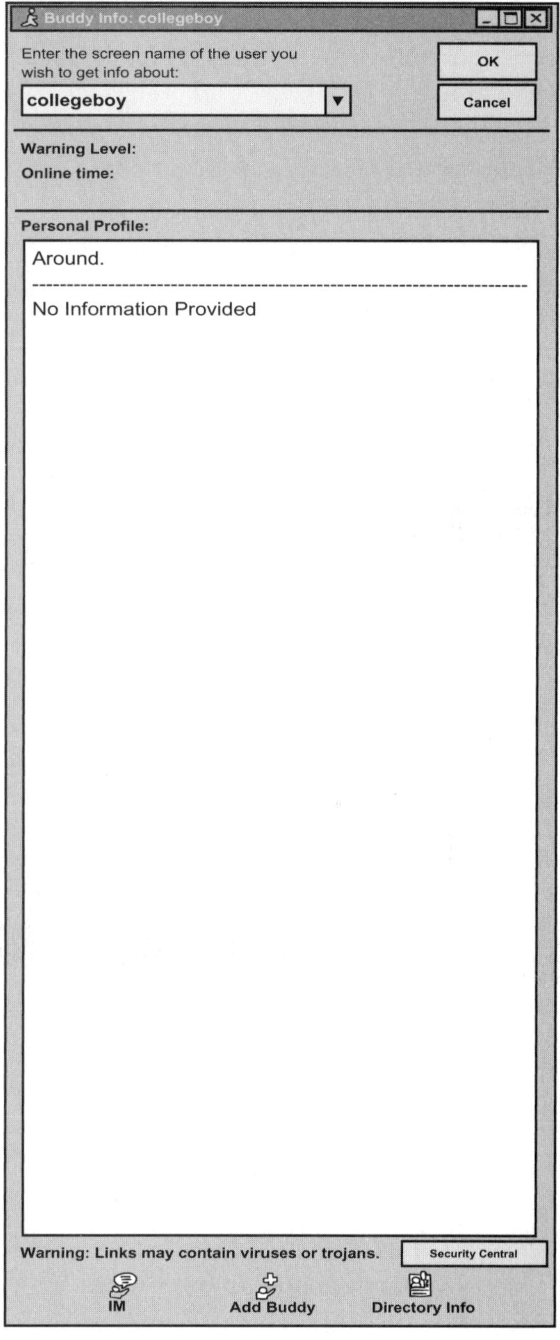

Holy shit, that's a great away message! So it was YOU who wrote the original screenplay for *Old School.*

Emoticons

Flirting with a girl over IM is dangerous. Subtle sexual text flies back and forth between screennames, each not knowing what the other really means. Emoticons provide the user with a tool to decipher hidden meanings in these pseudo-romantic statements. If your "friend" uses an emoticon, just check the guide below to see if you are one step closer to non-cyber sex:

Smiley: I like where this conversation is going.
e.g.:

LAX224: hey babe.
Stargirl9: hey :)

Winky Face: What I just said didn't seem sexual, but it was.
e.g.:

Stargirl9: Well, i'll see you later. I'm off to the library.
Stargirl9: ;)

Angel Face: What I just said seemed sexual, but I am trying to counterract my sluttiness by harkening upon the image of St. Peter.
e.g.:

Stargirl9: i like to do more than just cuddle.
Stargirl9: () :)

Big Smiley: What I just said was explicitly sexual. You probably have an erection, but I am trying to remain cute by double-smiling.
e.g.:

Stargirl9: i can't wait to feel you on top of me tonight.
Stargirl9: :))

Angry Face: I'm fake angry at you because I'm not getting what I want. Also, I have one eyebrow.
e.g.:

Stargirl9: you said you were coming over!
Stargirl9: l:(

Round-Mouth Smiley: I'm either shocked at what you just said or offering a beej, or sometimes even both!

e.g.:

Stargirl9: I can't believe you think I'm that type of girl!
Stargirl9: :0

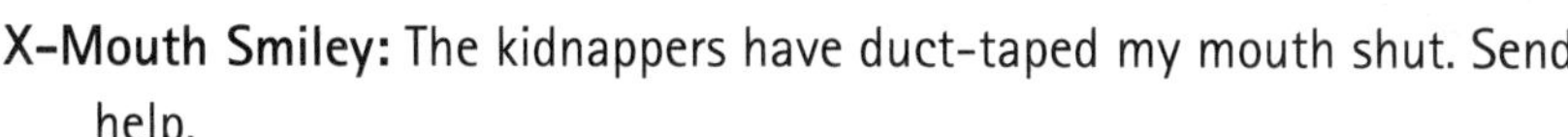

X-Mouth Smiley: The kidnappers have duct-taped my mouth shut. Send help.

e.g.:

Stargirl9: Autoresponse from Stargirl9: Please Daddy, just pay them what they want.
They have a knife.
Stargirl9: :-X

Money-mouth Smiley: Put your money where your mouth is or put a horizontal symbol for money there.

e.g.:

Stargirl9: If you think you've got a better emoticon for "put your money where your mouth is" then . . .
Stargirl9: :-$

An easy way to double your vocabulary is putting "e-" before every word you know to make it about the Internet.

European History 306 Classroom

File Edit People View Help

ProfessorCoolGuy: Welcome to the chatroom for European History 306, The Protestant Reformation and Modern Society. Just to get the discussion rolling, how was this week's reading affected by the Protestant Reformation?
TruDat84: a/s/l?
AandFGrrrl87: lol
ProfessorCoolGuy: Guys, c'mon, focus. I know you guys read the chapter, you all aced the online quiz.

TruDat84 wants to send file funnyboobs.jpg to ProfessorCoolGuy
ProfessorCoolGuy rejects file funnyboobs.jpg

ProfessorCoolGuy: Guys, we go through this every week. I can't accept .jpgs from you.
KirkRULESpicardDROOLS: The Reformation sent shockwaves throughout the hierarchy of the Catholic church and paved the way for secular art.
TruDat84: fag.
GratefulHempBracelet: You guys would not believe how baked I am right now. Seriously, I am so baked. Right now. Really.
ProfessorCoolGuy: Why would Henry VIII want to break with the Catholic church?
TruDat84: For the POONTANG!!!
AandFGrrrl87: lol
KirkRULESpicardDROOLS: Martin Luther's 95 theses changed the course of the medieval times and their effects are still felt today.
TruDat84: I got 95 theses but a bitch ain't one. BRB, gotta drop a major deuce.

ProfessorCoolGuy: I fail to see what that has to do with the material.
SExxxYVIOLETsONLY18: Click here to watch my webcam! Me and my slutty roommates go ALL THE WAY!
KirkRULESpicardDROOLS has left the chat room.

GratefulHempBracelet: See the thing about the Protestants is they believe in god. But god's like just an illusion, man, you know. There's something out there, but like what it is doesn't matter. It's all about love.
ProfessorCoolGuy: That's vaguely on topic, maybe you could expand on those ideas Connor?
GratefulHempBracelet: Dude, what are you talking about?
ProfessorCoolGuy: Expand on the ideas you present.
GratefulHempBracelet: The present? It's going to be the past to us in a few minutes. It's already the past. Dude, we're stuck in the stream of history, and the current keeps pulling us along.
ProfessorCoolGuy: Dead fucking wrong.

GratefulHempBracelet has left the room.

AandFGrrrl87: lol-apalooza!

AandFGrrrl87 has left the room.

ProfessorCoolGuy: TTYL class. TTYL.

1 person here

ProfessorCoolGuy

IM Ignore Talk Get Info

A | **B** *I* u | link

Send

Lessons from a Pro: How to Extend Your Paper Deadline by 72 Hours via E-mail, by Ricky

I had a friend in college who made it his mission to work as hard as he could to avoid working hard. That may sound counterintuitive, but it's true: in the amount of time he spent plotting out how to turn a paper in late, he could have written the paper twice. Here is his most clever method of getting a professor to extend a deadline:

Thursday, 4:45 p.m. The paper is due in fifteen minutes over e-mail. You haven't even started. Send an e-mail to your professor that goes like this:

> *Here's my paper, hope you enjoy! See you in class!*

However, do not attach anything to the e-mail. Immediately put up an autoresponse e-mail message that says something like, "Visiting Kelly, be back Sunday night. Call my cell if you need me."

When your professor writes back to tell you that you forgot the attachment, he'll get the autoresponse that says you're out of town. On Saturday, check your e-mail and respond to the professor with something like this:

> *Whoops, my bad! I'm at my girlfriend's school, and the paper is on my dorm computer. I'll send it as soon as I get back. Thanks for understanding!!*

Send your actual completed paper to him Sunday night or Monday morning. Good job, you just extended your deadline three days!

Screennames are a great way to tell how original your friends are. The higher the number at the end of their screenname, the less creative they are.

Desktop vs. Laptop

Each type of computer has its advantages and disadvantages, but it's good to get a computer to match your personality. Here's a basic composite sketch of a desktop vs. a laptop user:

Desktop User: A typical desktop user is fat. Really fat. This 400+ pound behemoth likes nothing more than pizza and computer games. He uses his keyboard as a plate and as such, many of the letters don't even work anymore. He types with his pinkies because his hands are usually greasy from eating pizza. He fantasizes not of real women, but of women in the computer games he plays. He says there is a frame in Mario Kart where if you pause it just right you can see Princess Peach's nipple. He's lying. That's completely fabricated.

Laptop User: A typical laptop user only wears turtlenecks. He wears glasses but doesn't need to because his vision is 20/10. That's better than perfect. When leaving his room, he'll say, "Excuse me? Close the door please!" even though it's one of those doors that closes automatically. He wipes his mouth with $20 bills, which is very disconcerting because he's not very rich. In fact, he's stealing those twenties from his roommate. Ask him to high-five you and his eyes will begin watering and he'll tell you that he can't high-five you, and that it's a long story. It's not a long story, though. He once high-fived his dad off a cliff.

Practically speaking, signing an Internet petition is the adult equivalent of writing a letter to Santa Claus.

The Only MATTBLOG on the Entire Web!

April 10, 8:52 p.m. What is a blog? Well, Webster's Online Dictionary defines blog as "Word Cannot Be Found," but I believe there's so much more to it than that. Got my tests back: yup, two F's.

Comments (0)

April 7, 6:23 p.m. Sorry for no posts for a while, what a crazy couple of days. I had two tests. I guess that's not really crazy, but you can see why I didn't have time to post! I'm pretty sure I failed both of them.

Comments (0)

April 5, 5:32 p.m. I have no stance on the following debates:
1) Paper v. plastic
2) The Pepsi Challenge
3) Versus v. vs.
4) Brown v. Board of Education

Comments (0)

April 3, 11:13 a.m. I don't want to get political or anything, but I really can't see why these Israelis and Palestinians can't get along. I mean, I had an Arab friend in elementary school and we had a falling out, but in seventh grade we were best friends again! Well, he was Asian, but the message is the same. Also, people shouldn't blow up cars. I'd kill for any wheels right now. (Not literally.)

Comments (0)

April 2, 9:03 p.m. Went on a date tonight. Well, it wasn't really a date, but I went to Starbucks and she was working. Everytime I go there I try to do something exceptional with my ordering so she'll notice me. Today I ordered 11 Frappucinos in Latin and left before I even picked them up. I'm quite certain she now thinks I'm cultured and rich. Little does she know, those 11 drinks set me back lunch money for the next five days! Oh God, I'm so alone.

Comments (0)

March 31, 7:48 p.m. Soon, blogs will become so popular that they will render these following items obsolete as well: Typewriters, Books, Refrigerators, Candy Stores, Aeroplanes, Gravity, and lastly, a mother's affection for her newborn baby son. I for one am happy to be part of the future! THE FUTURE OF BLOGS!!! BRB, my SpaghettiOs are done.

Comments (0)

LINKS!

- MATTWORLD
- MATTWORLD
- MATTWORLD
- Google
- Mapquest
- Amazon

A Word on Google

It's generally a bad idea to tell a prospective girlfriend that you've Google-image-searched her.

SO YOU'VE DECIDED TO
Set Your Computer on Fire

"Stupid computer! I wish I could set you on fire!" Well, now you can.

What you'll need: A computer, four drums of gasoline, a giant empty drum, a girlfriend

What you do: Empty the four drums of gasoline into the bigger drum. Throw your computer into the giant drum. Throw a match into the giant drum (preferably in slow motion). As the gasoline ignites, stand far away from the flames but look intently into the fire. Look into your girlfriend's eyes and mouth, "Fucking computer." Then passionately kiss her.

According to *The Jetsons*, computers should be so evolved by now that we should have flying cars, robot slaves, and machines that create dinner at the touch of a button. Well, zero out of three ain't bad.

Welcome to the tech support family! In all things, remember our motto: if someone says "Thank you," you haven't done your job correctly.

How to Handle a Student Call

Answer the phone in your most disinterested voice. Say, "Welcome to the Tech Support Hotline. For training purposes, your call may be recorded. Now, make it snappy, my food's about to get here. Seriously."

As the student on the other end begins describing their problem in great detail, which they almost always will, interrupt them and say, "Whoa, whoa, whoa. Slow down, nerdbrain. I'm not a rocket scientist. Start over." After they end their second explanation of the same problem, say, "Start over" again. If they repeat their problem again, you know you have a dedicated customer on the other end, and it's time to start helping them.

First, you are going to need to know what computer and operating system they're running. If they say anything other then a Dell running the latest version of Windows, tell them, "That's your problem right there," and hang up quickly. If they do tell you that they're running a Dell with the latest version of Windows, it's time to earn your wage.

Remind the caller that whatever's troubling their computer is probably their fault. "Were you using this computer to browse the Internet or check e-mail? Nice going. Why don't you throw it out of a moving car while you're at it?" If they seem confused, just sigh for several minutes while muttering, "What to do . . . what to do . . ."

It is now time to suggest basic troubleshooting techniques that they have probably already been attempting: "Have you tried restarting your computer? You have? Why don't we go ahead and try that again?" "Have you tried cursing under your breath? Have you tried saying, 'Fucking computer. My computer sucks'? You have? Hmmm, okay then . . ."

If none of this seems to work, it's time for you to say, "Can you hold on for just a moment?" and hang up on them. If they call back for more help, answer the phone with, "You again?" and slam down the receiver before they can protest. The important thing is, you tried. You can't help anybody who doesn't want to help themselves.

Parents and Computers

When it comes to computers, your parents are good at one thing: buying you one. After that, they get a little weaker and know only what they read in *Newsweek*. If your dad awkwardly IMs you in telegram style, it can get a little annoying. STOP.

However, since your parents don't know the difference between a mouse and a keyboard, you can have a little fun at their expense. See which of these computer lies you can get them to tell their tennis partners:

"No, you can't get e-mail if your computer is turned off. It's lost forever."

"Google Sandwich is being beta-tested as we speak. You'll never have to look for a sandwich again."

"The 'e' in 'e-mail' stands for 'e-mail.' "

"The name 'PowerPoint' is slang for a sexual maneuver common in porn films. The program was named by a perverted Microsoft developer."

"Child pornography is legal if you don't keep it in your 'My Documents' folder."

"The explosion of the laptop industry has required so much lithium for batteries that the world's supply of the element will run out in 2012."

"The first computer was largely inspired by an episode of *The Jetsons*. It was named Rosie. It made you dinner instantly."

"Before mp3 caught on as a file format, mp1 and mp2 were huge failures."

"The company is called 'Apple' because it originally made computers for fruit farmers."

"The inspiration for the character Leisure Suit Larry died of AIDS in 1998 after sleeping with over a thousand women."

"If you read it in a blog, it must be true; the government monitors them for factually correct content."

A Final Note on Computers

You should keep your computer porn in a well-hidden folder. And no, a folder called "Not Tittyfuck Vids" on your desktop isn't well hidden.

12 EXTRACURRICULAR ACTIVITIES

Introduction

In college, there are two extremes: classes and parties. Somewhere in between these two lies the gray area known only as "extracurricular activities." We know what you're thinking: "Academic meetings AND pizza?" It's confusing at first; there's no question about it.

Most universities have about as many clubs on campus as they do students. These veritable Mad Libs of quasi-academic gatherings are seemingly created out of a grab bag of adjectives, races, and causes. "Blue Asians for Health Reform," "Strong Russians for the Dolphins," "The Gay and Lesbian Association"—yup, college has every club you could think of.

So what exactly are extracurricular activities? The easiest way to figure it out is to break down the words into their Latin roots. "Extra" means "outside" and "curricular" means "of or relating to curricula." Glad we got that settled. Moving on . . .

Picking the right club for you is tough. Once you've narrowed your top fifty choices down to an elite four, it's important to choose one or two that you know you will be staying in for multiple years. Clubs are rapidly evolving organisms where you can go from intern to president in three years or less, so don't choose a club you wouldn't mind running in a few short semesters. Oh, and every club, for some reason or another, has a "treasurer." Don't be that guy. It may sound like pirates' booty, but being a treasurer is a lot like being an accountant: boring and Jewish.

Another club certainty is the "hot shot." Every club will have one person that devotes his entire life to being its greatest member. He spends every free minute he has in that small little club office and is the envy of all the girl members. He becomes obsessed with the club because outside of it, he is powerless and nobody notices him. After graduation he'll come back because he realizes that in the real world, clubs don't exist; the Burger King Kids' Club rarely holds meetings. A few years pass and every member finds it odd that this random thirty-five-year-old is jerking off during meetings. Moral of the story: have fun in your club, but don't become infatuated; college is about other things, too.

All of this information is not meant to imply that the only worthwhile extracurricular activities are school-sponsored clubs. They are, however, the only ones that effectively pad your résumé. It's not that napping six hours a day isn't an impressive activity, but employers are generally looking for someone who can remain awake and upright for more than half an hour at a time. Also, don't list "hanging out" as a special skill; that's practically as common on résumés as "proficient at Microsoft Word."

Please don't let us discourage you, though; some informal activities really take off. Everyone is going to be truly impressed by your college band and is just hoping you'll invite them to your "breakout gig" four towns over. Keep giving your demo to everyone you make eye contact with on the street; all of the great acts have gotten discovered like that.

The last rule about extracurricular activities is that you don't talk about extracurricular activities. If your friends gave one good goddamn about whatever little club you're in, they'd join it. If they wanted to hear about what went on at the meeting, they'd contact the club secretary and request a copy of the official minutes, and after the sergeant at arms signed off on this request and their $2 printing fee was processed (payable only in cashier's check), they'd find out for themselves. Otherwise, keep your mouth SHUT about what went on at the Jolly Jugglers Jamboree this afternoon; we're trying to watch TV.

Student theater: where only the audience's tears are convincing.

A Crapella

Hey, man, do you want to come see my a cappella group perform? No, no, we're not the Broken Amps, we're Rhythm and Booze. Yeah, we do things a little differently . . . We like to get funky. Like, for this show, we're going to sing "Hey Ya." Ya, I know it's a few years old, but we just got this new beatboxer. He's a freshman from Detroit, and he's incredible. I even get to do the "Don't want to meet your daddy" part. Wanna hear it? Okay, cool, you're waiting for the show.

Yeah, it's at the coffee shop on Thursday and we're going to have our CD for sale. It's twelve bucks, eight tracks, a little Ben Harper, a little Dave Matthews Band. Dude, we recorded it in my dorm room, but the sound quality's so good, you can barely tell we four-tracked it. This freshman producer is amazing, dude. Some of the cross-fades . . . Well, I don't want to spoil it for you.

You think you'll make it out? Drag. Well, you don't have to call it "a crap-ella." Do you know how many times I've heard that? Until you start throwing beer bottles, like at that show we played at Oberlin, I'm not even going to notice. Oh, sure, walk away. You want some traveling music that's not impeded by instrumentation? Well, too bad!

It's not that the Make-A-Wish Foundation can't give you any wish, it's just that they're out of twenty-third birthdays this month.

Conservative Political Group

Young Republicans
Association

Putting the conservative back in the liberal arts

Dear Student,

Our records show that you are a registered voter, but we haven't seen you at any meetings of the Young Republicans. We feel that you may be a good fit for our group. Do you use the word "fag," but not to be ironic? How would you complete the sentence "Big business is ______ for America because it fuels the economy while maintaining a well-funded arm of the collective conscience"? Does it still make you mad that Standard Oil was broken up right as it was getting off the ground? Do you know your monocle prescription?

If you answered "yes" or "Jesus's special gift" to any of these questions, it's a great time to join the Young Republicans. We meet each week in the Hall of Injustice and there's always sausage and ham pizza (can't have any Jewish "people" lurking around).

Majority rules, minorities don't,
Chip Wellington Jameson IV

Chip Wellington Jameson IV

President
Young Republicans

Liberal Political Group

YOUNG DEMOCRATS

Hey Man,

Our friends told us that you didn't like war so we thought we'd give you a shout. So, if you don't already know from the letterhead, we are the Young Democrats and you might be just right for our political action group. Do you find yourself spending hours feeling guilty for things your ancestors did? Did you grow up upper middle class, not upper class, and harbor resentment about that? Are you Jewish, Catholic, Black, Hispanic or different in any way?

If you answered "dunno" or nothing at all, then you are probably a good fit for Young Democrats. We meet somewhere every now and then, and you can come. Remember, united we whine, divided we fall.

Mike
President

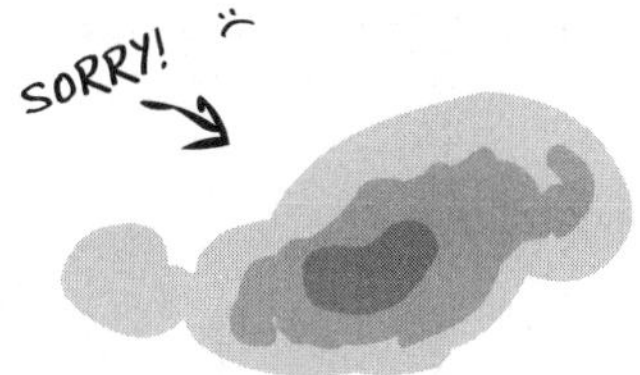

And now a word on college improv: "PROCTOLOGIST!!!!"

The Pious Adventures of

THE GOD SQUAD

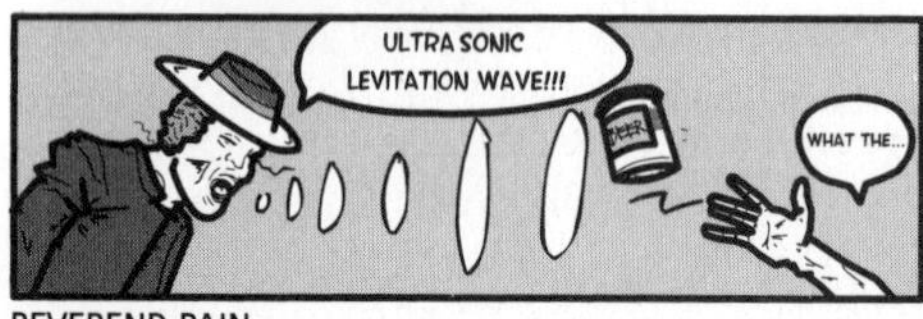

REVEREND PAIN

TRUE LOVE WEIGHTS

ABSTINENCE GIRL

Haitian and Asian sound alike, so you want to verify which one he is before forcing him to do your math homework.

Welcome to the home page of Napping, Every University's most popular student organization!

4,590,302 Members and growing strong!

Napper of the Week:

This week 's spotlight napper is Josh Harrison, who managed to reach REM in 3 MINUTES flat, while dozing on the main quad between classes yesterday. Now THAT'S NAPPING! Everybody give a big round of naps for our friend Josh here.

Upcoming Activities:

A mid-afternoon nap, and another before dinner. Possibly a pre-party nap, followed by a during-party nap, a during-nap nap, and a post-nap nap.

Freestyle Napping: The world of hip-hop and sleeping are back together! Slumber and rapping join forces for the first time since nursery rhymes in this three-hour tour-de-snooze. Bring a pillow—this will get ugly!

New Members? What took you so long?

For those of you unfamiliar with our club, we're glad you finally decided to leave your position as ruler of Nerdtopia and join the rest of us in Coolville, USA. Napping is not for the weak of heart. It requires 100% determination to be as lazy as physically possible for the rest of your college days. Think you're up to the challenge? Then read on, warrior.

Rule 1: You must embrace the fact that Napping can happen anytime, anywhere. It's not just for kindergartners anymore. If you find this concept difficult, take some time to reflect on the official Napping mantra:

"Napping in the morning, napping in the evening, napping at suppertime. When napping's on a bagel, you can eat napping anytime."

Rule 2: Size doesn't matter! Sometimes the shortest nap can have the greatest effects. One of our founding yawners, Bob Starks, spent 30 years of his adult life without sleeping! His secret: 15-minute powernaps. He would group 32 of these powernaps together every night and embrace the rest of his day fresh as a daisy!

So go for the gold and nap whenever you want, for as long as you want, as often as you want! Though remember, napping for over 6 months at a time is not recommended and may perhaps mean that you are a bear.

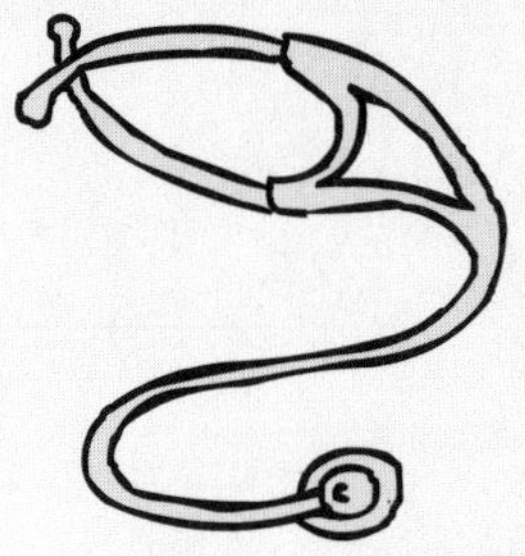

Laughter may be the best medicine, but *flyering* is the best preventive medicine!

Hello and welcome to the third annual peer health educator recruitment week. I say nothing gets the word out quite like flyering, and I'm sure you guys all would agree.

They say there is no cure for mononucleosis, but I've got one right here! It's a red piece of paper that says, "JUST SAY NO TO MONO!" with ten easy ways you can avoid getting this debilitating illness. Mass-produced, these babies have ten times the potency of all the world's penicillin.

STDs, meningitis, skin cancer—with your support, and our flyers, these diseases can become a thing of the past! I know that I simply cannot place all of these condoms onto all of these vegetables by myself—I need your support. I hope you all decide to join us in eradicating illness on campus, because there are enough papers, copy machines, bananas, squashes, lubricated condoms, and staples for all of us to make a difference!

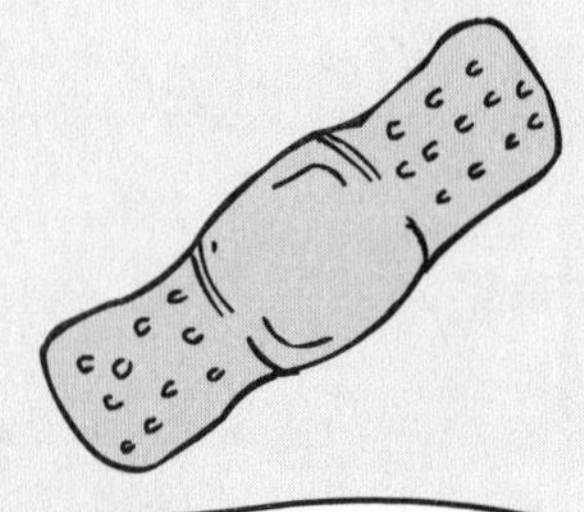

Campus Tour Guides

Being a campus tour guide is the most important extracurricular activity at college with the acronym CTG.

But how do you know if being a campus tour guide is right for you? Usually the university will administer an assessment exam to locate the top natural-born campus tour guides at your school. The exam will look something like this:

1. Do you prefer walking backwards instead of forwards?

a) Yes!

b) No.

2. Do you like saying "We all here? Great, let's get started. Firstly, my name is ____ and I will be your campus tour guide this afternoon. If you have any questions you can just—" and have several parents interrupt by saying "We can't hear you! Speak louder!"?

a) Yes!

b) No.

3. Can you tell that one kid, "Enough already with the SAT and GPA questions"; you don't know if he's going to get in!?

a) Yes!

b) No.

4. Will you attempt to slyly wink at fathers when talking about the girls' dorm?

a) Yes!

b) No.

5. On a scale of 1–10, how well do you deal with Jewish mothers?

Kids, check this out . . .

Ronny the ROTC Student!

He moves, he speaks, he dreads graduation!

Comes with: school-issued fatigues, practice rifle, deferred tuition bill, and ugly haircut!

Speaks up to four phrases!

- "I wish my dad hadn't got laid off right before I went to college."
- "Guys, keep it down, I have to wake up at 6 a.m."
- "Do you think the Middle East is as bad as everyone says it is?"
- "See you guys in four years . . . hopefully."

Warning: Ronny the ROTC Student is often foul-tempered due to drill. Do NOT attempt to wake, shame, or remind Ronny of his post-college plans in any way.

Starting a Band

From the primordial ooze of the first caveman college, four young Neanderthal rockers rose up and formed Urg and the Hunter-Gatherers, the first college rock band. Since then, guitars have merged with electricity to make rocking 38 percent easier and 24 percent more skull-crushing, so you almost have to start a rock band of your very own. Even no-rules rockers who don't play by anyone's rules have rules they must follow when starting a band:

1. The better the band name, the better the band. If you've picked up your instruments, you've already fucked up. Don't start a band without a bitchin' name for it. Your name should point out how cool and awesome your band will be, but it should also sound like you didn't put too much effort into it. For minimal effort/maximal awesomeness, just steal one of these:

    Latitude Problem
    Thanxgiving
    The Intern Ships
    Meal Plan Munchies
    Nevertheless But Thenagain
    ShredMonkey200
    The Dino Sores
    Womenorah

2. Write some hits. If your hits have anything other than power chords and blistering solos in them, they suck. Seriously, they're the worst hits ever. You expect to get on the radio with a suspended D minor? NPR, maybe. For those of you who don't want to fail, particularly awesome chords are E, G, C, A, and occasionally F.
3. Buy some threads. Your clothes are almost as important as your band name and your hits. What kind of band are you? Rockers always wear tight jeans, but knowing what type of band you are decides whether you wear ironic T-shirts or ironic dress shirts and ties.
4. Sign a record deal. Some little indie labels are going to try to sign you at first. Here's a good rule of thumb for how to handle these situations: fuck 'em. Don't worry about burning bridges; if they could afford a bridge, they wouldn't be an indie label. Hold out for a major-label deal and make sure you get tons of groupies in the contract.

5. Play some smokin' gigs. Now it's time for your band to perform its hits in other cities, or "take your act on the road." Make sure the light show is good and strobey. Only play in cities that consider themselves to be a metropolis or megalopolis. Anything else is just a waste of their, and more importantly, your time.

6. Break up. At some point, it will change and stop being about the music and someone will want to pursue an acting career. When this happens, say, "You've changed, man; it used to be about the music." This will be a very riveting scene in the behind-the-scenes VH1 show about your last tour. Record a solo album about the breakup and what a backstabber what's-his-name is. It will sell poorly, sending you spiraling into obscurity.

That's about it. It was a crazy ride on that magic bus, but you guys made it. Maybe you'll play some really fun high school reunions on the weekend and occasionally be referred to as "the guy that used to be Marcus from LOL and the Hotmail Gang." Rock on, man, rock on.

The Ghost of John Basedow

LOL and the Hotmail Gang

Palindrome Emordnilap

Black, White, and DEAD All Over

Reptile Dis Function

Your College Newspaper Takes On Music

Every single college in America (and one in Asia) has a crappy newspaper run by a wannabe William Randolph Hearst. And every crappy college newspaper has a music column written by some stoned-out loser who can barely spell and fancies himself the next Lester Bangs.

Trout Dog Live at Bunkiloo Festival

By Rune Winston, music critic and herbal enthusiast

Oh, man, I saw the best band last weekend: Trout Dog. They're this dank jam band from New Hampshire. I saw them at Bunkiloo, which is this sick festival on a dairy farm in Ohio. When they came on I was like, "Who are these guys?" cuz I was there to see The Cheese Consortium, but then they ripped into this country-infused dance jam and I couldn't stop my hands from twirling in the air. I remember turning to my friend Lars and I was like, "this is siiiiiiiick." And he just nods his head and we, like, connected. Then we ripped a bowl of sick nugget I got from this dude in the parking lot. I couldn't really concentrate on the nug though because The Trout went into this sort of tripped-out post-psychedelic atonal interpretation of "Ruby Tuesday," and I got so deep into it. I felt it moving through me and saying, "Rune, now is the time to dance." After an hour and a half, they finished the song and I was exhausted. Unfortunately, the suits made the Trout leave the stage after that because they had gone five and half hours over their allotted time slot. It was dank.

The results are in and for the fourteenth year in a row, the funniest political word is still "caucus."

Interested in getting involved around campus?
Want to be blamed for totally lame events?
Want to be cast as a complete social outcast?

Then come join

STUDENT UNION!!!

Seriously, please join. Please. We're begging you.

Here are JUST A FEW of the SUPER-COOL things we've done this year!

Late Night Sober Shuffleboard!

24-Hour King *of Queens* Marathon!

The Great Foxtrot-Off!

And don't forget all the GREAT bands!

Joan Jett and the Blackhearts!

Duran Duran!

Jimmy Eat World!

Come to our meeting next Wednesday to find out more!

FREE PIZZA!

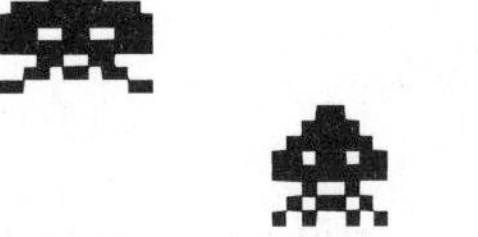

Ex-Box

A Brief Tragedy

She to me, "It's tearing us apart like a losing mutuel ticket at the dog track, and we're fluttering to the dirty ground in tiny bits."

Me to she, "This green reset button light illuminates your face perfectly. Green like the freshness of my blossoming feelings for you."

She to me, "Your feelings are all for first-person corridor shooters. Good-bye."

The door closes.

I to me, "Game over. Continue? Y/N." (silently) "N."

The worst part was, I knew she was right. The Xbox had four control docks. Her body had but three, and she wouldn't let me plug into one of them. The Xbox had thousands of games, and she had but one: deception. While the Xbox was created by Microsoft, a lumbering monopoly, she wouldn't even play Monopoly. Baltic Avenue reminded her of her Latvian grandmother. Drag.

It was then that I realized I'd lost everything at my plastic altar. I'd traded my roommate a GPA point for the latest edition of Madden. The registrar knew the score. Eagles 27–Ravens 19. He just nodded. But what else to worship? God? Did He have DVD capabilities? Could I sixteen-player multiplay with four TVs linked together against the apostles?

The cable wrapped easily around my neck. The controller caught fast on the pipe. This would be my last combo. X. Y. Trigger. Left. Right. Down. Down. Down.

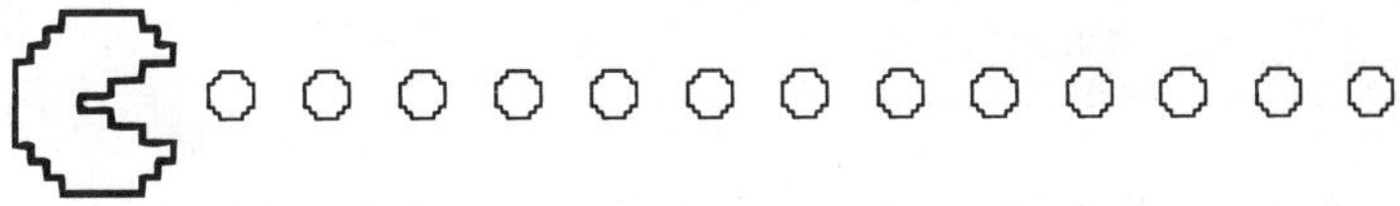

I've decided not to read any more books by authors whose names I can't spell. Good-bye, Fyodor Dostoevsky, hello, Lewis Black!

Secret Societies

There are three types of people in this world: people who are in secret societies; people who don't know about secret societies; and people who knew about them, didn't want to join, and are now dead.

Whether you know about them or not, secret societies exist on every single campus in America. They are named after two equally mysterious items, such as "Skull and Crossbones" or "Trout and the Flute from Mario 3." They meet in between the hours of 3 a.m. and 6 a.m., usually on a Tuesday, in a room that reveals itself after pulling on a candelabra.

Snacks are served at these meetings: secret snacks. Flavors of Pringles that you've never heard of flow like honey. It is not uncommon to hear somebody say, "Hey, pass the Teriyaki and Chives Pringles" or "Are there any Blueberry-Water Pringles left? I thought I brought enough for everybody."

Issues are discussed at these meetings: secret issues. Issues you had no idea were even issues. "First point of order is to discuss how we can get rid of all of these tigers eating our own campus policemen! Secondly, there is a grave overpopulation of black-and-white rainbows." You heard them correctly, black-and-white rainbows. Seven shades of gray that will melt your mind.

The worst thing about secret societies is that they are impossible to join; they join you.

Actually, that's the second worst thing. The worst thing is that they find out who's the closest to curing AIDS and then murder them. Talk about counterproductive!

My favorite Girl Scout cookie?
Masturbating after they drop them off.

A Final Note on Extracurricular Activities

There is a vast difference between extracurricular activities and "Extracurricular Activities." Extracurricular activities are your normal, run-of-the-mill, outside-of-classwork habits. However, "Extracurricular Activities" are what sarcastic professors use to connote something inherently immoral. Here are some basic examples:

EXTRACURRICULAR ACTIVITIES

- "Do you have any extracurricular activites that you're involved with? I only date goal-oriented females."

"EXTRACURRICULAR ACTIVITIES"

- "Welcome to the Young Christians retreat. I want to make one thing clear: there will not be any 'extracurricular activities' going around under my watch!"
- "During the test, I want zero 'extracurricular activities,' and I'm not talking about joining the newspaper, though I'm sure that's abundantly clear due to my use of sarcasm quotes."

A band called Blank CD-R probably wouldn't make very much money, since you can get their CDs in spindles of fifty for less than ten bucks.

13 SPORTS

Introduction

Let's clear something up: "college sports" refers to NCAA-sanctioned Division I sporting events, mainly men's basketball and football. Soccer and baseball kind of count, but "sports" never, under any circumstances, refers to anything else. Division II golf? Division III women's volleyball? Not even the players' mothers care about those games. Then again, it's probably the lack of maternal support growing up that led these normal athletes into a life of mediocrity in the first place. If your team is never on ESPN or in the NCAA tournament, you have two options: skip to the next chapter or transfer schools.

For many college students, especially male ones, sports are a huge part of life. They watch *SportsCenter* six times each morning, even though in their heart of hearts they know that it's the same highlights over and over again. "Let me just get through this 2 a.m. *SportsCenter*, then I'll start studying. That is, after two back-to-back half-hour editions of

Fun Fact: If you watch a NASCAR race in the Southern Hemisphere, the cars go in the opposite direction!

ESPNews. Oh wow, they're replaying the Cal-Stanford 1983 game on ESPN Classic at 4 a.m.! Forget college—at this rate I can have Stuart Scott's job in a year."

A large part of this obsession may stem from the fact that the players may be in your class or down your hall. You may never be able to catch a touchdown in a bowl game, but you can help your team by shouting "CATCH IT!!!!" as loudly as you can at your television. Somebody give Champ here a varsity letter!

School spirit is the most important manifestation of this obsession. If you're not willing to camp out for months on end to get tickets to a single home basketball game against Central Oregon Tech, you're not really a fan. If you're not willing to paint your chest and walk all the way to Alaska-Anchorage for an away football game, you're not really a fan. If you're a central air conditioner . . . Well, you get the point.

It's important to remember that varsity athletes are the gods of your campus. In fact, when Jesus Christ makes His triumphant return, it will have to be after the homecoming parade; otherwise nobody will even notice. If you see a varsity athlete, you should stop whatever you are doing and stare. If he asks to sleep with your girlfriend, just nod and don't say a word; if he wanted to hear normal people talk, he wouldn't have been a gifted athlete. Also, isn't it great how he grew up in poverty but can now suddenly afford a Lexus? Guess his parents put away a lot of money in his college fund!

Of course, college isn't just about watching sports. You can play them on intramural teams or club teams. Anyone who's on a club team will tell you that these teams practice just as hard and travel just as much as any varsity team. Anyone who's not on a club team will tell you these people are full of shit and didn't make it through the cuts to become a walk-on on a varsity team.

Intramurals are more fun; they give you an opportunity to compete against other students on campus in all sorts of sports. While most schools have all the big sports, in recent years, something of an arms race has developed among schools to offer the most intramural sports. Did you notice how every school you toured boasted that it offered ninety-two intramural sports? Half of those were variations on checkers. It's still basically the same game if you play with blue and green checkers, but don't tell that to the athletic department at Vanderbilt! At most schools the team that wins the intramural championship in a sport receives free cool T-shirts, and everyone else will tear their ACLs while trying to play defense.

There will be some people on your campus who are even below intramurals; they like playing sports just for fun and without any competition. These people are obviously wimps

---

You're really great at fantasy baseball. Have you given any thought to reality talking to girls?

who are afraid of losing, and it's your job to bully them. "If this is 'ultimate' Frisbee, I'd hate to see the inferior versions. How can you make this less fun? Lighting yourself on fire?" This is a good line to use if you want to have a bunch of hacky sacks thrown at you.

The lowest form of campus sports is the ones you make up yourself in the dorms. Think you can throw that tennis ball over that pipe? Think you can skateboard luge down the hall without hitting the walls? Think you can fingerbang five girls at once with only one hand? Congratulations, you're eligible to play "Fingerbang Ballboard," the most sex-driven death-ball sport in Noe Hall history!

Whatever your level of fandom, whatever your sport of choice, competition is a necessary part of college. There is nothing like the thrill of victory and the agony of defeat. Except, of course, for Fingerbang Ballboard tryouts.

Being a Fan

Being a college sports fan can get very intense. You will need to display unconditional love for all of your school's teams. Though there is ONE condition: that your love is unconditional.

You can either be a die-hard sports fanatic or a casual sports fan, but you should make that decision within the first week of school so you can choose your friends accordingly. Here is a basic fan rubric: as a general rule, you should only associate with people one level above or below your own.

Hierarchy of Fandom

Level 1: "We have a football team?"
Level 2: "Did we win today? Whatever."
Level 3: "No, I didn't see the game, but I heard about it."
Level 4: "Did you see that game!? It was awesome!"
Level 5: "Dude, I just shat our school colors."

Golf clubs take up a lot of space in a tiny dorm room. Achieve the same results by hanging a small "I'm a douche bag" sign.

Camping Out for Tickets

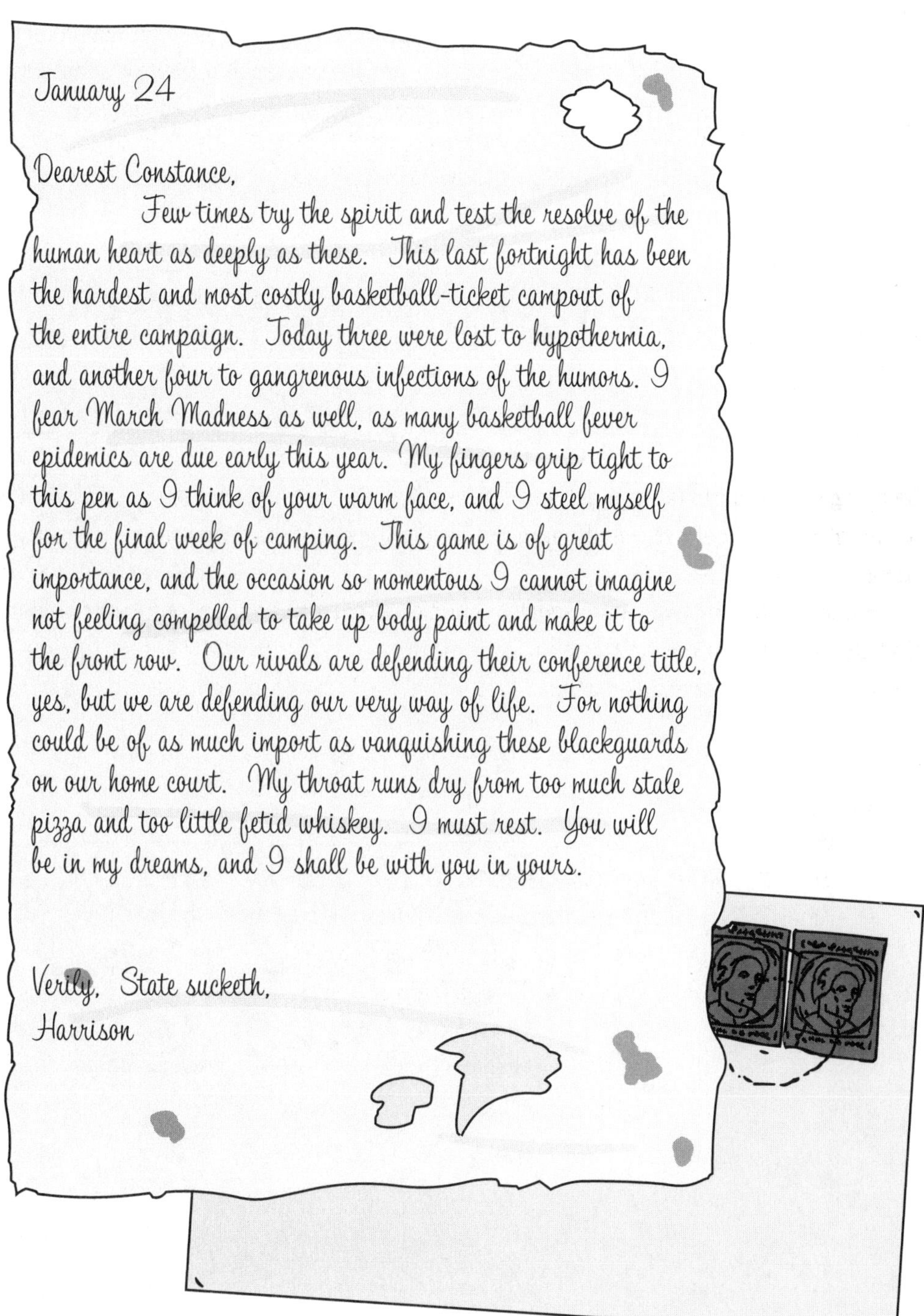

January 24

Dearest Constance,

Few times try the spirit and test the resolve of the human heart as deeply as these. This last fortnight has been the hardest and most costly basketball-ticket campout of the entire campaign. Today three were lost to hypothermia, and another four to gangrenous infections of the humors. I fear March Madness as well, as many basketball fever epidemics are due early this year. My fingers grip tight to this pen as I think of your warm face, and I steel myself for the final week of camping. This game is of great importance, and the occasion so momentous I cannot imagine not feeling compelled to take up body paint and make it to the front row. Our rivals are defending their conference title, yes, but we are defending our very way of life. For nothing could be of as much import as vanquishing these blackguards on our home court. My throat runs dry from too much stale pizza and too little fetid whiskey. I must rest. You will be in my dreams, and I shall be with you in yours.

Verily, State sucketh,
Harrison

Making a Sign for a Sporting Event

If you get on TV, you become a better person. While most of us don't keep it real enough to become reality television stars, all it takes to get on TV at a sporting event is some poster-board, a marker, and a little creativity. Actually, creativity is the last thing you need. A good sign is as formulaic as possible.

For example:

If the game is on ABC:

You can't yell "brick!" to distract a basketball opponent anymore. Screaming "vinyl siding!" is pretty confusing, though.

Victory Celebrations

Most students are pretty good at victory celebrations. However, they have a serious problem deciding what victories are worth celebrating. Just as you don't get high fives from your buddies after hooking up with a beast, you shouldn't storm the court or field after every single victory. Before storming anything, ask yourself this:

1. Does the team you just beat have a losing record?
2. Is everyone on the opposing team white? Or, in the case of polo, is everyone on this team nonwhite?
3. Does the university's name end with "School for the Deaf"?
4. Does the university's name begin with "Harvard"?
5. If you had started at quarterback, would your team still have won by a large margin?

If you answered "yes" to any of these questions, the victory is not worth celebrating. Instead, find something your team did wrong and complain about it. "Sure, 17–2 seems like a dominant hockey score, but I just feel like we lost our championship poise late in the third period."

However, if you beat a good team, you should celebrate accordingly.

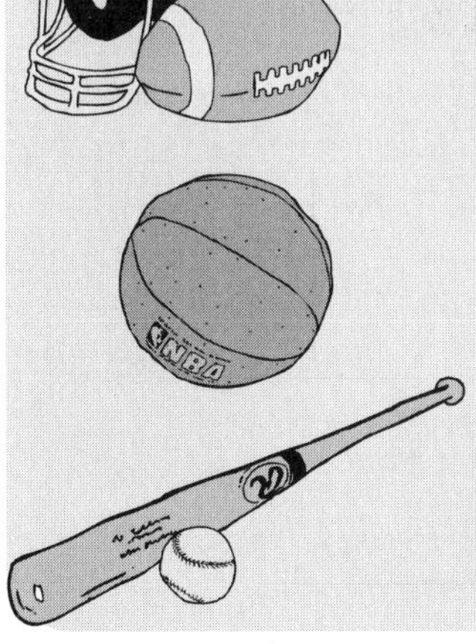

If the victory was in football, you should riot on the field and pull down the goalposts. Letting tear gas or riot cops deter you is for pussies. 70 injured. 4 dead. 1 victory.

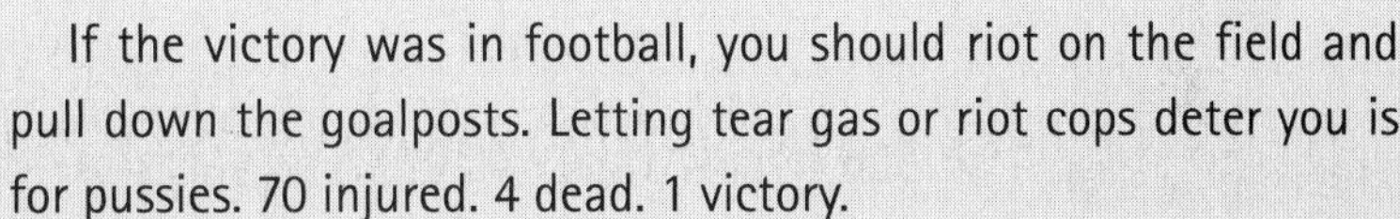

If the victory was in basketball, you should storm the court. Run as hard as you can to press through the crowd and get to center court. Have smelly people's shoulders hit you in the mouth. Wonder why you made such a terrible decision.

If the victory was in baseball, stand up quietly and high-five yourself. You are officially the first person to ever stay through an entire baseball game, and the players should be celebrating your endurance.

Away Games

Anybody can root for their college during home games, but it takes real moxie to don your college duds and walk into the opposition's arena. The key to attending your team's away game is to get your ass kicked. If you come home with a black eye and bloody nose, you were officially the fan of the game. But getting the shit beat out of you by rival fans is much harder than it seems; it is necessary to achieve a certain level of nuisance that pushes the outer limits of fandom.

Initially all you need to do is plant the seed of hatred. When walking to your seats, you will get booed. The key here is to remain calm and casually scream toward the audience, "Fuck you guys!!! FUCK YOU GUYS!!!" An occasional crotch grab never hurt. Nobody likes being told to "Suck my dick!"—especially not those darn Rival U students!

As the game wears on, it's time to kick up your obnoxiousness as well. Throwing water, beer, or a handful of AAA batteries at older, innocent bystanders usually ticks people off. If they politely tell you to stop, tell them to go have sex with themselves and high-five your buddy.

If by the fourth quarter your face is still in good shape, it's crunch time. Racial slurs, discharging firearms, and threatening murder are all fair game. Any of these usually results in a good punch in the face.

When you get home battered and bruised, tearfully tell your friends that those jerks punched you just for wearing the wrong colors. As they hug to console you, smile to yourself and relive the exact moment when you grabbed that Korean lady's boob and called her a "dirty Mexican."

Fans of Special Olympics football have touchdown syndrome.

Gym Sociology

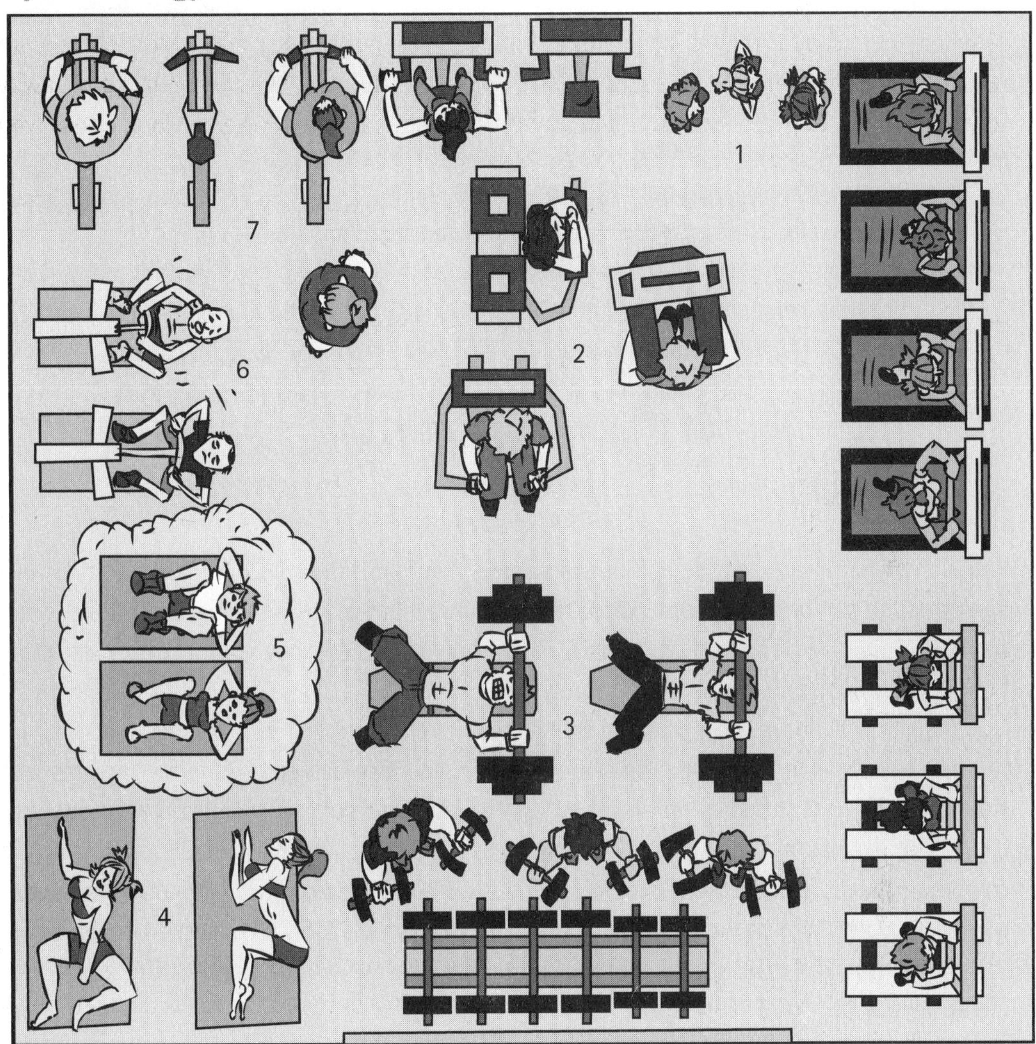

1. Hot girls waiting for cardio machines.
2. Gym rookies using machines that are for "pussies" according to the giant buff gym experts.
3. Extremely large men lifting the weight of their frat house to kill time before their next ox testosterone injections.
4. Hot chicks stretching, preparing to have sex with anybody but you.
5. "Oh no, I didn't fart, it's just this new type of sit-up I'm doing."
6. Old men using machines that were popular when they went to school in the 40s.
7. Fatties burning half the calories from last night's Ben & Jerry's party. Fatties . . .

Dude, Can You Spot Me?, by Blake

Hey, dude, can you spot me? Oh, thanks a lot, bro. Yeah, I've got some serious weight on there. What? No, I'm not on the football team, but people ask me that all the time. I probably could be, but it would get in the way of my weight-lifting. To be honest, I don't even really need a spot; I only asked because the kid that works here gets real uptight about it. I know it sounds insane, but this isn't a lot of weight for me. I've done waaaay more than this before, but I still appreciate you spotting me. Do you want me to spot you after my set? It wouldn't be a problem. No? Okay. Actually, dude, could you move back a few inches? I can see up your shorts. Yeah, it makes it hard to concentrate. That's better. Okay, bro, ready? On three. One . . . two . . . BLAKE!

Intramural Sports

You know what impresses the hell out of people? Your "Intramural Champion" T-shirt. You walk through campus and people know that within, or "intra," these walls, or "murals," you were the very best at a sport. It doesn't matter how you get it, but you have to wear that 50–50 cotton/poly blend wreath of laurels.

You can play dozens of intramural sports, but there are only three that really matter: flag football, basketball, and softball. Lap swimming, lacrosse, flag basketball, and the rest are just ways to make lesser athletes feel involved and to give tour guides a way to brag about the eighty-five intramural sports offered on campus. These three are the pinnacle of intramural competition and should be taken extremely seriously. If someone tells you that intramural sports are "only a game," punch them in the throat. Then tell them it's "only a collapsed trachea."

Intramurals differ from real sports in a number of ways, all of which can be exploited in the pursuit of your athletic glory.

Real sports are refereed by referees. Intramural sports are refereed by a kid from your Bio class working for five bucks a game. Real refs can't be pressured, but intramural refs are pretty easy to work over. Lines like, "What are you, blind?" can start to swing calls in your favor, especially if you go to a school for the blind and the ref can't hear you getting fouled.

If the And 1 Mixtape Tour has taught us anything other than hot moves and how to give yourself a nickname like "Spyda," it's that sportsmanship stopped being cool in 1996. However, intramurals still enforce sportsmanship rules, so you have to be a little more subtle. If you dunk on a guy, don't scream in his face. Quietly run back down on defense. If an opponent falls to the ground, politely help him up and see if he's okay. After the game, sleep with his girlfriend. Sportsmanship grade: A–/B+.

Naming Your Intramural Sports Team

Unlike real sports teams with their "serious" names and "groupies," intramural teams are all about having fun, so naming your team should be fun, too! The better the name, the more notoriety you'll experience around campus. For instance, "Substance Free" = LOSERS! "Free Substance" = RAD! In fact, we're so concerned with making your team the best at school, we've provided you with some great time-tested examples:

Pop-Culture References

- The Ralph Wiggums
- Turd Fergusons
- More Cowbell

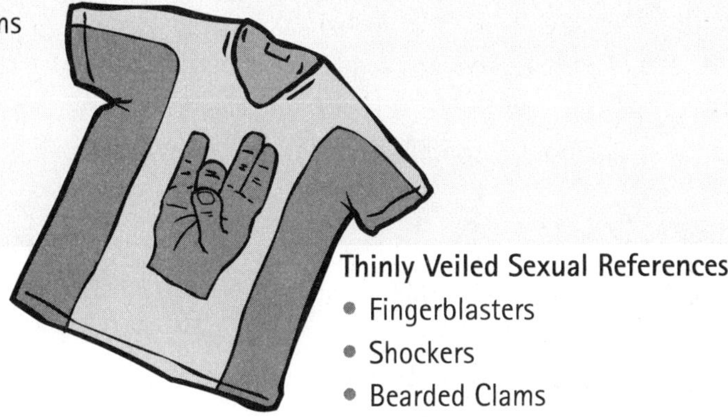

Thinly Veiled Sexual References

- Fingerblasters
- Shockers
- Bearded Clams

Corn-Related Team Themes

- Niblets
- Team on the Cob
- Cream of Team

Vague Drug References

- Best Buds
- Puff Brothers
- Portland Blazers

Overt and Blunt Drug References

- Fourth-Floor Marijuana Users Intramural Softball Team
- We're Currently on Cocaine
- Heroin. Yup.

Intramural Trash Talk

Everything about intramural sports is a watered-down version of the real thing, including the trash talk. Here are some mediocre lines to try to slightly rattle your opponents:

Chanting "overrated" after your school beats a top team is like saying, "You're the ugliest model I've ever fucked."

The Legend of the Greatest Intramural Team in History

When most people think of dynasties, immediately their thoughts drift to professional franchises that play at a level higher than their peers for three, four, maybe five seasons. But the Fourth-Floor Deek Sluckers of Southern University dominated intramural broom hockey from 1972 to 2003, a feat unsurpassed in modern athletics.

"I covered the Steelers in the seventies, the Lakers in the eighties, and the Bulls in the nineties," a famous reporter once wrote in his book, "but this team—this team was something special."

Special indeed. The Deek Sluckers went undefeated in thirty-one consecutive seasons, with an average margin of victory exceeding eighteen goals. In a broom-hockey era dominated by defense and tenacity, the Sluckers gracefully danced their way to a thirty-nine-goal-per-game average.

"They dominated all facets of the game, both defense and offense. These guys were seriously intimidating!"

Intimidating indeed. The average height and weight of a Deek Slucker throughout their thirty-one-year reign was seven-foot-five and 590 pounds. Even more impressive, for lunch, each Deek Slucker would eat one ham and one turkey. For dinner, they would eat their opponents' lunches.

"And what people didn't really pay attention to was the fact that these guys weren't twenty-one-, twenty-two-year-olds like the other teams, these guys were young!"

Young indeed. No Slucker ever exceeded the age of ten. This statistic is exceptional when you realize that the same players who played in 1971 were still playing in 2003.

"In 2003, the team broke up so each of the twenty-three Deek Sluckers could go pro in a different sport. For fans, the news was just devastating."

Devastating indeed. On the way to meet their new pro teams, each Deek Slucker was killed in a separate car accident. This record, too, will never be broken.

Sports Gambling

As moneymaking schemes go, sports gambling is perhaps the most foolproof. In fact, it's mathematically impossible not to make a mint by betting on sports games.

Sports gambling is illegal in most states, but the Internet provides a lawless frontier

---

You will play racquetball at least once in college and then never again. Scientists still don't know if this is nature or nurture.

where anything goes. If you thought porno was racy, wait until you're picking the ponies. Two hundred to one on "Blue Suede Booze" to win, place, or show!? Thanks, you'll take two!

A lot of people will tell you that betting on sports events is a good way to lose all of the money you would ordinarily spend on boring stuff like insulin, but nothing could be further from the truth. Gambling makes bad sports exciting; it can turn the Arena Bowl into the Super Bowl, and women's basketball into men's basketball.

If you're not comfortable with Internet gaming, you can probably find a local bookie on your very own college campus. Bookies are generally easy to find, so just ask any varsity athlete for one's cell number. Make sure you find an honest bookie, though, because some teams, like Arizona State or the Washington Generals, will not hesitate to shave points in order to keep money in bookies' pockets.

Most students participate in an NCAA tournament "March Madness" bracket, so named because of the month of the year and the high prevalence of rabies among players. If you don't have any friends who run a pool, you can even play against yourself. Just fill out who you think will win the games and then put $10 in your garbage disposal. Man, that was great; bet you can't wait for the NHL play-offs to start!

So that's all you need to start gambling. How much fun will you have? We'll bet the over!

Poker: The Lost Sport

Back in the 1600s, if somebody wanted to play poker, they would have to invent it. Today, poker is everywhere! Over twenty network and cable television channels have bought into the craze. There is *The World Series of Poker* on ESPN, *The Iron Chef Plays Poker* on the Food Network, and *Black People Playing Poker* on BET. With this televised onslaught, kitchen tables are turning into poker tables, frat houses are turning into casinos, and casinos are turning into even more populated casinos.

If your intramural team sucks, just steal the quarter at the pregame coin flip and run. You'll forfeit the game, but in a typical 0–8 season you can make up to two dollars this way.

Most professional poker players will tell you that 10 percent of poker is knowing how to play, and 90 percent is knowing the slang terminology. This list of poker jargon will ensure that even the suckiest of poker players will win the World Series of Poker Main Event at least twice.

"Pocket Rockets" = Pocket Aces (See also: "Pocket Smockets")

"Brothers Karamazov" = Pocket Kings. (See also: "Pocket Kockets")

"QQ Netanyahu" = Pocket Queens (See also: "Pocket Queefs")

"Pocket Curvy Dicks" = Pocket Jacks (see also: "Fishhooks")

"Dead Man's Hand" = Two Pair: Aces and Eights

"Live Man's Hand" = Anything that's not Two Pair: Aces and Eights

"Jew" = A Jewish poker player

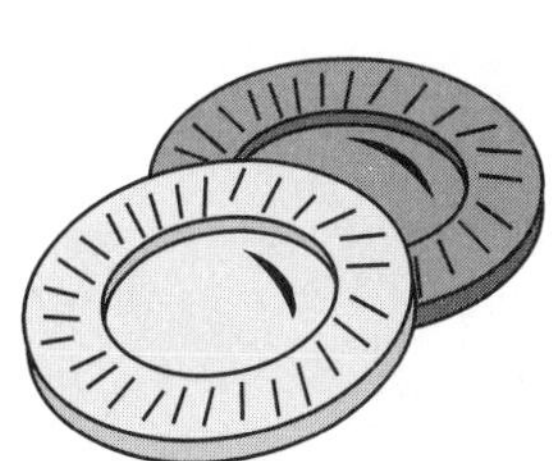
"Check to the Raiser" = Checking to a player who's recently raised

"Check to the Raisin" = Checking to a giant raisin

"Tuition Buster" = When a player loses his college savings on one hand. The player is then given five minutes to leave the game and enroll in a nearby city college.

A Final Note on Sports

If some fanatics used half of their enthusiasm for sports on academics, there would be millions more smart people in this world. Though the line of people camping out to take midterms would get rather annoying.

Bloodless coups are for student governments that didn't raise the price of basketball tickets. Get your flaming sod hook.

14 SPRING BREAK

Introduction

SPRING BREAK!!!!!!!!!!!!!!!! (Editor's note: We can't really print three pages of "!" This will have to do.)

For as long as there has been college, there has been Spring Break. Quoth a young Thomas Jefferson, "I just wanna drink some brews and see some titties. I got a pocketful of two-dollar bills with my name on 'em, baby!"

For one week in March or April, students everywhere give up the celibate drudgery of regular college life and cut loose on the beach to sleep with strangers from colleges they've never heard of, binge drink, and write "FAG(got)" on each other's chest with sunblock. You'll come back with a case of antibiotic-resistant something, a T-shirt commemorating your wild nights at Señor Frog's, and a lifetime's worth of memories that you can't remember.

Spring Break is all about knowing your limits, then pushing past those limits. Think a four-person hotel room in Key West can only sleep four people? You have to multiply the suggested number by five. Hope you have nineteen friends who like partying and using a hotel towel as a blanket. If you think you can't drink an entire fifth of Jim Beam in one day, you should drink a gallon or two. When the doctor brings you back to life, you'll know you did it, champ.

Of course, this kind of debauched Spring Break mayhem isn't for everyone. Some students—losers, for example—think that "Spring Break is just so stupid; it's all about drinking and having sex with people you don't know. I'd rather go home and see my friends." Nobody's fooled into thinking you have friends, but nice try. Oh, and piling friendship bracelets on your arm doesn't convince them otherwise; it just slows down your hand gestures.

Now that we've gotten rid of those dorkasauruses, let's talk companionship for Spring Break. You'd think going with your best friends would be the best idea for having fun on Spring Break, but nothing could be more wrong, except for possibly a hamster having sex with a cat. You want to go on Spring Break with casual acquaintances who party really really hard. You don't want to like them too much, though, because if they get thrown in jail for punching a cop, you don't want to waste valuable partying time going to six different ATMs trying to get enough pesos to pull him out of a Tijuana jail.

Once you pick a group of traveling partners, you have to pick a destination. Get out a map. Point to your school. Now drag your finger five inches south. That's where you should go. Topeka sounds shitty to you? Maybe you shouldn't have gone to school in Minnesota.

There, you're ready for Spring Break. Now which way to the KEGS?!?!?!?!?!?!?!?!?!?!?!?! ?!?!?!?! (Repeat till the page is full, printer.)

"How do you know we're a Dave Matthews cover band? How do you know Dave Matthews isn't covering Crash into Me's songs?" That's never fooled anyone.

Packing for Spring Break

Chicks!

- [ ] Coordinated bikini/towel/purse/shoes/hair color for each day
- [ ] Laxatives and diuretic to keep in swimsuit shape
- [ ] Diaphragm (particularly popular if Spring Breaking in 1960s California)
- [ ] Self-tanner
- [ ] Backup self-tanner
- [ ] Danny Tanner
- [ ] Designer sunglasses, nose
- [ ] White teeth, All-American smile
- [ ] Lax morals

Dudes!

- [ ] Bathing Suit
- [ ] Beer

Red Bull and vodka is a good beverage choice for students who want to stay up all night writing an essay but at the same time don't want to do too well on it.

And Now a Word on Packing Liquor

Everyone makes a run to the liquor store to stock up before Spring Break. This makes about as much sense as flying giraffe cars: very little. Unless you're Spring Breaking in Utah, they will sell liquor wherever you are going. Also, it's illegal to transport more than a small quantity of liquor across state lines. Do you want to end up in a Delaware jail? They're the first state in prison beatings, too! So instead of buying seven handles of Captain Morgan in Boston and hauling it all the way to Miami, just trust that they'll have it in Florida.

True College Stories—Last-Minute Exercise, by Sarah

I knew it was pointless. I knew it was futile. I knew there was no way I was going to lose ten pounds in a week, but that sure as hell didn't stop me from hitting the gym with a vengeance when I finally realized that my senior-year Spring Break was just eight days away.

"Holy shit!" I yelled. "I can't believe Spring Break is already here!" But the truth? I believed it.

Yet somehow I had managed to waste another entire year without planning for this moment. I remember the lame excuses. Back in September it was, "Nah, I'm not gonna start going to the gym today. Spring Break is ages away." Then in December it was, "Nah, I'm not gonna start going to the gym today. It's Christmas morning." Then February came and it was, "Nah, I'm not gonna start going to the gym today. I have a bad feeling about it." That last decision was the best of my life. The gym burned down that day.

But for some reason, all excuses just seemed to melt away once the urgency of Spring Break was upon me. No amount of laziness could hide me from the fact that in eight days I'd be forced into wearing a bikini. When all my friends started hitting the gym, the pressure grew even stronger. Soon enough it became a competition to see who could squeeze the most ridiculous amount of exercise into the least number of days.

ME: Hey, Katie! Coming back from the gym?

KATIE: Of course! I did cardio for an hour and then hit up Ab Attack. You?

ME: Yeah, about the same. Only I did cardio for three hours and then took four straight classes of Butts and Guts. No big deal, just a warm-up, really. Now, if you'll excuse me, I have to go vomit blood.

I tried to blend in with the crowds of anorexic aerobaholics as best I could, grabbing an elliptical and setting it to the highest incline. So what if I immediately lost the pace and fell off? The important thing is that I tried. And that the doctor says I can still go in the ocean with my cast as long as I wrap it in a garbage bag first. At least I burned those nine calories. Way to go, me.

When you think about it, this last-minute frenzy of hard-core exercise does not only prove hopeless, but utterly idiotic. You're leaving for a week of binge drinking, cheap beer, drunk eating, and plates upon plates of Mexican monstrosities. So even if you lose that extra five pounds before you leave, ten Natty Lights and a Nutella and graham cracker sandwich later, you're back to square one. It's like a boxer putting on makeup before he goes into the ring.

So, girls, take my advice here. If you haven't been exercising four times a week for the last three months, a six-pack isn't going to develop magically in the next three days. There is just no way to make up for two and a half months of considering Smartfood White Cheddar Popcorn a dairy product (which I seriously do). Instead of killing yourself for the week before Spring Break, I suggest going on an eight-day bender. Because nothing says, "I'm passively trying to kill myself," like sixteen straight days of drinking.

What happens at Spring Break stays at Spring Break, including your reputation as a girl who doesn't fuck on waterslides.

Spring Break Hot Spots

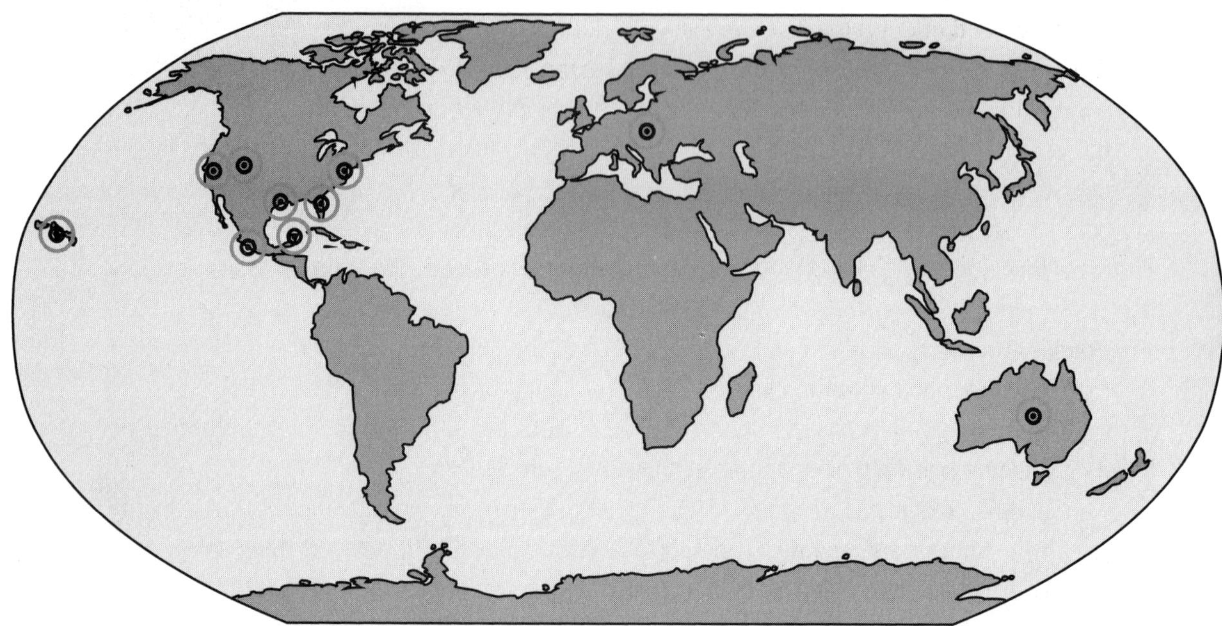

Cancun

Pro: Cancun is one of the leading places to see girls and drink beer. Nude beaches cater to Mexico's number one export: titties.

Con: Nice "Save water; drink beer" shirt. Is it 1987 already?

Florida

Pro: Hot babes, and your primary competition is seventy-eight-year-old dudes. Though they sure can dance.

Con: No matter how you slice it, you're going to have to drive through the Deep South to get there.

LA

Pro: Come see the city the Beatles once performed in!

Con: The smog will penetrate your girlfriend and then never call.

If a class is taught by an instructor and not a professor, it means he doesn't have a Ph.D. Bring that up during office hours.

Aspen

Pro: If you haven't skied in Colorado, then you havent skied. And if you have skied in Colorado, then you've only skied once.

Con: Being cold on Spring Break. Having to hear your friends repeat *Dumb and Dumber* quotes. A lot.

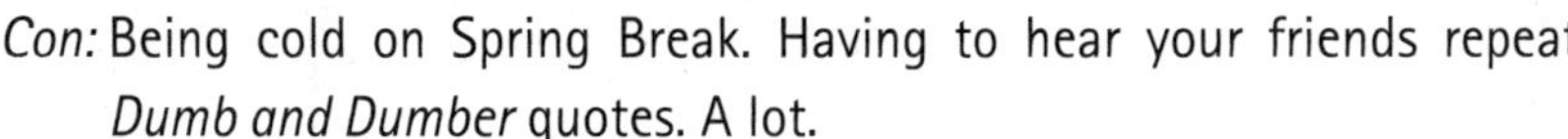

Europe

Pro: You'd be surprised at what's legal in Europe.

Con: It's terrorism. Terrorism is what's legal.

Hawaii

Pro: If you lose your virginity, Magnum, P.I., can track it down and look damn fine doing it.

Con: Magnum was actually a character played by Tom Selleck.

South Padre Island

Pro: It's the Hawaii of Texas.

Con: It's still Texas.

Myrtle Beach

Pro: You can see where your dad got arrested on his Spring Break in 1974.

Con: South Carolina just outlawed slavery last week.

Australia

Pro: Usually when you get drunk and see kangaroos, it's a hallucination. Not this time, friend.

Con: Long flight. You actually only get to see the airport.

Acapulco

Pro: Lots of things that are illegal in the United States, like bungie jumping with lots of rubber bands tied together, are legal.

Con: Probable death.

The earth's equator is so big that if you laid it out flat, it would circle the earth approximately one time.

Customs

Foreign countries are great destinations for Spring Break. Hotel rooms and liquor are cheaper, and if you want to pay to see a man wrestle a mule, no one's going to stop you. You can even pick up some off-brand pharmaceuticals and liquor made in a dirt-floored shack. You're going to have to sneak these things past Customs to get them back to school, though, so try one of these handy lines to get past the officer questioning you:

"Look, I don't have time for this, I'm trying to ride my high until the plane's in the air."

"Hey, just want to let you know, I'm severely allergic to dogs and so is my backpack."

"Well, it's MY custom to not have my bag inspected!"

"A body cavity search? What are you, some kind of homo?"

"What's the big deal? If I fire it while we're in the air, I'll die, too."

"I know someone who likes you but I'm not allowed to tell."

Great Spring Break Pranks

Nothing says, "Hey, we're on spring break!" like a good prank. It's important to note that Spring Break pranks require a lot of extra yelling and drinking, so standard on-campus pranks like lighting a financial-aid student on fire don't cut it. You have to take your pranks to the next level, because beach life is EXTREME. Here are some classics:

Beach-a-Go-Go: Hide the ocean with a tarp that looks like sand. Stand idly by cracking up everytime somebody asks, "Hey, where's the beach? All's I see are sand dunes!" Dumb crackers.

You Win Some, You Loosen Some: Loosen the tire mounts on every car in your Spring Break city. Then take your spot atop a city street, grab a beer, and watch complete chaos ensue. Note: You will need a place to hide the hundreds of thousands of lug nuts that you collect on your way. May we recommend a lug nut storing facility?

Hot-Blooded: Set up a traveling blood donation center. Tell Spring Breakers that there is a shortage of blood for hungry kids in some African country. They will all want to help. After you get 1000 pints of blood, travel six miles up the road and shoot the horror movie you've always wanted to make. Critics will note that while the script was lacking, "the blood looked so real. It felt like I was there." Welcome to IMDB, prankster!

Extreme Botox: To complete this prank you will need a syringe filled with local anesthetic, available at most emergency rooms. Challenge somebody to a one-on-one game of beach volleyball, loser has to tread water in the ocean for ten minutes or so.

Then, as the game takes place, inject the anesthetic into your opponent's neck and watch him fall to the floor rather instantly and complain of nausea and complete body numbness. At this point, decline his request for a cancellation and kick his ass at beach volleyball. You'll win, and you'll win big. Then call some friends over to help you lift this empty shell of a human and throw him into the ocean for his "ten minutes" of embarrassment. Laugh as his face slowly sinks into the bottom of the ocean and saltwater fills his lungs. You are the new king of Spring Break.

The SPF your skin requires is inversely proportional to how much fun you'll have on Spring Break.

Hotel Tetris

Spring Break is only great if you enjoy it with thirty-two of your closest friends, but who's got the money for all those hotel rooms? Just get one and arrange yourself for maximum efficiency.

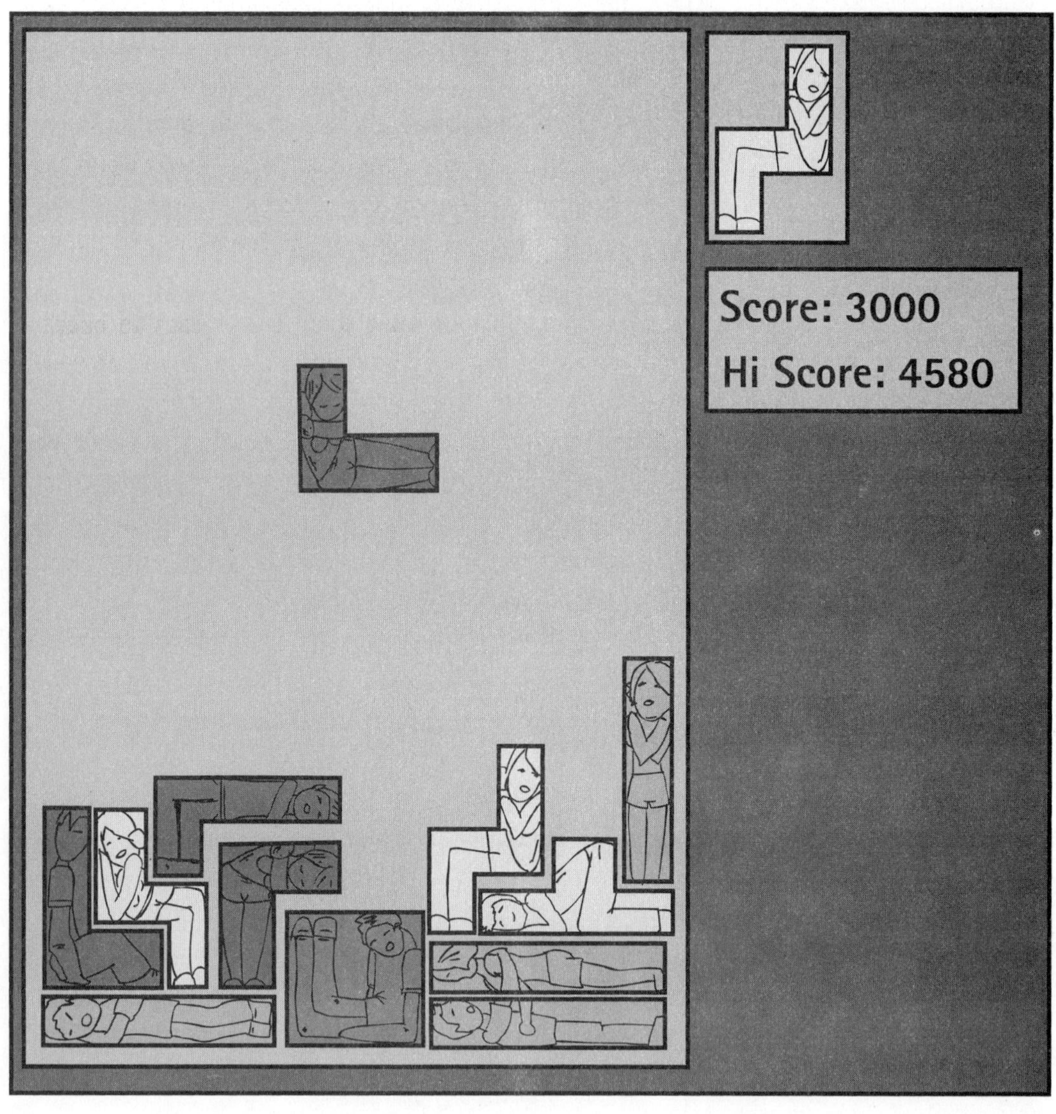

Beach Football Rules

Many male students and mannish female students like to toss the old pigskin around at the beach over Spring Break. It seems pretty easy: pick up ball, throw ball to friend, catch ball thrown by friend, drink beer, repeat. Believe us—it's not that simple. First, there is way more beer drinking involved, and second, there are a few unspoken rules when it comes to a beach football pass.

No punting: Every time a group of guys get together to throw a football, there's always one for whom throwing a ball is not enough. No, this young man needs to punt, and he needs to do it at the beach. His punt, obviously, will not go anywhere near its intended target and could even end up in the water, where scary fish live. Be an American and throw the ball, leave the punting to the Europeans, who hate you.

No "go long" fakeout: Everyone's favorite joke as a kid often comes back to haunt Spring Breakers. The old I-tell-you-to-go-long-and-when-you-get-real-far-away-I-throw-the-ball-to-someone-else is a common practice among pricks, assholes, and redheads. This isn't eighth grade anymore, guy; making your friend look like a loser doesn't hold the same sexual pull it once did.

No no-look pass: Crowded beach + beer + you trying to look cool + friend looking the other way = broken nose.

No long "li'l help": You shall never request that someone give you a "li'l help" in retrieving your ball if the ball lies more than ten large steps from the chosen helper or in an obstructed area such as a bush or volcano.

Dude, Did You See That Catch?, by Blake

Dude, tell me you saw that catch. What catch!? The fucking sick one I just made, that's what catch. Bro, I had to, like, run and dive for it. How did you miss that? I never miss a catch; everyone knows that. I can catch anything; it's like a God-given talent, I guess. Remember freshman year when that Steve kid threw that apple down the hall and I caught it? Remember that? Yeah, that was fucking sick, too, but not as sick as the catch I just made. I'm normally pretty modest about all the amazing stuff I do, but for that awesome catch I'll make an exception. Dude, aren't you so pissed you didn't see it? Now there's a huge hole in your life where my sick fucking catch should be. Oh well, bro, that's why you gotta pay attention. I'm open!

Club Promoter Date

The following is a conversation overheard between Armani "Sweet J" Johnson, a beach club promoter in Fort Lauderdale, Florida, and his date, Linda. They were dining at a very fancy restaurant.

LINDA: Armani, this is a very fancy restaurant, but our relationship just isn't working for me. We need to break up. I feel like there's no communication.

ARMANI JOHNSON: YO, YO, YO, LADIES DRINK FREE TILL TWO AT CLUB ATMOSFEAR. GUYS, FIRST DRINK FREE WITH FLYER!

LINDA: See? That's what I'm talking about. All you care about is getting everyone to show up for the Wednesday-night Foam and Fingerfucking Party.

ARMANI: NO BULLSHIT, NO GIMMICKS! FIVE DOLLARS AT THE DOOR! LADIES, WIN ONE HUNDRED DOLLARS IN THE WET T-SHIRT CONTEST EVERY NIGHT!

LINDA: You're not even listening to me! I'm a woman. A woman with needs! Put down that bullhorn and listen to me!

ARMANI: LADIES, LADIES, LADIES, FOAM PARTY TONIGHT AT CLUB ATMOSFEAR. FIVE DOLLARS AT THE DOOR. NO BULLSHIT, NO GIMMICKS. FREE T-SHIRT FOR EVERYBODY.

LINDA: Okay, I see where you're coming from. Maybe you're right after all. I mean, you do have a job that helps people.

ARMANI: BODY SHOTS! CAGE DANCERS! FREE HAND JOBS FOR EVERY GUY THAT BRINGS TWO GIRLS! CLUB ATMOSFEAR!

LINDA: Oh, Armani, you're the perfect man!

Your Spring Break Hookup

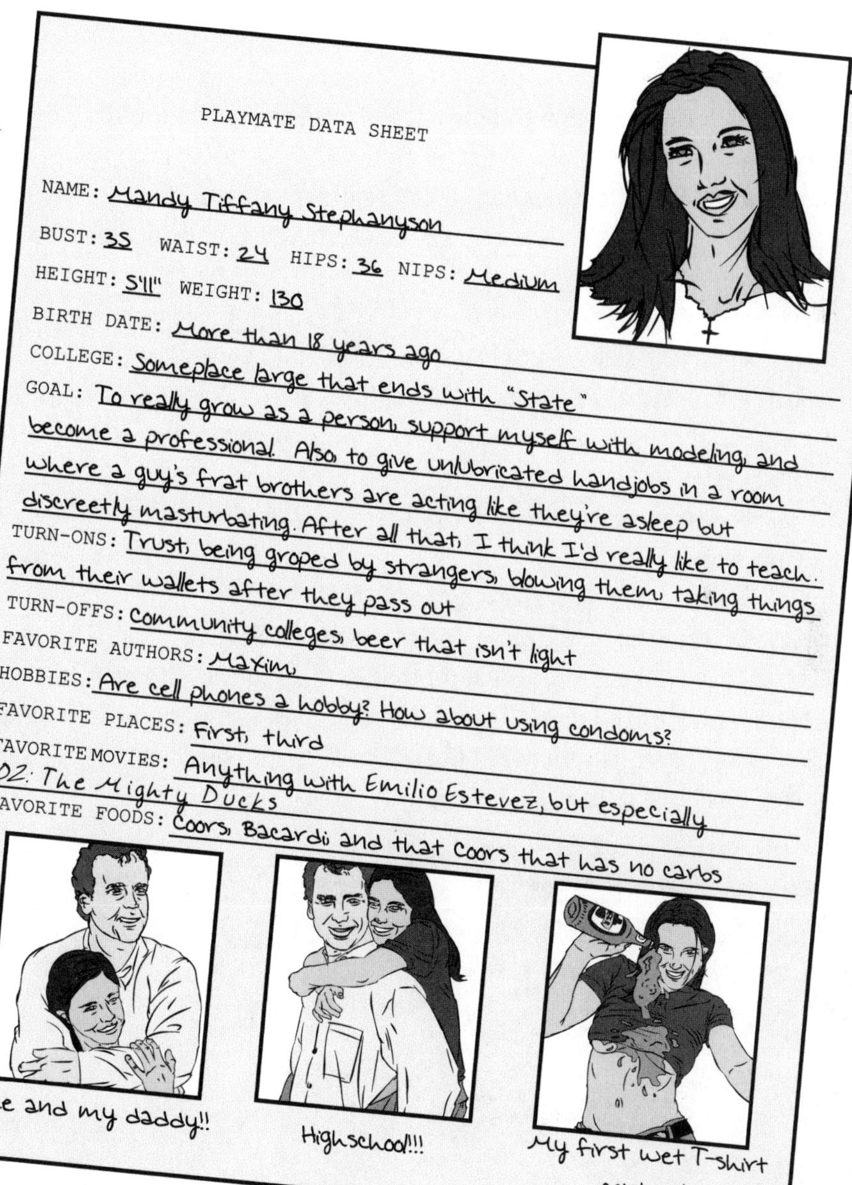

PLAYMATE DATA SHEET

NAME: Mandy Tiffany Stephanyson

BUST: 35 WAIST: 24 HIPS: 36 NIPS: Medium

HEIGHT: 5'11" WEIGHT: 130

BIRTH DATE: More than 18 years ago

COLLEGE: Someplace large that ends with "State"

GOAL: To really grow as a person, support myself with modeling, and become a professional. Also, to give unlubricated handjobs in a room where a guy's frat brothers are acting like they're asleep but discreetly masturbating. After all that, I think I'd really like to teach.

TURN-ONS: Trust, being groped by strangers, blowing them, taking things from their wallets after they pass out

TURN-OFFS: Community colleges, beer that isn't light

FAVORITE AUTHORS: Maxim

HOBBIES: Are cell phones a hobby? How about using condoms?

FAVORITE PLACES: First, third

FAVORITE MOVIES: Anything with Emilio Estevez, but especially *D2: The Mighty Ducks*

FAVORITE FOODS: Coors, Bacardi and that Coors that has no carbs

Me and my daddy!!

Highschool!!!

My first wet T-shirt contest!

True College Stories—Skinny-Dipping, by Streeter

I may be one of the best skinny-dippers in the world. I can convince anyone to shed their clothes and join me for a nude swim. I use many methods to achieve my goal, but the most reliable is the old "we're just friends so it doesn't matter" routine. I've skinny-dipped with literally dozens of women, but I'll never forget my first time. Her name is Vanessa and she was a friend of mine. I recently got in touch with her to ask for her thoughts on our first skinny-dip, which occurred during Spring Break of our freshman year.

STREETER: Vanessa, first off, did you enjoy skinny-dipping with me?

VANESSA: Yes, I did. It was fun.

STREETER: What was it about what I did or said that put you at ease?

VANESSA: Well, I suppose it was the way you weren't forceful about it. You were like, "I'm gonna take my bathing suit off because it feels better to swim naked." So I did, too. There was hardly any pressure. It was all so friendly and casual. Plus, you were right, it does feel better to swim naked.

STREETER: Was there anything sexual about it for you?

VANESSA: No, I thought we were just having fun. Why, was it sexual for you?

STREETER: Definitely.

VANESSA: But you said it was just for fun.

STREETER: Yeah . . . I lied.

VANESSA: So you were, like, checking me out?

STREETER: Oh yeah, for sure. You've got a killer ass, too.

VANESSA: I can't believe you would do that, you asshole. I felt comfortable and you betrayed my trust. I didn't know I was just a sexual object for your amusement. You said, "We're just friends, it doesn't matter." You fucking liar!

STREETER: Deal with it, baby.

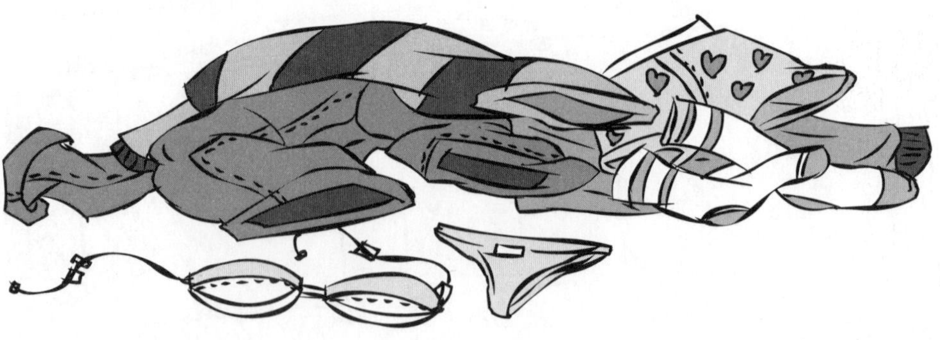

You see, works every time. Sure, she'll never talk to me again, but the point is I got to see her naked, and that lasts longer than friendship. So remember, if you want to run naked through the waves with a hot lady this Spring Break, never pressure, always encourage, and by no means suggest that the skinny-dip is sexual. Follow that and you'll find yourself swimming in an ocean . . . an ocean of hot wet naked girls who have no idea that you're inspecting every inch of their hot, wet, naked bodies, that is.

VANESSA: I still cannot believe you would lie to me like that, you dick.

How You Are Going to Explain Your Tattoos to Your Children

Spring Break tattoos are a great way to say, "Hey, I'm so drunk and stupid that I have zero concern for any long-term consequences." But there will come a day when your kids stare at that ink drawing of a shark jerking off that was etched into your abdomen and ask you what you were thinking. Here are a couple responses to guide you along your way:

Daddy got on a hot streak one night and won fifteen games of beer pong in a row. I realize now how silly that sounds, but when you're older you'll realize what a HUGE fucking deal that is.

Look, there's no easy way to say this. Mommy liked to sleep around.

Daddy used to be a huge nerd. Now keep it down, I'm trying to get through Final Fantasy 29 on my PlayStation 8.

Stupid? Maybe. But can you name one other tattoo that's both badass and magically delicious?

That's the Chinese symbol for "Go do the dishes!"

Hootie & the Blowfishe 4EVA

Your mother and I fell in love to "Only Wanna Be with You." What? It was a catchy song!

"Spring Break? No wonder. Mattress sucks!" said the Navajo Indian who partied too hard.

Spring Break Community Service Trip

To Marie From Diana

Dear Marie,

SPPRRRINNNGG BREEEAAAK BIOTCH!!! Hahahaha. Miami is fucking AWESOME. We stay up all night partying and sleep for like 2 hours, then it's back to the beach to party more! Yesterday I was sooo wasted, me, Kelly, and Tracey did a three-way kiss for free Marga-hitos (this weird green drink) all night at Pancho Sangria's. We miss you, girl! Hope you're having WAY fun building houses!

Lurrrrrrrrv, Diana

PS. OMG, Tracey is slizuttin' it up big time with this hottie from UDel. I'll send pics!

Love ya, biotch.

To Diana From Marie

Dear Diana,

Our Spring Break service trip is off to a great start! Yesterday was the 14-hour bus ride to the Appalachian Mountains. It seemed a little long, but we passed the time by discussing our favorite Psalms. I simply cannot wait to build some houses for these poor people. I must go, the Internet cafe here is pretty much 15 Lite Brites hooked up to an Etch A Sketch, so I hope this e-mail reaches you.

Love, Marie

To Marie From Diana

SUP BIOTCHHH!!!!

OMG, Spring Break is gonna be UN-EFFING-FORGETTABLE (if I can remember it, LOL). Last night, in like two hours, I won a wet T-shirt contest, a creamed-corn wrestling match, the Third Annual Miami Banana Blow Job–Off, and a Pulitzer Prize. Just kidding about that last one, but I did win this banana contest and now my tonsils are sore, LOL. Which reminds me, last night I banged the two hottest guys in Miami; I've never felt so respected in my entire life! G2G, I'm supposed to be at Panama Pete's for this nude body shot contest thingy. Lata, Sk8a.

Love, Diiiirrrtay D (lol)

To Diana From Marie

Diana,

Sounds like you're having a really, um, sexy time. I too am having a rewarding experience. Building houses is like having a really small orgasm. So small you can't feel it. Miss you girls . . .

—Marie

To Marie From Diana

Marie,

Spring Break is almost over and I'm totally bummed. But I made so many great memories with the girls, we're so much closer now. It's weird, but there's something about licking whipped cream off your best friend's nipples that really brings you together. I'm kinda psyched to get back to campus and talk about break with the girls. We have like SOOOO many stories and inside jokes and stuff. I dunno, I guess you won't get it cuz you weren't there, but whatevs, we can still talk about guys we met. Wait, were there any boys on your trip? Can't wait to see you, biotch! Whipped-cream kisses! Diana

To Diana From Marie

Diana,

Today while building houses I got bit by a zambuto spider. I couldn't feel the left side of my body for 10 hours, and my ankles swelled to the size of a grapefruit. But I guess it's worth it, as long as these people get homes! I'm missing my girls . . . sounds like you're having . . . fun. Maybe I should have gone with you?

Marie

Spring Break at Home

Not everyone needs to drink nonstop, get laid, and have the best time of their lives to have a good time. Stuck at home? How about one of these activities:

Catch up on your schoolwork
What you will need: Your textbooks from school, hopelessness
Remember how you skipped the weekly reading, faked your way through class, and got away with it, promising yourself you would return to catch up when you got a chance? That chance is upon you; you've got an entire week to not go to the beach and to read instead. Doesn't that sound like fun?

See how hard you can bite down on your finger before you can't take it anymore!
What you will need: Your finger, your teeth
Ever wonder about your pain threshold but never had the time to explore it?

Watch MTV Spring Break
What you will need: One television, one bag of Cheetos, lack of self-respect
It's like you're there! Plus, can people who are REALLY at Spring Break read *Entertainment Weekly* while they watch an unreal collection of girls in bikinis lick peanut butter off each other? Probably NOT.

Pretend Budweiser is sponsoring something around your neighborhood
What you need: A Budweiser banner, delusions
Hang a Budweiser banner on your local library. Offer people who walk by a chance to switch clothes behind a curtain in exchange for free T-shirts.

Catch up with old friends
What you need: Cell phone, desperation
Who are you kidding? All your friends are on Spring Break! No one actually goes home.

A Final Note on Spring Break

You know you have a crappy professor when he assigns a project due the day you get back from Spring Break. However, you know you have an awesome professor when that project is "Gettin' Laid!"

15 ALL THINGS HOME

Introduction

"FRIENDS FOREVER!!!" That's the rallying cry at high school graduation. If you guys were even a little bit honest with yourselves, the rallying cry would be "FRIENDS UNTIL THE END OF SUMMER!!! THEN INTERMITTENTLY THROUGHOUT FRESHMAN YEAR!! THEN EVEN LESS SOPHOMORE YEAR!!! THEN BY OUR THIRD YEAR I WILL DELETE YOUR PHONE NUMBER FROM MY CELL TO MAKE ROOM FOR SOME KID IN A GROUP PROJECT OF MINE!!!"

Your relationship with everyone you know starts to change pretty dramatically the second you pack up the minivan and head out to college. Your friends become nothing more than e-mail addresses, your parents become nothing more than a phone number, and your dog becomes nothing more than a doodle of a dog you once drew. Ears are the hardest part.

It would be convenient if everyone you knew before leaving for college just disappeared from your life, but they don't. Like the herpes virus, they resurface every few months

You truly haven't lived until your parents have sex.

to make your life unpleasant. Thanksgiving, Winter Break, summer . . . these all become socially awkward trips through a Paxil-fueled hell. It's a little-known fact that the original working title of Thomas Wolfe's *You Can't Go Home Again* was *I Don't Care if They Lock Up the Dorms over Winter Break as Long as I'm on the Inside.*

You'll go to high school parties and answer what your major is four thousand times. 3,954 of those will be to that nosy parrot your friend bought, but it's still rude to just ignore him. Kids who are still in high school will ask you how college is and if you've "gotten laid." Tell them they "don't even know." It's not a lie because "know" sounds like "no."

Don't expect your family to be any help, either. Your parents will have used all the free time from parenting to take up wine-making, redecorate your room, and sometimes even reproduce. Your house will be full of siblings you've never even met. You leave for one semester and all of a sudden you have a sixteen-year-old little brother? Granted, you just failed your Bio final, but this sounds highly implausible.

Your extended family is even worse. All college kids have crazy, crazy grandparents. You may remember your grandfather as a lucid, jolly guy, but at Thanksgiving dinner he'll look deep into your eyes and say, "Bologna mausoleum munchkin." Then he'll bite the hand that feeds him: yours. Your cousins are all in jail now for crimes they "didn't commit." Your aunt Harriet? Turns out she's actually a dude from Detroit named "Slice." We can keep going, but your family dice game is about to start. Don't bet a nick on eight, whatever you do.

Hiding Homesickness

Everybody misses their parents at some point, but not everybody cries about it like you do. Don't get us wrong—it's totally fine to miss your parents, but your tears might as well scream, "I'm coming out of a pussy's tear ducts!" as they roll down your pussy cheeks. It's impossible to prevent your emotions, but it's not impossible to hide them!

You can begin running very fast every time you cry, so people mistake your tears for sweat. Some recommend developing an obsession with washing your face, muttering to yourself, "Clean skin, clean skin, you're never clean, never ever clean skin," as you wash your tears away. You can tell people a family member died so your tears are slightly more warranted, or perhaps even develop a fake allergy to something very accessible like "dorm beds" or "freshmen." Also, it's normal for people's eyes to water after eating spicy foods, so eating a handful of habanero peppers can disguise your crying ways and make you look like a badass. Spending all of your time in the pool will hide your wet cheeks fairly well. Your skin can begin to prune after two months of constant swimming, but your triceps will be amazing.

Some advanced methods include dyeing your face "aqua" so that the tears just blend in. Or you can learn how to cry upside-down tears so that they fall out of your eyes and float toward the roof, transforming your crying into a party trick. You can learn to cry syrup, develop a pancake addiction, and tell people to mind their own business. The possibilities are endless, but the reasons are singular: if you let them see you cry, your nickname throughout college will be "Sir-Cries-a-Lot," and nobody likes a sad knight.

Billy the Bigot

"Why do Jewish people get to go home for Thanksgiving? They weren't there."

Your First Thanksgiving at Home

Thanksgiving break your freshman year is your first opportunity to impress your family after being at college. Do not blow it. Here are some surefire tips that will have Grandma saying, "Oh my!"

- Ride your motorcycle into the living room without opening the front door. Your family will be impressed by your reckless disregard for authority. Then spell your name with tire marks on the carpet, toss the helmet to your mom, and ask her, "What's for dinner, lady?"
- Tell your dad you made him a bookmark for Father's Day. Then give him a picture of you banging two girls. Tell him the way it works is that you put that picture in between the pages where you stopped reading.
- If a relative asks you how college is going so far, open your mouth and respond in a single tone, as if you are singing. Hold that note for three minutes. If the relative tells you, "I don't get it," respond with a casual, "You wouldn't."
- Eat the whole turkey. And we're not talking about being a wussy and eating it piece by piece. We're talking about unhinging your jaw and swallowing it whole before your dad even gets to carving it. If your family asks where you learned that, say, "Math 1B." For dessert, eat your uncle.
- As the meal draws to a close, ask your mom if there will be any strippers attending the after-party. When they do come, don't act so surprised. You're in college now.

Dude, My Frat Is Crazy, by Blake

Dude, my frat is fucking crazy. Yeah, that's why I'm wearing my letters; I'm a Zeta for LIFE, MOTHERFUCKER! Bro, the Zetas at my school party harder than anyone in the world, ever. Yo, but my chapter isn't even the craziest; the Zetas at State all have rabies, bro. It's, like, part of their initiation or some shit. You should party with them. They're motherfucking wild, son! What? The Zetas at your school are nerds? No way, bro, I don't think so, you must be confused. Zetas don't let nerds in. I would know, bro; I was pledgemaster this semester. It was, like, a big honor to be chosen as pledgemaster. It was like all my Zeta bros were like, "Blake, you're the fucking MAN," right? What? Your cousin is a Zeta at Western? The one I met? No way, he didn't seem like Zeta material. Yeah, I know he knew the handshake, but whatev, he wasn't a Zeta . . . he didn't fucking party hard enough. Bro, didn't I just tell you all Zetas are crazy?

Impressing Your Friends from Home

A necessary part of visiting home is convincing your friends that your college is the best, even when it clearly isn't. This will require some embellishing, a little fibbing, and a lot of outright lying.

You know you've been at college for too long when you visit home and refer to your mom as your RA.

TRUTH	INFLATION
"I attended a very large party at my school where alcohol was served."	"I was at a kegger—you know, just a regular kegger like we have every night—and there was this old guy there. I asked him what he was doing, and he goes, 'I'm from the *Guinness Book of World Records*. You guys just made it for partying the hardest.' "
"*The Princeton Review* rates my school's food as 'very poor.' "	"The FDA had to come to our cafeteria with biohazard suits because someone spilled a cup of soup. Scientists called it 'more dangerous than a category-five hurricane.' Their words, not mine."
"My fraternity hazing ritual was bad, but I was able to complete it."	"I talked to one of the older brothers after I was in, and he said that our hazing was the worst he'd ever seen. So I called about forty other chapters around the country, and they all agreed. I wasn't allowed to eat for a month."
"My school is locally known as a fun place to be."	"*Playboy* won't even consider ranking my school on the biggest party school list because it would win every year. . . . That's why it's not on there."
"This semester I was single but sexually active."	"I had so much sex this semester I had to go to the health center. They claimed I wasn't sick; my genitals were merely exhausted."
"I experimented with drugs this semester."	"I was legally dead for three minutes. When I came back to life, the doctor was like, 'You did so much coke, I'm not even gonna call the cops. That's how impressed I am by you.' "

Hoodie Parties

Hoodie Party: noun; hoo-dee par-tee—A gathering of recently returned college students over the Thanksgiving and/or Christmas break. So named because all in attendance will be wearing their school's hooded sweatshirt and lying to one another about how crazy their college is. "Three chicks, dude . . . three chicks."

Old Flames

We do not condone cheating on your college girlfriend. However, is it technically cheating if you are sleeping with your old high school girlfriend during Winter Break? While you contemplate the answer to that brain buster, here's a guide to sleeping with your old high school girlfriend during Winter Break:

Phone Call: Establish communication with ex. Suggest "grabbing a cup of coffee" or "a drink or two" in local establishment. Refrain from asking if she wants a "cockwich." Not because that's too forward, but because cockwiches are full of sodium and carbs and she'll probably refuse.

Pseudo-Date: Meet at prearranged location for aforementioned coffee/drink. Reminisce about high school, gossip about friends, exchange college stories, etc. Avoid the following "red-flag phrases": "My gossip has been better than yours thus far." "Yeah, whatever." "So I'm like banging away, right?"

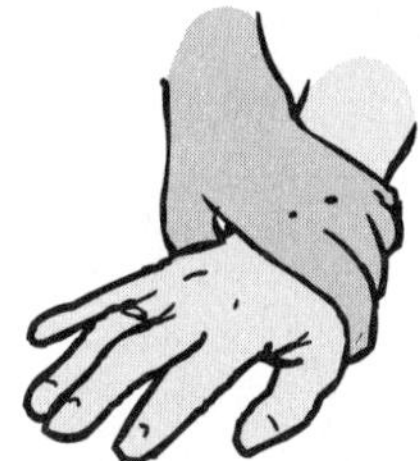

Hint Drop: As the conversation winds down, bring up your old relationship. Confess that the sex you had with her was "the best ever... really, unbeatable." When she says you're lying, grab her wrist, look her dead in the eye, and say, "No, really" repeatedly, or until she says something romantic like, "I think my wrist is broken."

Suggestive Behavior: Suggest moving the pseudo-date to your home or hers after the sun goes down. Once at new location, joke about all the different places you two "made love." Tell her how much you missed "talking" to her. Don't worry; she doesn't know you're lying. You will now start making out.

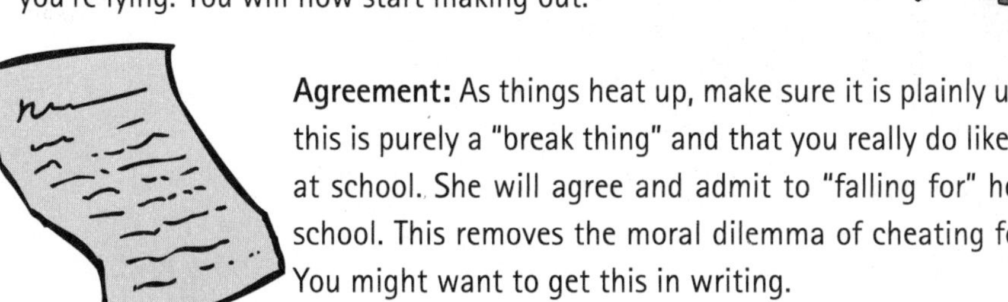

Agreement: As things heat up, make sure it is plainly understood that this is purely a "break thing" and that you really do like your girlfriend at school. She will agree and admit to "falling for" her boyfriend at school. This removes the moral dilemma of cheating for both of you. You might want to get this in writing.

Do It Well: Make sure to perform at the utmost level of perfection. This will ensure that you have a reliable break hookup for years to come—more like "four years to cum"!

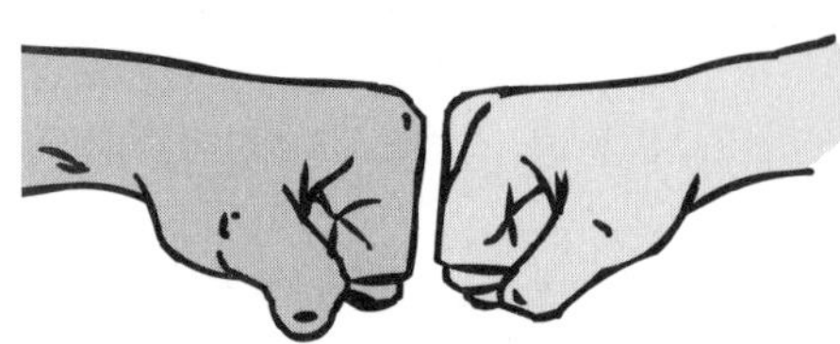

Aftermath: Continue to hook up over the break and hang out. When it comes time to return to school, bid farewell with promises to "keep in touch." Don't hug; instead, tap closed fists. Explain that you "gotta keep it gangsta." You will both understand the emptiness of these promises and realize that the fling is now over . . . until summer, that is.

Your Old Room

Don't know what your parents really think about you? You can tell a lot about your relationship with your parents by what they do with your old room:

Younger Sibling's Room: Out of sight, out of mind. Your parents are basically uninterested in your well-being now that you're of college age. Your younger brother or sister is the wave of the future here. Hope you don't mind sleeping in a race-car bed. We recommend letting your legs dangle over the plastic hood; it's more comfortable that way.

Gym: If your parents turn your room into a gym complete with dumbbells, yoga mats, and exercise balls, they are basically saying, "We love you, but not as much as we love being in shape." They would sell your soul to a personal trainer if it were legal.

Garage: Nothing says, "We don't love you anymore," better than converting your old room into a garage. This is even more telling if your room was on the second floor. "You can sleep in the car, dear! Oh, and leave the engine running. Mommy will wake you up in the morning."

Sublet to a Tenant: Remember when your dad bought all of those gumball machines and said it was a better investment than buying Microsoft stock? Yeah, the April Fool's edition of *The Wall Street Journal* ruined a lot of family fortunes.

Siblinguistics

Many college kids have a younger sibling. Sure, Mom and Dad say little Scotty looks up to you and wants to be just like you, but that's not true. He wants to be better than you. He's learned from all your mistakes. He's seen you fall again and again. He is prepared to steal your parents' love away from you. Don't let it happen.

When you visit home, your younger siblings will be very curious about college. They'll ask question after question about your school and your major. Your goal is to steer them in a bad direction so they'll never accomplish more than you. Control their feeble minds with any of these sayings:

"Man, if I could do it all again, I'd have been a Creative Writing major . . . that's where the real money's at. Write that down."

"Look, I didn't want to say anything, but I heard Mom say that she'd start drinking again if you ever leave home."

"You want to go to Yale? That's for people who couldn't get into the U.S. Army, which, incidentally, is looking for new recruits. Here, read this pamphlet."

"Right before Grandpa died, he told me that his greatest wish was to see you become a landscaper."

"GPAs are like golf scores: the lower the better. Study hard and you can get that hole in 1.00!"

"I hear really good things about those online universities. I wish my diploma was e-mailed to me as a PDF attachment."

"Forget college, man, your band is one of the best I've ever heard . . . and I have like ten thousand mp3s."

Schedule for Spending a Day at Home

When you go back to school after a break, people will ask you what you did. You'll thrust your hands into your pockets and say, "Nuthin'."

"Surely you did something!" they'll say. No. You did nothing. In fact, your schedule probably looked something like this:

1:30 p.m. Wake up. Fucking sun.
1:35 p.m. Hot Pockets!!!
1:49 p.m. Hmm . . . next time you're gonna heat them up before eating.
2:00 p.m. Search through digital cable guide to see if anything's on. *The Shawshank Redemption* is on, just watch that for a couple minutes . . .
4:00 p.m. God, you fucking love that movie.
4:05 p.m. Nap time!
6:03 p.m. Wake up from nap as parents arrive home. Quickly change out of pajamas.
6:05 p.m. Your dad notices that you are wearing shorts over your pajama bottoms. My God, you're lazy.
7:00 p.m. Dust off the old Nintendo. Beat *Super Mario Bros.* again. This time, no warping.
9:45 p.m. Fuck it, you can warp.
10:00 p.m. Beat the game. Time to check your e-mail.
11:00 p.m. Back to the TV. Sweet, an episode of *The Daily Show* you've only seen once!
11:25 p.m. Oh well, the interview is a repeat. Time to begin your day.
11:45 p.m. Sneak into Blockbuster just before it closes, much to the dismay of the Blockbuster employees.
11:58 p.m. Leave Blockbuster with *Mallrats*, again.
12:15 a.m. Make self dumber with chemicals, watch *Mallrats* with remaining home friends.
2:00 a.m. Obtain White Castle.
2:20 a.m. Vow to never again eat at White Castle.
2:25 a.m. Finish the two burgers your friend ordered and didn't want.
3:00 a.m. Talk about stuff. You know, important stuff.
3:30 a.m. Bedtime!

Your mother's birthday is not a "Hallmark Holiday." Just admit you forgot to get her a present, dick.

Parents Weekend

Parents Weekend is a difficult time, and it's hard to know exactly who to blame for the difficulty. No, wait, it's your parents' fault for being such a couple of embarrassing jerks. Your parents will do the following things to mortify you on Parents Weekend:

- Confuse North Quad with North-Northwest Quad and ask for directions. Is this TOURISM season? PUT ON YOUR DISNEY HATS.
- Attempt to photograph you with a nondigital camera. WHAT, NO DAGUERREOTYPE OR CAMERA OBSCURA IN THE MINIVAN?
- Talk to your RA and say he's such a nice boy. They might as well jerk you off in the middle of the hall because that's how embarrassed you are.
- Forget to pump the keg after their kegstands. They're called freakin' manners, MOM.
- Attempt to hug you when they leave, like a couple of fags from the Hug Patrol. Christ, is this *Teletubbies* or college?
- Be way more successful than your friends' parents. Middle class means fitting in.
- Ask to meet your friends. Why don't they make some friends of their own? Because they're embarrassing pieces of shit, that's why.
- Want to see your dorm room or the buildings where you take classes. Those are for students, not washed-up old bastards.

Hey, Parents!

Feel obligated to send a care package, but don't really like your kids that much?

Well, stop worrying, because now there's a solution:

Careless Packages!

Available in four flavors:

EMPTY BOX!

EMPTY BOX
full of packing peanuts!

EMPTY BOX
with an empty toilet-paper roll and broken lightbulb!

MANILA ENVELOPE with
laser-printed form letter!

Sure, other moms send cookies and little basketball hoops or candy, but other moms haven't been in and out of jail for the last eleven months. Nothing says, "Here's to another Thanksgiving at the orphanage," like a careless package!

Honey, Do You Want a Beer?

At some point in college your mom will say, "Honey, do you want a beer?"

Act cool; this is not a trap. Don't do anything too rash. You don't want to shotgun the can and smash it on your forehead, and you don't want to place a citizen's arrest on your own mother for dispensing alcohol to minors. Just sit back and relax, enjoy some drinks with your parents. The first time you drink on your parents' dime is a wonderful, intoxicating experience, so don't let their little rules about drinking anger you. Ninety-four percent of mothers don't allow you to drive after you've been drinking. Under normal circumstances, this is a pretty solid policy, but for a mother, the period known as "after you've been drinking" is ninety-six hours or fourteen episodes of urination, whichever comes last.

One last thing: getting drunk on your parents' dime has its downside. As the old saying goes, "*En vino veritas*," which is Latin for, "After she has three wine coolers, you're going to hear about Mom's miscarriage."

Holiday Gifts from the Bookstore

Nothing says, "Thinking of you, but only at the last minute," like a holiday gift from the college bookstore, purchased with your meal plan.

Summer Jobs

BARTENDER WANTED

Nice cans a must. Painful insults probable.

SUMMER-CAMP HELP

Want to act like a kid while promising not to touch one?
Positions available in arts, all positions in crafts are filled.

HORSE WHISPERER WANTED

Must have hidden secrets.
Having once killed a man a plus.

INTERNSHIP AVAILABLE

Get your foot in the door while getting me coffee.
And it damn well better be decaf!

BE A HUMAN FLY

You supply the dreams, we supply the suction cups.

EARN $10K SELLING COSMETICS

Just kidding.

SEASONAL BAKED-GOODS SALESWOMAN

Cookies salespeople needed for month of March.
The younger and more uninformed, the better.

EGGS NEEDED

Blond, Ivy League preferred. Tall, blue eyes a plus.
$320K, confidential.

SEMEN NEEDED

Not currently stoned preferred. Recent employment a plus.
$13, semi-private.

Summer Road Trips

The summer road trip is a venerable collegiate tradition. Driving cross-country is like running cross-country, but on a much longer course, in a car, and without boring friends with stories about the time you almost tripped and fell, but didn't.

The only problem with traveling from sea to shining sea is that the douche bags who designed the country, like Benjamin "It's All about the Me's" Franklin, forgot to put anything interesting between Philly and Vegas. This is understandable, because they were still skeptical about the recently invented motorcar, which they referred to as the "Teapot Dome Scandal." Seriously, driving through the white middle of the American Oreo is about as interesting as a three-day tour of a dictionary factory. And not a Spanish-English dictionary factory, either.

However, there are some saving graces of Middle America, so throw these spots on your itinerary:

National Pun Museum, Omaha, Nebraska: The NPM has a wall of fame that displays puns throughout history, including the earliest pun known to man: "What caveman favorite sandwich? Club." Which was written on a stone wall with blood in 1900 B.C.

Birthplace of Scott Bakula, St. Louis, Missouri: Take a "quantum leap" to the boyhood home of St. Louis's favorite son. Highlights include both of the actual tickets sold to *Necessary Roughness.*

Raccoon Hunt, Sharkey, Kentucky: Watch every Saturday night as a dozen men with guns, dogs, and Budweiser try to outsmart a nocturnal scavenger. Some weeks they win!

Famous People Did Stuff Here Museum, Conroe, Texas: Come visit the gas-station bathroom that David Robinson once peed in! Marvel at the book that Matthew McConaughey thumbed through once as a preteen. David Duchovny never visited, but rumor has it he thought about coming once.

Navajo Casino, Pearlman, Wyoming: Adjacent to the American Museum of Stereotypes is this haven of quality buffets, loose slots, and eight kinds of table games. Marvel at how seamlessly Native Americans transitioned their stereotype from "buncha drunks" to "buncha gambling junkies." Can "buncha middle-class people with full voting rights" be far behind? These writers think not!

Wichita, Kansas: The city so nice they named it once! Wichita has lots of great attractions, and the vibrant community will suck you in so far that you'll never want to leave. Contact the tourism bureau for reservations; the summer fills up fast!

A Final Note on All Things Home

They say you can never go home again. But that's loser talk. You put on a fake mustache and walk back into that house. "Wanted Dead or Alive?" Ha! You'd like to see them try.

A great way to get beer at a bar is to ask an older friend who's leaving for his wristband. Another great way is to have boobs.

10 FINANCE

Introduction

There's only one thing that separates college kids from homeless people: having a home. Being poor in college is a sacred rite of passage. You would be cheating yourself out of a great life experience if you ever had more than $15 to your name during college. Of that $15, at least $5 of it will be in the form of a blackjack debt from that kid Brian on your hall who swears he's good for it.

Yes, between spending upward of $35,000 a year on tuition and student loans, you're not going to have a ton of money sitting around. However, if you do want to have a ton of money sitting around, we suggest pennies. They're pretty heavy and very cheap; you could get a ton for less than a grand.

Even from this relative poverty, you know you've reached *extreme* poverty when you have to say, "Mac and cheese? What am I, a Rockefeller? It's mac OR cheese here." Oh, and by the way, putting red food coloring in water doesn't turn it into "Gatorade," but nice try, you fooled that girl you like at the gym. When this time comes, you're going to have to cut some corners. Natty Light is for people who can afford to walk to the gas station; you can just dump some rubbing alcohol in whatever liquid's in your dorm's gutters for the same effect. Don't have health insurance? There are very few gashes that can't be repaired using a little fishing line and a needle or, failing that, a Swingline stapler and a stick to bite on. Pain was a white man's invention, but so was sterilization.

Once you become accustomed to thinking like a poor college student, there's nothing you can't do, unless it costs more than 17 cents. Just learn how to say, "I'd rather stay in and study than go out. I've got a lot of work to do. Hey, are you going to just throw away the rest of that Popsicle? Give it here!" Licking sticks for nutrients provides just as many health benefits as a multivitamin, with the added benefit of eating wood.

The watershed moment of your college financial career will be when you are so broke you have to cash in all your change. You'll get a bucket, search under the futon for every last nickel, and strain against the grueling weight of all those coins as you take them to your local Coinstar machine. When you get your money, you will say something to the effect of, "That was a lot of work for nine dollars." Hey, Pennybags, if that was too much work for nine bucks, can we get a loan? Seriously, we all split one envelope of ramen and a sleeve of saltines yesterday as our only meal. We called it "brinner." For dessert we coughed.

Asking Your Parents for Money

Well, it's that time of the week again. You're at college, you're young, and you need a way to weasel some more money out of your parents. Just follow these seven easy steps and you'll be well on your way to buying that new Xbox game you've been wanting. Follow them thirty times a semester, and you'll be well on your way to buying that small, remote island off the coast of Delaware you've been wanting. It will be a place where society can start over from scratch, without capitalism or greed.

So remember these steps by using the handy acronym "B.E.E.E.E.E.R.," and you'll be getting free money in no time!

Note: keep this page open for easy reference while on the phone with parents.

BEGIN SLOWLY. Don't start the call by asking for money! This is the number one mistake people make. Let them think you love them, even if you don't. They knew they were running that risk when they sold your puppy to pay the cable bill.

EGO STROKE. Even though you're drunk when you make the call, an "I miss home" never hurt anyone. Actually, being drunk may even help you seem sincere when you say, "Daaaaddddd... this guy... man, he's the best guy... You're all right, Dad. I mean that. I really mean that."

ENTERTAIN WITH POSITIVE STORIES. Mention any good grades you've recently received, and if you haven't received any grades recently, just talk about a paper that you managed to finish. Parents want to know you're doing something productive at college besides seeing if vodka is a suitable replacement for milk on your breakfast cereal. Parents are funny that way. Also in the knock-knock-joke way.

EASE AWAY FROM BULLSHIT. Here's where you really earn your paycheck that you actually didn't earn. You need to go from casual conversation to the big question without shifting gears. For instance, let's say you are talking about that nasty midterm lurking over the horizon. Casually mention how after you finish up your academic responsibility, there is a girl in your class that you would like to take out to a really nice dinner to celebrate. This works particularly well for males asking their mothers for money, even though it is clear to both parties that the girl is fabricated. Come on, 36–24–36 measurements AND a Harvard doctorate? You got greedy.

EXPLAIN YOUR CASE. Let's say you are talking about the weather (and if your parents are old, oh boy will you be talking about the weather). You can turn it around with, "I've been feeling a little sniffly lately, maybe I need a new coat." That's a lot better than, "Send me three hundred dollars by next Thursday or I'm sure the bookie will send you one of my thumbs. No, you can't just use it as a bookmark!"

EXECUTE! When you ask for money, be sure to highball them. After all, this is business. If you need $250, ask for $500. That way, when they negotiate you down to $250, they'll feel they're setting proper boundaries and you'll feel like a con man. Good luck sleeping tonight. Note: Jewish parents will be impressed with your shrewd negotiations. Gentile parents will be confused by your frequent use of Yiddish.

RECOGNITION. Be a gracious loser. Your parents have done a lot for you, and despite what you think, they don't owe you any money. If they won't budge, say thanks anyway and you understand. The goodwill might pay off when you need more money next week. Be an even graciouser winner! If they say yes, you want to really pile it on. This probably won't be the last time you'll need their help.

Squeezing Your Last $10

You only have ten bucks left of the $200 your parents give you every month and it's only the eighth. Although you're not quite sure where that $190 went, you think it may have something to do with the brand-new kegerator that you bought two days ago for $190. Is it possible to make it through on only your post-kegerator assets? You bet! (But don't bet. You only have $10.) Here's how to make those last one thousand pennies count:

Tip 1: Never mind Easy Mac, Top Ramen is cheaper than salt. In some supermarkets you can buy twenty Top Ramen for $2. One a day is plenty to live on. If your urine appears to be highlighter yellow, change flavors from "chicken" to "Oriental."

Tip 2: For entertainment, we suggest standing outside of your local movie theater and asking the patrons as they exit what their favorite part was. That way you can tell your friends you saw a movie today, and when they ask you what your favorite part was you'll have something to tell them. Remember, 90 percent of the joy of watching movies is being able to answer your friends when they ask you what your favorite part was.

Tip 3: Pizza is for aristocrats—you'll just have the toppings. Each slice is two or three dollars, but the toppings are only 50 cents each! Why get two slices and waste half your bankroll when you can get a handful of mushrooms and olives for $1? Extra cheese? Don't mind if I do! The weird look you're getting is that of jealousy . . . and pity.

Tip 4: Laundry machines are a waste of quarters. Why pay a machine to do something you can do in a lake for free? You wouldn't pay a robot to pee for you, would you? Didn't think so.

Tip 5: Postage stamps are for people who can afford 39 cents. For the next couple weeks it's all hand delivery. Need to send your father a card for his birthday across the country? Well, start walking.

Tip 6: How much did you pay for the shirt you're wearing? If your answer was more than "nothing," you're paying too much. College campuses are the world's leading exporter of free T-shirts, narrowly edging out Sri Lanka. If you run out of clothes, don't do laundry; just go to a sorority event or fill out a credit card application.

Tip 7: Ordering soda in a restaurant? Maybe when you're a billionaire! Until then, ask for one of those ludicrously undersized cups for tap water. Then fill it with Sprite. If the manager spots the carbonation bubbles from his post across the room, well, you'll go to jail knowing you were beaten by the best.

Tip 8: Your days of eating bread that was baked recently ended when your parents' bread factory exploded. If you're willing to eat three-day-old bagels, you can get them for free. You still have to steal them, but it's easier on your conscience this way.

Tip 9: Negotiate on everything. Price tag on that DVD says $20? Offer ten bucks. The guy at Target will be confused and have to go ask the manager. This opens a great opportunity for you to walk out the door with it. They'll wish they had that ten-spot now!

Credit Card Debt

They lured me in with a free T-shirt that said, "Boobs: It's What's for Dinner." At the time, it made sense. Credit card application completed and funny-ass shirt in hand, I strutted back to the roaring sounds of the monster-truck arena, feeling on top of the world.

I was happier 'n a hog in mud when my MasterCard showed up in the mail. Now, I'm a community college student with no job, so I don't know how I got instantly approved for a $1000 line of credit, but, hell, there it was. And it had a picture of Ric Flair driving a Camaro on it, part of MasterCard's new "Takin' It Greasy" collection.

At first I tried to be responsible and only buy things I really needed: haircuts, groceries, that sort of thing. But then I started getting things I just really liked. I visited my brother, and on my way through Tennessee I picked up some great fireworks. Them Jupiter Jubilees were four bucks apiece, and it looks pussy if you don't got at least ten of them. I spent a lot on my two best friends: Jack Daniel's and Jim Beam. You get it? They're liquors that are named after people. Shit, I should write a country song about that on my new guitar.

Soon I had maxed out my card and was a grand in debt. My friends told me that if I paid off the minimum each month it would go away. Not true; that shit's harder to shake than herpes. I had to quit answering all three of the cell phones I'd bought because the collection agents kept calling. They staked out my dentist's office, so I couldn't get the rest of my gold caps put on. You know how many girlies wanna jitterbug a man with half a gold grill? None, son.

Eventually, though, they tricked me again. I should have known that there wasn't going to be a wet T-shirt contest at no Olive Garden. Even if there was, wasn't nobody going to invite me. I showed up, and they took everything, even my shoes and my shirt about eating boobs. Guess it shows you there isn't no such thing as free money. Hell, it sure ain't free from those MasterCard boys.

Emergency Credit Card

If you're like most college students, your parents will probably give you a credit card that is for "emergencies only." So in order to make sure you don't take advantage of this generous service, we've set up a little quiz for you that we like to call, "Emergency or Not an Emergency." Just read each situation and try to determine which of these two labels best describes it before reading the very next line, which contains the answer. This is also a test of willpower.

You are in the middle of nowhere without any cash or anything to eat.	⚠EMERGENCY!
You really, really, really, really want a Snickers.	⊘Not an emergency
Your girlfriend is pregnant and abortions are charge-only expenses.	⚠EMERGENCY!
Your girlfriend has dandruff and not enough cash for "Head & Shoulders."	⊘Not an emergency
Grandma's funeral is across the country and you need plane tickets.	⚠EMERGENCY!
"Grandma's Funeral," your friends' morbidly named band, is playing and you need tickets.	⊘Not an emergency
You're on a hot date and when the bill comes you notice you're out of cash.	⚠EMERGENCY!
Stripper wants another drink. For her friends, too. Now.	⊘Not an emergency
You find out you're allergic to kiwi. The hospital only accepts credit cards.	⚠EMERGENCY!
You eat another kiwi just because you have a crush on your nurse.	⊘Not an emergency
Advance token to the nearest Railroad and pay owner twice the rental to which he/she is otherwise entitled. If Railroad is unowned, you may buy it from the Bank.	⚠EMERGENCY!
You are assessed for street repairs—$40 per house and $115 per hotel.	⊘Not an emergency

At your first crappy job, say, "Four years of college for this?" a lot. It's not like you didn't know the risk of majoring in "making copies" when you went in.

Easy Money

You'll hear a lot in college about "get-rich-quick schemes." There are many crooked businessmen out there looking to take advantage of susceptible college kids. They understand that college kids are predominantly poor and always searching to make an easy buck. Let us make it abundantly clear: there is NO WAY to make a quick buck in America . . . until now!

How would you like $5000 in cash, today? How would you like to tell your mom, "Hey, Mom, I'm not a loser anymore!" Americans are defined by their financial dependency, and using our foolproof technique you'll have as much freedom as a hundred Emancipation Proclamations! How would you like to be able to keep your money in wads instead of coins? Ever wanted to fill up a Jacuzzi with "dollar dollar bills"? Well, now is your chance!

Introducing: Cash-o-matic 4000! That's right, you read correctly: Cash-o-matic 4000!

FACT: Cash-o-matic will get you laid.

FACT: Cash-o-matic will make you rich.

FACT: Cash-o-matic will bring back a dead relative. But only one. Cash-o-matic is great, but it's not magical.

Cash-o-matic was developed by astronauts who went crazy—crazy with their love for making you rich! But don't delay, call within the next fifteen minutes and we will throw in a Mini Travel Cash-o-matic absolutely free! Cash-o-matic is fun, free, and affordable. Don't be a moron and order one today.

Please send blank checks to: Me.

Being Rich in College

The modern stigma around college kids is that they are relatively poor penny-pinchers who do their damnedest to squeeze every dime of their paycheck in order to live comfortably.

But not you! You're rich! Why should YOU have to suffer?

Being rich in college is fantastic; we cannot stress that point enough! Restaurants, entertainment, and gasoline prices: they're all catered toward the rich. Two dollars for a slice of pizza? Thanks, you'll take eight, please. Concert only costs $39? I'll take four tickets! One for me, and three to make a paper hat!

Another wonderful thing about being rich in college is all the friends you'll make after purchasing cool expensive gadgets. Nothing says "coolest guy in your hall" quite like a seventy-inch plasma TV scraping against the walls of your seventy-one-inch dorm room. Not that nine-inch Quasar TVs don't serve a purpose; you should have ten, and burn them to keep warm.

The greatest thing about being rich in college is that relative to all the poor kids, you are EXTREMELY rich, and that image is exactly what you need to get blow jobs from hot moneygrubbing whores. Sure those other kids are "nice and friendly," but who's gonna buy you dinner, baby? Whoa, not so fast! My balls need to get dry sometime, Jesus!

So while it may seem like most kids are poor and you want to fit in, just remember: Be yourself. Your filthy-rich self!

Top 5 Signs Your Roommate Is Rich

1. Has own butler named Cadbury who calls him "Mawster Richie."
2. Foppishly dressed in blue shorts, white shirt, red bow tie, black blazer, and knee-high white boots.
3. Was once played by Macaulay Culkin in a poorly grossing feature film.
4. Featured in a long-running comic book in which he thwarts thieves and pirates.
5. Is something of a "poor little rich boy."

Scholarships for the Rest of Us

Whether you need to pay for your own tuition or you are having your parents pay, scholarships are a great way to ease some of the financial burden. Most college kids are familiar with popular scholarships based on "academic [nerd] merit" but there are thousands of other types of scholarships, for almost any talent or ability. Here are a few that may or may not be offered at your college:

JUDAH B. TINSLEY AWARD FOR ACADEMIC MEDIOCRITY

Requirements: The student needs to maintain a B average. Exactly a B average. Any B+ or B– will be counted against you. Judah B. Tinsley maintained a "perfect" 3.0 grade-point average at his fiftieth-percentile school and is looking to give $2000 to any student who displays simliar mediocrity.

ARTHUR R. WIGGLEBOTTOM AWARD FOR PRIME SOCIAL SECURITY NUMBERS

Requirements: Is your Social Security number divisible only by 1 and itself? If so, you are eligible to receive the Wigglebottom scholarship. Arthur R. Wigglebottom has generously donated $11,731 to fund this scholarship in search of students whose Social Security number is also a prime number.

THE RAMIT SANGRAVANIAN "DRINK THAT SHIT, DUDE" PRIZE

Requirements: Imagine half a glass of lemonade with relish, mustard, poppyseeds, a stick of butter, chewed gum, mud, and ham in it. Would you drink that shit, dude? This prize of over $25,000 is given once every two years to a college student who can, in fact, drink that shit, dude. Past winners include the guy who played Waldo Faldo on *Family Matters* and Jeremy Piven.

THE BRENHEIM AWARD

Requirements: Once every ten years the Brenheim Institute grants one student full tuition if he can correctly identify which hand Wilson Brenheim, the Institute's president, is holding a quarter in. Over the past seventy years, the quarter has been in the left hand 20 percent more times than the right.

Failed Dorm Businesses

If we were all rich, then there would be no more poor people to make fun of.

Fortunately, we're not all rich, and to scrappy go-getters in your dorm, this will be inspiration to start a dorm-room business. Some are successful, but some end up in the

HALL OF BROKEN BUSINESSES

'Crazy' Matt's iPod Charging
"I Won't be Undersold"
Next day pickup available

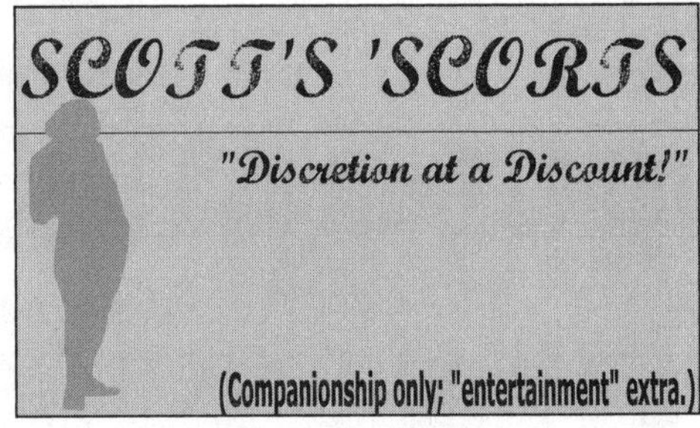

Making your checkbook stand up on its side doesn't count as balancing it. You're now $4000 in debt.

Tired of minimum-wage jobs? Busting your ass day after day only to receive the least possible income for your tireless efforts? Well, now those horrible days are over!

INTRODUCING: INTERNSHIPS!

Internships are a great way for you to use phrases like "learning experience," "yes, sir," and "foot in the door." Perhaps best of all, internships are unpaid! We know what you're thinking: "Unpaid? That's ridiculous, and practically illegal." Ha! More like so much fun, it should be illegal! But it isn't!

You see, unpaid internships are legal because they're technically accepting you as a volunteer! Which means all of the fun responsibility of a normal job, and none of the annoying hassles of getting paid!

How often do you find yourself thinking, "This job sucks. And to make matters worse, on Friday, I have to go all the way to the bank and deposit this damn paycheck!"? Internships get rid of the lame hassles of paychecks, and rely solely on direct depositing all the money you don't make straight into the most important bank account of all: your conscience.

Internships were first developed by scientists who needed coffee but lacked the funding to train monkeys. Using a space-age method of guilt, they were able to coerce overqualified college students to perform seemingly menial tasks. The result: a neo-futuristic form of legal slave labor that can thrive in nearly every state and field of study imaginable! Before long, hundreds of thousands of college students everywhere were spending their summers in large office buildings gaining zero money but tons and tons of invaluable experience!

So what are you waiting for? Don't delay, don't get paid today!

Job Disclaimer

The jobs you have in college won't be the most desirable ones. In fact, most of them will be fairly dangerous and involve warnings before you sign your contract. See if you can match the disclaimer to the job!

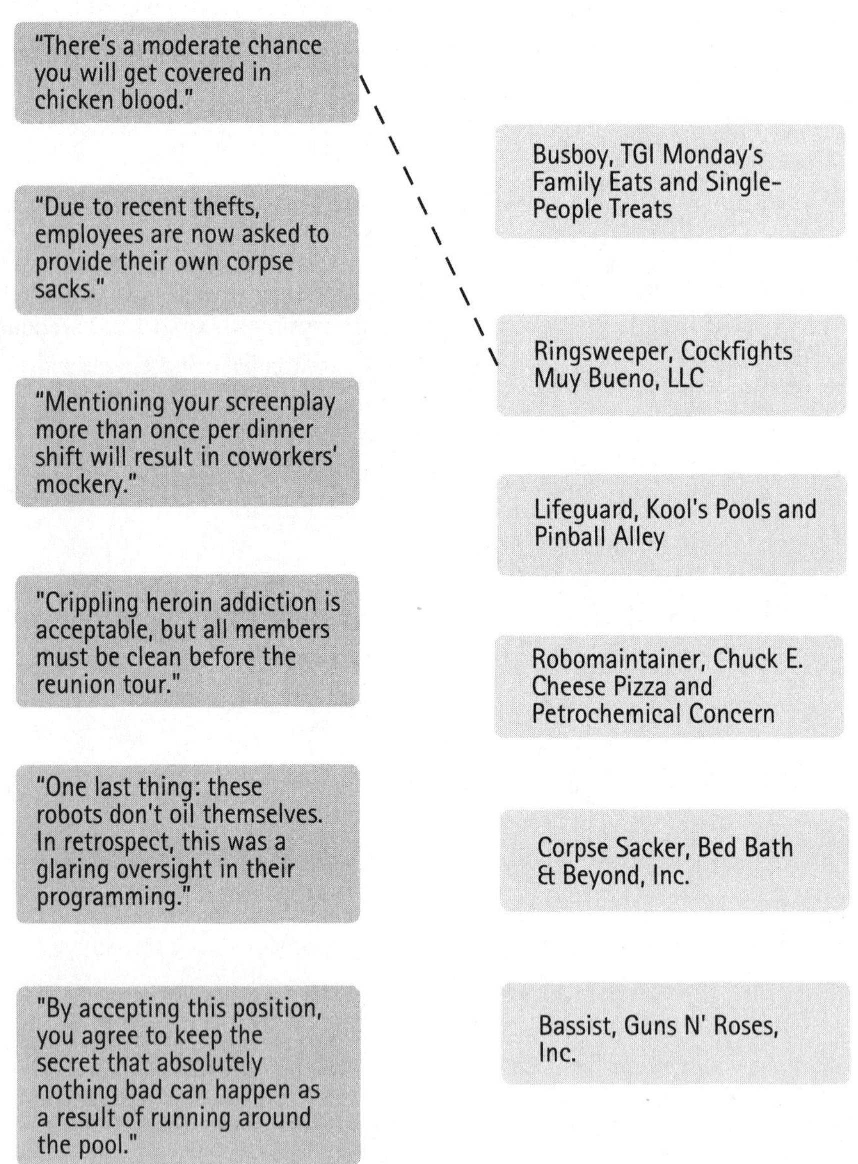

Work-Study

The common perception is that work-study is for suckers. However, after a little exploration of the facts, I think you'll realize that a job at the library or the Administration Building is actually the highest-paying gig in town.

Let's say, for example, you earn $6 an hour for your work. What people don't realize is that you only have to work about two minutes every hour. The other fifty-eight minutes are spent browsing eBay for odd items, perusing craigslist for free items, and checking/rechecking away messages. "Hmm, LizzieKat943 is still 'Chillin'. Wonder how long she can keep that up!"

So with only two minutes of real work every hour, that means it takes thirty hours of "fake work" to accumulate one hour of real hard-core working. However, the school is going to pay you for those thirty fake hours. This translates to $180 (30 × $6/hour) for only one hour of real work. We defy you to find a job that pays higher than $180 an hour!

Note: since this book was written, LizzieKat943 has stopped using her computer and is now considered idle.

A great way to make money is by counting cards. Bicycle is always looking for people to make sure there are fifty-two cards in every deck before wrapping their product and making a shipment.

Padding Your Budget

A Final Note on Finance

Make sure to spend all your money at the beginning of the semester, as it tends to run out by the end.

17 SUMMER SCHOOL

Nice one, retard. If you need us, we'll be at the beach.

18 STUDY ABROAD

Introduction

When you tell your parents that you have decided to study abroad for a semester, your dad will likely say something to this effect: "Just one? I studied lots of broads when I was in college!" Do yourself a favor and laugh at Dad's feeble attempt to be original, because he's the one who is going to fund your intercontinental four-month vacation.

Studying abroad offers college students a great opportunity to travel the world, become immersed in a different culture, and brush up on their language skills. With this sort of cultural bounty available to students, it's no wonder that over half of them go to that most foreign of cities, London. Nothing says, "I'm expanding my horizons," like studying in a city with more Starbucks than black people. As soon as study abroad in Vancouver gets fired up, everyone will end up there. (Sorry, Canadian readers! Here's a consolation joke: what's the DEAL with nationalized health insurance?) Sadly, your American passport may make you the target of some ridicule among Europeans, so throw it away as soon as your plane lands. You can't put a price on saving yourself from mockery.

When you study abroad, you do more than just jet around on a Eurail pass, send mass e-mails home, and eat McDonald's but act like it's some foreign exotic version of the Filet-o-Fish. You learn how to seriously annoy everyone in the entire North American continent upon your return. Remember, if you call an elevator a "lift," everyone will think you're cultured and British, not some idiot from Alabama. Oh, and please don't forget to tell us how rickety the stairs were at Il Duomo in Florence. Oh, and the food! It never fucking stops. If we wanted to learn about foreign cultures, we wouldn't have let our *National Geographic* subscription expire; at least that had tribal boobs in it. If you go abroad and you don't want your friends to hate you, never, ever talk about having gone abroad. If people pry, say, "I was molested by my host dad, okay? Don't ever say the name Carlos around me again." That ought to shut up their nosy yapping.

But study abroad isn't all about feigning nonconsensual sex. It's also about taking photographs. You can use them in a screen saver to make everyone you know jealous, or you can bind them into photo albums so that people will sigh and say, "Okay, I guess I can look at one or two . . . Look, I gotta get up early, I better go. No, DAVID, I DON'T want to see another goddamn photo of you at the Eiffel Tower!" *(sound of David being stabbed)*

Listen to us going on about what you shouldn't do! What about what you *should* do? Well, you should take easy study-abroad classes to pad your GPA; don't worry, the law school admissions officers have never seen that trick before. You should allow your worldview to be really expanded, but only to the point where you say, "After studying abroad, I know the world is just so big" in a lot of irrelevant contexts. You should take a trip to Amsterdam and do the following things: smoke "the best pot you've ever had, just some serious quality shit," tour the Heineken brewery, and consider getting a hooker in the red-light district before pussying out at the last minute. You really did it: you studied abroad.

Finally, remember that learning how to say, "Which way to the Internet cafe?" in a foreign language is for nerds. Just keep yelling it in English; once you get it loud and slow enough, they'll understand.

When studying abroad, be wary of any country that not only has an Internet cafe, but also an electricity-and-running-hot-water-cafe.

Study-Abroad Destination

United Kingdom: "Pound sterling for pound sterling, the world's best."

What's the Deal?

Would you like to study abroad, but not deal with the hassle of learning a new language? Then the United Kingdom is for you! Whoa, is that an apartment or a flat!?!

Things to See:

- London. Then it's just France before a woman's underpants. Schoolyard chants don't lie. Now, how about that place in France where the naked ladies dance?

Things Not to See:

- Wales. Has nothing to do with *Free Willy* and everything to do with a shitty country full of sheep and textile mills.

One Great Item to Bring:

- Handgun. You'll have the only one on the whole island, and you will be their master.

France: "No, we don't call French toast, 'toast.' "

What's the Deal?

The French love nothing more than not loving you. Don't get mad if a Frenchman gets angry at you; he's just naturally mad because his car is small, his house is crooked, he stinks of brie, and his daughter finds you irresistible.

Things to See:

- Normandy. See where Grandpa orphaned twenty German children with one well-placed grenade toss.

Things Not to See:

- EuroDisney. There's nothing stranger than a Frenchman in a Goofy costume. Goofy indeed!

One Great Item to Bring:

- Your Republican National Committee membership card.

Italy: "Once great, now dirty."

What's the Deal?

The ancestral homeland of Danny DeVito is one hot place. Make sure to bring plenty of sunscreen and gypsy repellant if you plan on seeing the sights.

Things to See:

- Pompeii's ancient whorehouse. Come see the exact spot where the world's oldest professional blow job was given back when you could give a whore three rocks for oral sex and she'd gladly accept. A generous tip was a handful of dirt.

Things Not to See:

- Pisa. Everyone's first thought when they see the leaning tower: "Hmm, I wonder if it will fall today." Answer: no.

One Great Item to Bring:

- Pizza Hut coupon. Redeemable for one confused Italian cashier.

Spain: "The England of Mexico."

What's the Deal?

The average American takes six semesters of Spanish in high school but will still be reduced to yelling, "Which way to *el baño*!" on their Spanish vacation. Remember to look around and say aloud, "This shithole controlled the world for centuries?"

Things to See:

- Ibiza. Drugs? Sex? Techno music? It's as if Tara Reid's mind created an island.

Things Not to See:

- Madrid. The Newark of the Iberian Peninsula.

One Great Item to Bring:

- Hammock. Bring this fine piece of lounge equipment along and you can participate in the national sport—laziness!

Japan: "We know what your tattoo means."

What's the Deal?

The Japanese are a lot like the Chinese, but don't tell them or they'll karate kick you to outer space. Or is that the Chinese? See!

Things to See:

- Tokyo. There's only one city in the world where you can sleep in a tube, and we're not referring to a homoerotic metaphor.

Things Not to See:

- Sumo match. You'll become depressed when you realize that the Sumos aren't that much bigger than your fat American ass.

One Great Item to Bring:

- Used panties. Sell them on the street for some extra cash. . . . Seriously, they buy that crap over there.

Australia: "England's Alabama."

What's the Deal?

If you're looking for kangaroos or sand, this place is a done deal. A crocodile done-deal.

Things to See:

- The Great Barrier Reef. This is the largest living thing on earth. It is your job as a native Kentuckian to try to kill it.

Things Not to See:

- Great white shark. You see, you die. They keep things simple down there; no rules, just right.

One Great Item to Bring:

- A shiv wrapped in a bandana. This is a country originally founded by prisoners, so you can never be too careful.

How to Look Like a Canadian

America is the best country on earth, but, unfortunately, only we know it. Occasionally—like the last two hundred years—this has made people hate us. They find our appetites gluttonous, our voices loud, and our women crude. Sure, we could just bomb them or take over their country, but that might make your study-abroad trip less than enjoyable. Luckily, America has a neighbor to the north that nobody ever thinks about, ever . . . Canada. Since they never do anything, nobody hates them. Plus, since they're all copycats and stole our racial features, they look just like we do. Disguising yourself as a Canadian can save you a lot of trouble and keep you from answering McDonald's-related questions for the whole semester.

You'd trot the globe, too, if you were from Harlem.

Gypsy Journal

Everyone dreams of going abroad and making wonderful foreign friends who will enrich their lives. Then they go abroad and realize that every third person is a filthy gypsy who wants nothing more than to steal their passport, wallet, and gallbladder for use in a potion. Although gypsies have gotten a bad rap in American culture, much of this press is unfair. Let's separate fiction from reality in a little section we like to call:

GYPSY MYTHS AND GYPSY FACTS

Gypsy MYTH: Almost all gypsies are bloodthirsty thieves who only want to steal.
Gypsy FACT: All gyspies are bloodthirsty thieves who only want to steal.

Gypsy MYTH: Gypsies have magic powers and can curse non-gypsies.
Gypsy FACT: Gypsies can fucking fly. I swear to God.

Gypsy MYTH: Gypsy children are often used as decoys in elaborate scams.
Gypsy FACT: Gypsy children are actually tiny gypsy adults and should be shot on sight. Gypsies do not have children.

Gypsy MYTH: Gypsy women can tell your fortune by reading your palm.
Gypsy FACT: Gypsy women don't need to even touch your palm to tell your fortune. They just need human contact every once in a while.

Gypsy MYTH: Gypsies can't run or jump.
Gypsy FACT: There have been over five hundred secretly gypsy athletes in American history, two of which have been named Orel Hershiser.

Gypsy MYTH: If you shoot a gypsy, he will die.
Gypsy FACT: A gypsy once wrestled Jesus Christ in an eight-round cage match. Who won? Let's just say they made up that "death by crucifixion" story to save Jesus some embarrassment.

Dude, That Chick Has Pit Hair, by Blake

Dude, did you see that chick? Bro, she had, like, fuckin' pit hair. That's nasty, yo. If I took that bitch home, I'd be like, "Yo, ho, shave that shit . . . NOW!" Right, son? Word. Dude, do you think she even knows that pit hair is for dudes? Maybe I should tell her . . . Sike! I'm not talking to that freak. She'd be kinda hot if she stopped being disgusting, right? She's like this bitch Sarah my boy Beandog bones at school. She's, like, hot but one time I saw that she hadn't shaved her legs in a few days and I was like, "Beandog, your girl is a she-beast." He got all pissed, so I go, "Bro, is it a full moon? Cuz your bitch is turning into a wolf." He hasn't talked to me in a few months. Bro, look, she's bending over . . . sick. I bet she has ass hair too, right? I should be like, "Hey, if I wanted to see a hairy ass I'd look at mine . . . NOT cuz I shave my shit up nice." Seriously, bro, these foreign chicks are nasty. What? You don't speak English? What are you, retarded?

Hostels

Hostels (super-cheap accommodations for international travelers and backpackers) are a great way to save money on weekend trips around Europe. The problem is that you often get what you pay for and end up stuck in a complete shithole. Of course, the hostel is not going to warn you of their less-than-mediocre status. The trick here is to figure out the truth (in parentheses) behind a hostel's self-written description:

I wanted to study abroad until my dad pointed out it would be like spending a semester at Epcot. I really dodged a big, boring, golf-ball-shaped bullet there.

Albo D'Ara Campsite in Venice, Italy

(a bunch of tents in the middle of nowhere, possibly near Venice, Italy)

Welcome to Venice! Our cozy cabins are the perfect Italian getaway, surrounded by Italian scenes of family, fun, food, and culture!

(Glad you didn't die on your way out here! Our cabins barely have enough room for you to move and the walls have no windows, just crayon drawings of pizza and spaghetti.)

Our campsite is located right near the heart of Venice, with a personal shuttle service directly from the Plaza to our front door. There is also public transportation that leaves from across the street every hour on the hour.

(We are about forty-five minutes outside of Venice on the side of an unlabeled highway. The personal shuttle service only runs every third Tuesday and is driven by a blind man. The public bus rarely shows up, and when it does, a one-way trip costs 87 euro.)

Albo D'Ara is a common getaway for international backpackers, so stop by the on-site bar and exchange stories!

(If you look in the garbage, there might be some half-empty beers you can drink. Oh, and while you're doing that, other backpackers will be stealing your personal belongings.)

We offer the following services to our guests:

-A 24-hour doorman

(a dead pigeon on the ground at the entrance)

-Secure storage facilities

(a couple empty refrigerator boxes, sealed with Scotch Tape)

-Internet access

(a single computer with dial-up Internet at the front desk, which costs 20 euro for every five minutes of use)

-Bed linens included

(which you're pretty sure are just a bunch of paper towels sewn together)

Study-Abroad Friend

The evolution of a study-abroad friend is a very formulaic one. From its conception to its death, each study-abroad friendship follows relatively the same trajectory. Why? Because we said so, that's why.

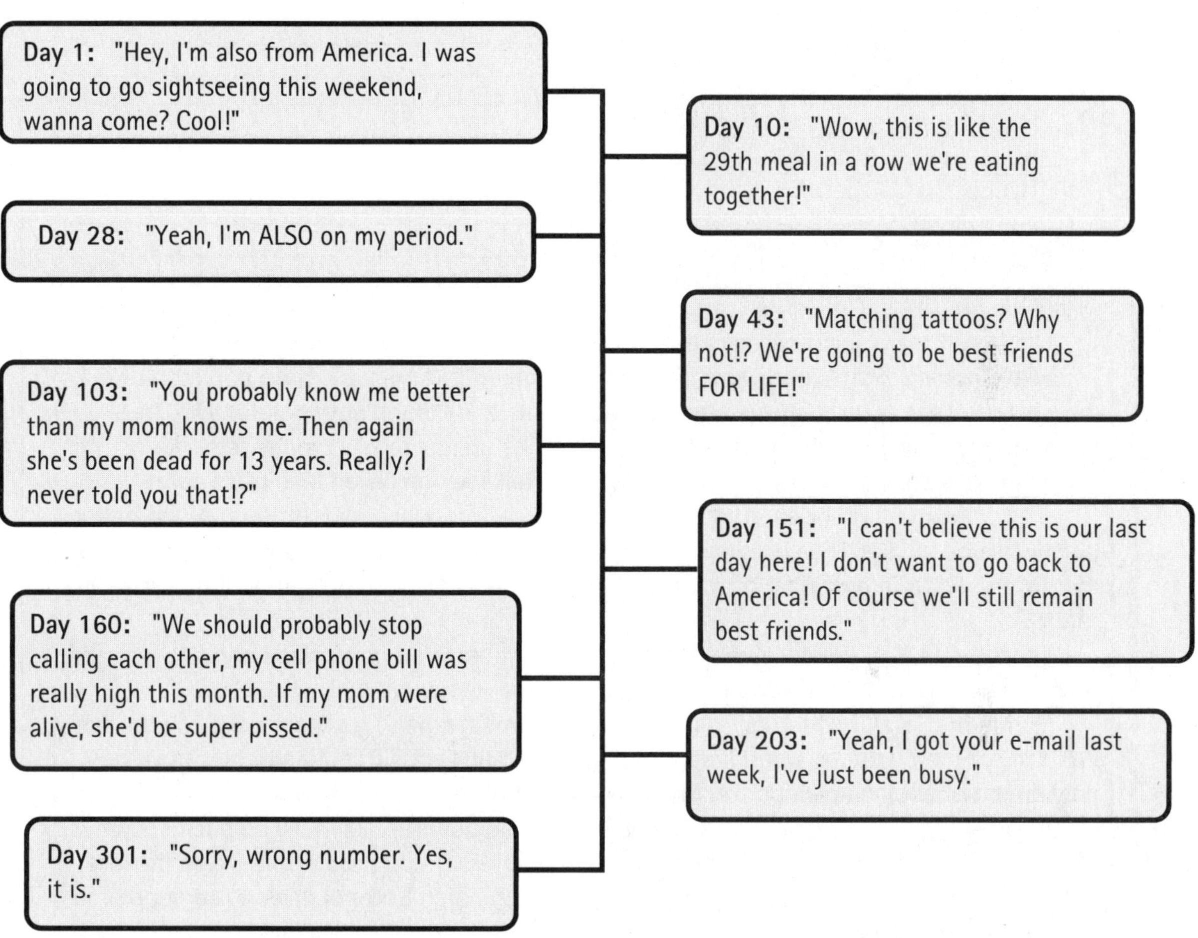

How to Write an E-mail from Another Country

The most important part of studying abroad is making your friends as jealous as possible through e-mail. Sending a weekly e-mail to your friends boasting about your fanciful excursion isn't as easy as it sounds, so here is a generic guide:

To: Everyone You Know

Cc:

Bcc:

Subject: Update from [Your Host Country]!

["Hello" in Your Host Country's Language]

Life here truly is [positive adjective]. I honestly cannot imagine myself anywhere else, especially not in [Town Where Your College Is Located in America]. The people, the food, the weather, it's truly uniquely spectacular and unable to be found anywhere! People here go to bed at [a particular hour in the morning] and wake up [some point in the late afternoon]! They say New York is the city that never sleeps—well, we don't even take naps here!

This weekend I attended a [famous sport, soccer probably] match! Sooo much better than what you guys did this weekend. We get drunk every night and alcohol here costs less than water! For a [metric unit] of wine it'll run you about [a very small amount of local currency].

I hope you guys are enjoying your [semester or quarter]. I go to class once a week for an hour. And I've only taken one test all year and everybody got 100.

During the week I spend time at [several local museums]. I go there so much the docents know me by name. I see firsthand paintings by [Ninja Turtle Names] that you guys only dream of seeing in textbooks. My eyes thank me on a daily basis.

Anyway, I hope everything is okay in your sad little pointless town. I'll be back soon but only for a little while; I definitely want to move here after I graduate. Oh and be on the lookout for this awesome song called [Song Currently Popular in Europe]. It won't be popular in the States for another [number of months], but you're totally going to love it when it eventually gets there.

I love you all, but not as much as I love [The Country You Are In].

—[Your Name]

Send | Save Draft | Attach | Tools | Cancel

Note: Be sure to replace the generic phrases between the [ ] with your unique particulars; otherwise your friends might think you're a robot.

Photo Guide

Studying abroad isn't about personal growth and forced introspection through cultural isolation; it's about taking as many photos as possible to point out just how much more fun you're having than those bums back at "normal" school. For maximum effect, attach said photos to previous e-mail template. Make sure the recipient list on the e-mail is no fewer than seventy-four people long.

Now that we've settled that, you just have to take the pictures. What works best? Here's a handy guide!

HOW TO KNOW THAT THE PICTURE IS WORTH TAKING:

Will seeing it make others cry about how terrible their semester has been? Will they say, "You're so beautiful and well traveled, and I'm stuck here in this hole, trying to get out of credit card debt and using watercolors as eye shadow?" Good. They asked for it.

Is there a large monument or building in the frame? If not, is there a large open space where one could be Photoshopped in? "The Eiffel Tower isn't located in this vast German plain, is it?" The answer is, "Shut up."

Will anyone know what the building is? If not, then snap away. When friends say, "I don't know what that building is," condescendingly reply, "So what else is new?" Then flip quickly to the next photo. That'll teach them to not study abroad in Australia!

Take pictures of all the food you eat, so your friends can see how authentic it was. If you forget to do this, go to the Olive Garden directly from the airport when you get back into the country. Take pictures of every iteration of the never-ending pasta bowl. Now you've got never-ending memories!

HOW TO KNOW THAT THE PICTURE IS NOT WORTH TAKING:

Are you trying to be creative or artsy? People don't want to see any of the shit you picked up in Photography 101. They want the most basic, mundane photos you can get. Are you at Pisa? Then take a picture of you holding up the tower. HAHAHAHA, you were the first person to do that!! Are you at Oktoberfest? Take a picture with a beer and an oompah band. Make sure everyone can see how drunk you are! Sarajevo? Blow off half of your legs with a leftover land mine. Smile and give the camera two stumps-up.

Are you actually in downtown Cleveland? That isn't studying abroad. That's failure.

Nobody wants to see pictures of paintings. Same goes for statues. And if you think we are going to be lenient on lithographs, think again.

Domestic Study Abroad

"I'd like to study abroad, but the idea of going to a foreign country makes me uncomfortable and sad." Is this you? It must seem like there's no solution. But wait, there is!

Introducing Domestic Study Abroad!

There are just too many steps to going abroad in our go-go society. You have to apply for a passport, take passport photos, get your passport out of the mailbox when it comes, and those are JUST the passport-related steps. What about getting a travel visa? DON'T GO THERE!

America, on the other hand, is a huge country, almost as big as Europe, and all you need to travel it is a car and some energy.

Now, it sounds like some of you are saying, "But I heard you have to leave the country to study abroad." WRONG!!! That was all well and good for nineteenth-century authors like Henry James, but domestic study abroad is the wave of the future. Just look at some of the great benefits of studying abroad in the United States:

- Easy currency exchange rates. Would you rather multiply by 1.8 to do a pounds-to-dollars conversion or multiply by 1 to get dollars-to-dollars? Thanks a lot, Tony Blair, but we're not all math wizards!
- Free refills. Try getting a refill in Europe. I fucking dare you. What? You couldn't? Well, the important thing was that you tried. Tried AND FAILED.
- No problems getting through Customs. Try bringing pot back from Amsterdam and you'll find yourself in a windowless Swiss prison cell. You want to carry an eighth from Seattle to Portland? Have it your way: the American Way.
- No language barrier. Have you ever tried speaking English to a European? It's impossible; those people just don't get it. In America, they speak English everywhere except Texas. What a country!
- No mad cow disease. What do American cows have to be mad about? Having it too GOOD?!?!

There you have it: a definitive set of reasons why you should join the millions already taking part in domestic study-abroad programs. When you get back, remember to obnox-

---

Frank Sinatra once said, "I studied abroad every fuckin' day." He wasn't lying, either. He attended Oxford.

iously pepper your speech with local slang like "burger," "fries," and "shake." (These terms are, respectively, short for "hamburger," "French fries," and "milk shake.") What a time to go abroad!

A Final Note on Study Abroad

You have to sign up for most study-abroad programs years in advance, so don't choose a country that may not exist by your junior year. We don't care how appealing the Prussia brochure sounded.

19

LIFE BEYOND COLLEGE

Introduction

Well, you did it. You made it to the end of college. Or, failing that, you made it to the end of the book. It's time for you to leave the best four years of your life and begin the slow decline into the worst fifty-two years of your life.

From the beginning of senior year forward, all of your thinking should be geared toward your life beyond college. You can't stay in college forever, no matter how hard you try. Unless you become a dean or a professor, you will eventually have to say good-bye to your college campus. And trust us, with the pictures they have of you after four years of college, you won't become a dean or a professor.

On the plus side, post-collegiate life is not that much different from college. You're still poor, you still don't go to class, and you're still pretending to look for a job. Only this time, your parents won't accept your "busy schedule" as an excuse, since you graduated five years ago and the only thing on your résumé is "Professional Cereal Eater."

Choosing a career in the modern world can be tough. Technology is improving at such a rapid pace that students of today have a new, scary thing to worry about: robots taking their jobs. In this next decade, robots will have taken over most of our best jobs, including poet, leading to unemployment rates of up to 57 percent. The key to protecting yourself here is choosing a career that can't possibly be stolen by a robot. We suggest robot repairman.

For those of you brave enough to still get a job, you'll quickly fall into a routine of waking up early, coming home at five, and talking about how tired you are. Your boss will quickly turn into the "old man" who won't stop giving you "accounts" to work on. They'll dangle the brass ring of success over you, even though you're pretty sure you can't "make partner" at the Barnes & Noble in the mall. You will be grossly underpaid. Sure, $18,000 a year sounds like a lot now, but when you realize that you can't get a place to live for less than, at a bare minimum, $45 a month, you come to grips with the fact that you probably won't be buying that Bentley anytime soon. The Rolls should still be doable sometime next year, though, if you play the market correctly.

It's perfectly natural not to get a job, though. Some students just take some time off to find themselves. It's important to clarify that no one in the history of the world has ever "found himself" while living in his parents' basement, although they have found their old Super Nintendo and found they were much, much better at Mortal Kombat than they remembered.

Of course, some graduates decide that seventeen years of school was not nearly enough for them and continue on to grad school, law school, or med school. These schools have all of the bad parts of college—studying, professors, and homework—with none of the drinking or sex. This academic drudgery can get tiring, but remember the old adage that the last person in the med school class is still called "doctor." However, they call him "doctor at a small college's student-health infirmary." They also call the last person in a law school class "lawyer," but they call him at a number printed on the side of a bus. "*El abogado numero uno en todo el mundo*" indeed.

This chapter is a guide to life beyond college. Just because the fun will die doesn't mean you have to as well.

If you get married right after college, your wedding cake should be topped with a white flag.

Sample GRE Question

Toward the end of college, you might consider going to grad school. If you do, you'll have to take the Graduate Record Examination (GRE). The GRE is basically the SAT's older brother who takes steroids and knows that filtered cigarettes are for pussies. Here's a sample question:

37. Cat is to dog just as magnetic resonance techniques are to ____.

A) pig

B) Reagan

C) Dostoevsky

D) 2π

E) D, C, and A

F) E, but not C and A

G) J/K

H) All of the above

I) None of the below

Solution: J) Not enough information

Job Fairs

They come to your schools like nerd magnets. Every smart kid on campus is instantly drawn to their suits and cheap giveaways. They've got exactly what these kids want: a career.

For those of you still ignorant of the ways of recruiting, here is a basic breakdown of the process. Your college sets up a job fair of sorts, and representatives from companies large enough to sponsor a football bowl game set up their booths. When your friends ask you how the fair was, it's important to shrug and say, "Eh, fair." They won't laugh, but they'll know you're clever.

Hey, anarchists, smelling bad and listening to shitty music has never overthrown anything.

Each booth is a six-foot-by-six-foot cubical optimized for piquing your interest in a career at number crunching. They have brochures, videos, informational sheets, and most of all, they have trinkets.

That's right, trinkets. Trinkets are such a powerful draw that for every nerd looking for a job, there are three looking for a little basketball hoop and ball. Trinkets are the reason YOU should go to job fairs. One lap around these job fairs, mixed with conversations of feigned interest, can land you a king's ransom of crap. "Have I considered a career in financial accounting? Only like EVERY DAY! Say, is that a squirt gun? Let me get that. Seriously, now."

Bouncy balls, Silly Putty, stress balls, little parachuting men! Everything that costs 50 cents from an ice-cream truck is here and absolutely free! As long as you don't mind corporate logos screenprinted on these trinkets, there is no reason NOT to attend.

So whether you're looking for a career, or just looking for a little rubber thing that you can turn inside out, place on a flat surface, and watch bounce really high, job fairs are a great excuse to put on a suit and skip class.

Interviewing

During every interview, your future employer will ask you the following tricky question: "What's your biggest weakness?" It is imperative you try to answer as confidently and honestly as possible. Or you can just recite the following:

"What's my biggest weakness? Obviously, that I don't have an answer to this question! *(giggle)*

"No, but seriously, that's a good question. Well, I guess I tend to work too hard and care too much about things. It's like, sometimes I'll stay at work all night if I don't think something's perfect. I'm crazy like that. I really tend to get in the way of the cleaning ladies when I do that, but then I'm also too compassionate and way overly fluent in Spanish, so I always end up talking to them about how their lives are and how their kids have been doing in school. Those kids try so damn hard, you know? I just wish I could afford to give them the same economic opportunity with which I was blessed.

"Jeez, listen to me rambling on. I suppose that's a weakness as well! Anyhoo. Next question. And if it's 'Can you start on Monday?' the answer is '100 percent YES!' "

An alternative, slightly less effective reply:

"Biggest weakness? Chocolate cake. Next question."

Five out of five dentists are pissed they had to take such a long survey.

Résumé vs. Reality

Robert Hartford

RÉSUMÉ:

Education: Harvard University
> BA expected May 2006
> Intended Physics Major
> GPA: 4.13

Experience:

- Professional Life Mentor: Duties included providing spiritual and pragmatic guidance for underprivileged city youth. I don't want to brag, but these kids were drawing pictures of me dunking over Michael Jordan with crayons I bought them.
- Aquatic Filtration Assistant: Used personal H_2O filtering device to hydrate severely dehydrated organisms within the United States.

Special Skills:

- Extensive knowledge of Microsoft Office, HTML, and American Sign Language.
- Fluent in Hebrew.

References:
T. W. Walker, Esq.
San Francisco, CA

REALITY:

Education: Hartford University
> B.A. unexpected May 2009
> Actual Physical Education Major
> GPA: 1.43

Experience:

- Older Brother: My younger brother is so fucking annoying. He keeps doodling sketches of me being gored by a unicorn. What the hell is that?
- One time I drank from a water fountain.

Actual Skillz:

- Made a "God's Eye" out of yarn at summer camp.
- Attended a Bar Mitzvah in 1995.

Actual References:
My buddy Todd the Actor

Fuck Now, While There's Still Time, by Jay Pinkerton

As a young fuck enthusiast, you may be asking yourself: "Why am I reading this article, and not fucking?"

If you're not thinking this, you certainly should be. Joe and Jane College Fuckscene are, even as you read this sentence, pumping triumphant fists in the air while they make big heaping shitpiles of love in the dorms, student residences, and Wendy's bathrooms that surround you. So why aren't you? Right now? With the person to your immediate left or right?

As a member of that luckiest of breeds, the college student, you have an obligation to the rest of us. Though you don't realize it yet, it will never, ever be as easy as it is for you, right now, to get into the pants of absolutely everyone around you. As a college student, you are out of high school, out of your parents' house, and out on your own for the first time. You are surrounded by single people your own age who want to meet you and like you, and want you to like them. You could throw a rock and hit someone you will later be getting your naughty parts moist with, assuming you don't throw it too hard.

You should be doing everything in your power to get laid as often as possible, while this embarrassment of choice still exists. When not eating, sleeping, or going to class, fuck. Fuck often. Fuck hard. Fuck until your sex parts are numb and sort of bluish. Don't worry about rejection. Don't worry about reputation. Don't even worry about how ridiculous your penis/vagina looks (and sorry, but yes, he/she lied, it looks hilarious). Just fuck often and indiscriminately.

I'll tell you why: I've now been out of college for a few years, and I never see any of the people I didn't fuck while at college. On a few occasions, I refused to take care of business for what seemed like coherent and well-founded reasons at the time. I now see them for what they were: times I wasn't, but should have been, fucking.

Believe me, no one was more shocked than I was that I even got opportunities. I wore cheap, ill-fitting shirts. I got $10 Supercuts haircuts. I was one of those idiots who read philosophy and was always blathering on about some political stance or other that, looking back, you couldn't pay me to give a dick toss about.

I was poor. Ill-mannered. I smoked. I had the emotional depth and personal maturity of a can of salmon. If ever there was a candidate for the Lifetime No Fucking section, I was that candidate. I tell you these embarrassing truths for one reason: even I managed to get laid at college. My head reels to think about how well people without the above character flaws were making out, presumably like bandits.

I'm going to let you in on The Big Secret. I'm not supposed to, but here it is anyway: the future is a desolate wasteland entirely bereft of hope. The world you know now—where single, attractive people with nice teeth and intelligent things to say mingle by the thousands; where today's only responsibility is to attend a three-hour lecture and type out an essay about T. S. Eliot—does not exist out here.

Nobody gives a shit about T. S. Eliot. We certainly don't care about your postmodern feminist take on "The Waste Land." Out here we're burdened with responsibilities, bills, jobs, concessions. We have less time on our hands, and we spend what little time we do have going to places we don't like, in a desperate attempt to meet single people our own age.

Eventually you will have to leave college—because if you stay, you'll be one of those people, and you'll become unfuckable anyway. The second you leave college, you will get older. Your dating pool will start to shrink—rapidly and unmercifully, like a smelly geriatric. Your fantasy of nailing that nineteen-year-old frosh or taming that brutish quarterback into submission? That gets progressively creepier sounding and unrealistic as the years pass.

In short, my friends, enjoy the fuck-filled bounty that is college while you still have it. Fuck loudly. Fuck proudly. And if you can, try to nail that nineteen-year-old first-year with the tight little package so that I may live vicariously through you. Spare no details when you relate these stories to me.

Oh, and if you mix about a half cup of red wine, a half-cup of Worcestershire sauce, a quarter-cup of soy sauce, and a tablespoon of salt into a container, pierce a thick steak with a fork, let it marinate in the sauce mixture for a day, then cook it on a barbecue—man, that is good eating. This represents the full extent of everything I know.

Dude . . . Babe, Will You Marry Me?, by Blake

Dude . . . I mean, babe, will you marry me? I know things have been tough in the past, but I'm gonna change; it's only light beer for me from now on. I couldn't think of a better place to ask you than Fat Tuesday's cuz that's where we met on sophomore Spring Break. Yes? Really? Oh, man, this is SICK! Yo, dawgs, she said yes! Yo, everybody, I'm getting motherfucking married! Oh man, this wedding is gonna be fucking ridiculous. Babe, I'm gonna invite all the brothers and maybe a few pledges. We're all gonna get so shitty! What? But, babe, bachelor parties are, like, part of the whole wedding thing. Well, as long as we can have the reception at Alpha House, it's all good. Oh man, we are gonna fuck so hard that night!

Graduation Speaker Bingo

Every time your graduation speaker says a phrase that's in a box, check it off. If you get five in a row, stand up and interrupt the speaker with a thundering "BINGO!" Everyone will be glad you shut him up.

B	I	N	G	O!
"This is the end of one thing, but the start of another."	"Congratulations, class of ____!"	(any inspirational quote)	(any joke contrasting the speaker's own age with the age of the graduating class)	(any talk of how they don't want to give a regular ole graduation speech)
"The world is a tough place."	"Do the right thing."	"History has issued a call to your generation."	". . . proud . . ."	"Go forth."
"We stand here today . . ."	"But in my book . . ."	FREE SPACE—"ummmm"	". . . a brighter future . . ."	(any joke about the dean)
(any joke about the weather)	(any joke about the duration of the speech)	"We've waited a long time for today."	(any joke about a local bar)	(awkward mention of skyrocketing tuition)
"I am truly honored."	(any irrelevant anecdote)	"I offer you this one piece of advice."	(any insane piece of advice)	"Webster's Dictionary defines . . ."

TOP 5 THINGS TO DO AT GRADUATION

5 When your name is called and you're walking to get your diploma, trip over your own two feet, land headfirst, and remain motionless for what will seem like days.

4 When receiving your diploma (or the fake piece of paper they use for aesthetics), take the microphone from the dignified man handing out the papers and say, "Yo, yo, pass the mic. Aight check it, my name's Kid Fresh and I'm here to say, I love Fruity Pebb—" At which point you should be tackled by Security.

3 Hire two four-year-old girls to sprinkle rose petals on the floor as you walk to receive your diploma. When you get to the end of the stage, lift one of the girls up by the scruff of her neck and drop-kick her into the audience. Look the other four-year-old girl square in the eyes and tell her that she is lucky to be alive.

2 Hide a small person under your gown. When walking up to receive your diploma, stop short and let out a primal scream. Drop to the floor and have the second person, who should be naked and doused in pomegranate juice, spring forth from your gown and receive the diploma with his teeth; then have him scamper off into the distance. You'll know to meet him at the rendezvous point you two have set before the graduation. Come alone.

1 Tape dozens of hot dogs to your body in the fashion of a suicide bomber. When you walk to receive your diploma, throw your gown off and expose your fake dynamite vest. When the dean says, "It's okay, it's okay! Those are just hot dogs!" blow yourself up.

It's generally not a good idea to fill out your job application in crayon. Not because it looks unprofessional, but because you're applying for a job at a marker factory.

Things Not to Take with You

Unlike finals or losing your virginity, graduation is special because it happens only once in your collegiate career. You've spent four years accumulating knowledge, friendship, and a boatload of crap.

Packing is a long and arduous process. To streamline the process, here's what to donate to Goodwill for the next generation of little bastards looking for ironic gifts:

1. Your "shelving" made of concrete blocks and boards. In college, it made you look thrifty and awesome. In the real world, it will just make you look poor. And not the "I'm cool and artsy" kind of poor. The "I'm poor" kind of poor.
2. Any T-shirt from a college event. Nothing is sadder than walking through Target and seeing some balding middle-management type trying to coolly kick back in his "Pi Phi Phantastic Phuckphest '94" shirt. If it's less than fifteen years old, it's neither retro nor vintage, just kind of vaguely sad.
3. Your collection of beer bottles that almost circumnavigates your living room. Yes, it was a cool idea at the time, but look on the bright side, at 5 cents a bottle you have accumulated enough nickels to buy eight dimes!
4. Your college girlfriend/boyfriend. He's nice enough, but all of the sad, imagery- and angst-filled letters and three-figure phone bills in the world can't silence the message your heart has been texting your brain since May: that you can do better than a long-distance relationship. To borrow the immortal words of the troubadour Tom Petty, "I have never recorded a decent song."
5. Naps. The worst part of the real world is that sleeping from one to four every afternoon is no longer an option. If crankiness occurs, take two graham crackers and some juice.

"Aww, baby wants his bottle?" isn't sarcastic if you're actually talking to a baby that wants his bottle. Congrats, world's worst dad.

The REAL M.A.S.H

M.A.A.A.A.A.A.A.A.A.A.A.S.H.

Future Ex-Wife
1.
2.
3.
4.

College Debt
1.
2.
3.
4.

Type of Mazda
1.
2.
3.
4.

Failed Career
1.
2.
3.
4.

#Kids You Can't Afford
1.
2.
3.
4

Strange Disease your Health Insurance Doesn't Cover
1.
2.
3.
4.

What City in New Jersey Your Honeymoon Is In
1.
2.
3.
4.

Pints of Blood You Need to Sell in Order to Afford Dinner.
1.
2.
3.
4.

It's hard being a door-to-door salesman. Especially if you're selling doors. Because right away you know it's giving them something they already have.

Real-World Traveler

Gaze into this year's most popular post-graduation destinations!

Destination: Middle Management!

Enjoy unpaid overtime, cruel bosses, and more benefits than you can count on the first two fingers of your left hand! Sink into a negative work ethic and severe state of self-loathing!

Destination: Failed Marriage!

Have a blast in your first failed attempt at eternal happiness! Bask in the realization that your college girlfriend was a dirty slut and develop a healthy case of alcoholism!

Destination: European Trip!

Cling desperately to your youth by splurging on a post-graduation European tour! Avoid the real world as long as possible while contracting as many foreign STDs as possible!

Destination: Parents' Basement!

Re-create the definition of loser by moving back home after graduation! Hang out with your stoner friends in your parents' basement until they come through on their threat to cut you off!

Law School

All students consider going to law school at one point in their college careers. However, for every 1 million college freshmen who consider law school as a possible option, only one ends up actually attending. So what happens to the other 999,999 students? Let's take a look:

235,335 students change their minds when they realize there are no frats in law school.

125,910 students change their minds when they realize they'd rather do something "rad" after they graduate, like travel.

59,645 thought you meant "Jude Law School." Sorry about that.

307,477 college students responded, "Oh shit, really? Whatev," when they learned the LSAT application deadline was last Tuesday.

82,113 college students take the LSAT and do "pretty all right" but decide they would rather just get a normal job and watch *Law & Order* reruns to get the lingo down.

189,518 college students do so well on their LSATs that they decide to become LSAT tutors and make twice as much money as any lawyer.

1 student forgot to set his alarm and missed registration.

Which leaves exactly one student! One nerdy student who likes lawyer jokes.

Med School

You remember when you were a freshman and people asked you what your major was and you said "Pre-med"? Turns out that wasn't a major. Not your fault, but you should have figured it out more than a week before graduation.

Moving Back Home, or a Fate Worse than Death

You may not remember it, but at birth you and your parents signed a contract that makes them responsible for always providing you with free food in exchange for you posing for stupid pictures every now and then. With that in mind, let's take a look at the differences between living at college and life after moving back home:

In college . . .
One of your roommates was always ready to start drinking, anytime, anywhere.

In college . . .
Your bong was the centerpiece of the living room.

In college . . .
Pizza for two meals a day was an acceptable and common occurrence.

In college . . .
You saw more naked girls than you ever saw in your life.

In college . . .
When you got hungry, you would be lucky to find some ramen.

In college . . .
You had the freedom to do whatever you wanted, whenever you wanted to. And the freedom to be loud and stupid while you did it.

At home . . .
Mom can BARELY hold you up long enough for a kegstand.

At home . . .
Your bong is the centerpiece of under some old sheets in the back of your closet.

At home . . .
Nobody even delivers past 4 a.m.

At home . . .
Dad has decided shirts are more of an outdoor thing.

At home . . .
Well, actually, there's a lot of food. And it's all free. That part is pretty cool.

At home . . .
You have the freedom to only take a "no, thank you" portion of vegetables at dinner. Which is at 6:00.

Alumni Mad Libs

One of the toughest things to do when you meet an alumnus of your school is humoring him while he babbles on and on about the classes he used to take, his favorite makeout spots, and how great the sports team was "in his day." To get a feel for these conversations, complete this Mad Lib:

College Alumni Mad Lib

So a ________ university man, huh? GO ____________ ________! Haha!
(LOCATION) (VERB ENDING IN -ING) (PLURAL ANIMALS)

I graduated from there, too. Yup, class of _______. I bet things have
(NUMBER)
changed since then. Do people still ________ _________ during ________?
(VERB) (NOUN) (TIME OF THE YEAR)
What? They don't. Wow, things have changed!

Is the ________ ________ still open? We all used to go there to hang out
(ADJECTIVE) (NOUN)
after class, and sometimes during. Hahaha, things were a lot looser back then. It's a ___________ now? That's a shame, there's nothing
(TYPE OF STORE)
else like that place. They had the best ________ this side of _______.
(FOOD) (PLACE)

Does Professor ________ still teach there? He teaches Advanced ______.
(NAME) (NOUN)
Oh, you'd have heard of him if he was still there; everyone knows him. Once, he made his class _______ for an entire __________ just to
(VERB) (PERIOD OF TIME)
teach them about _____. That's the kind of teachers we had back then.
(NOUN)

Do you ever go see the __________ team? What—really? You couldn't
(NAME OF A SPORT)
even get into their games back when I ruled that school.

All right, I'll let you go now. I bet you think I'm an old _____, but in twenty-
(NOUN)
five years you are going to be me. That's just how things _______ .
(VERB)

And Now a Word on Alumni Associations

Money.

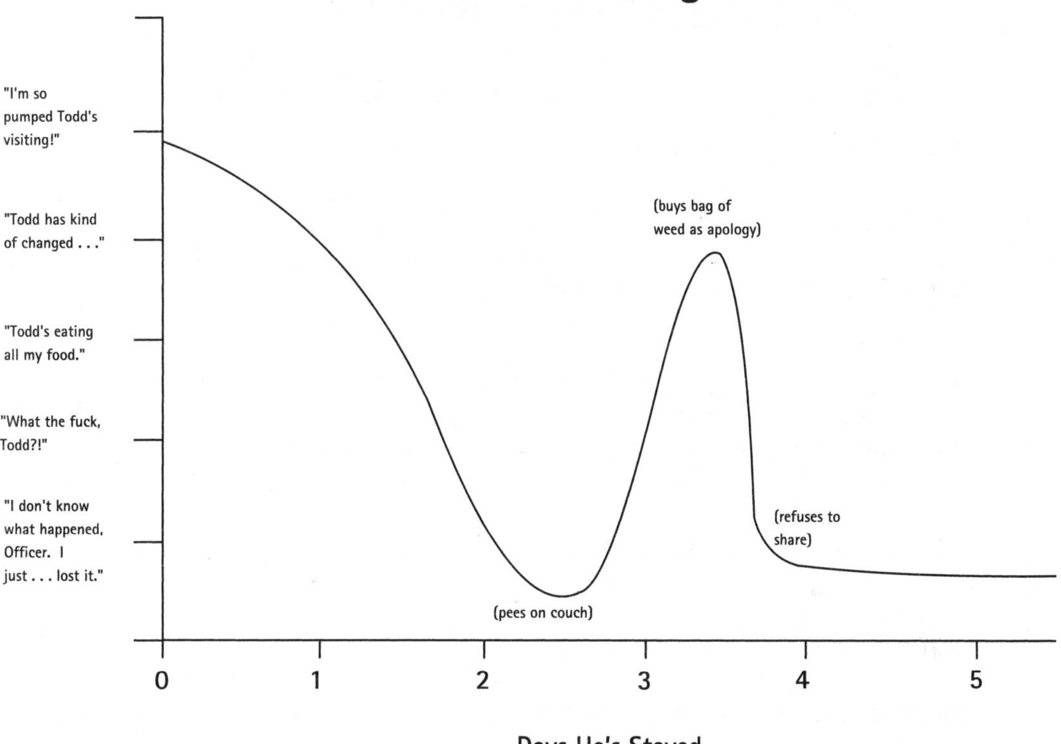

Did you hear about the senior who died? He called college the last four years of his life.

Nostalgia

Leaving college is depressing: your friends move away, you have to support yourself, and you begin to regret that Phi Omega brand you gave yourself junior year. However, many recent grads make their depression worse by becoming incorrectly nostalgic. They remember themselves in college being way cooler than they actually were, and this leads to a false sense of loss. Don't get caught in this trap—consult the Truth Check below:

Truth Check

- She was a backup cheerleader, not the captain.
- You weren't on the intramural lacrosse team; you went to two practices.
- That goldfish was already dead when you swallowed it.
- You never got a rash from not showering; it was a hereditary skin disease, and you still have it.
- Your freshman-year roommate wasn't that big of a dick; he just didn't share your enthusiasm for nightly *King of Queens* reruns.
- Actually, that fart may very well have been the smelliest thing ever.
- You didn't win a French-fry-eating contest. You just ate a lot of French fries, and everyone clapped because it was so gross they didn't know what else to do.
- You never wrestled a gorilla. It was an orangutan, and it beat you.
- Your Chem final junior year wasn't the hardest thing of all time. You're confusing it with being a slave in colonial America.
- You didn't drink an entire keg of beer by yourself that night; it was whiskey, you fucking PARTY ANIMAL!!!!
- You did not keep the Ark of the Covenant out of Nazi hands. That was Indiana Jones.

A Final Note on Life Beyond College

College was fun, but now that you've graduated there are a few things you can't do anymore.

Wearing a backpack is now considered odd, meeting with professors is now considered cultured, and hoping to bang a couple freshmen before they know better is now considered illegal. You have been warned.

There's nothing cooler than finishing your graduation and walking straight to a bus station, getting on, and leaving your college town forever. Either that or a nice family brunch.

CONCLUSION

Anyone who's ever written a paper knows that the conclusion is easily the least important part. While you probably spent hours picking the right font and laboring over the title page, your first thought about the conclusion usually comes fifteen minutes before you have to hand in your paper. That thought generally sounds something like, "Oh, shit, the conclusion . . . I'll just summarize what I already wrote. Yeah, that'll work. Now, where did I leave my beer?"

With that in mind, oh, shit, here's our conclusion:

If you're an incoming freshman, don't worry, this book is not exhaustive; you'll do lots more things than we could ever write about in three hundred or so pages. Many of these things will involve alcohol, but just as many will involve otters. Yeah, you knew even less about college than you thought.

If you're a current college student, we hope we offered you some valuable advice on how to maximize the rest of your college experience. We are sure we missed some totally awesome college antics that you and your buddies have done, and we're also sure that some of our stuff was "so fuckin' wrong, dude. Man, we could write a book better than that." By all means, do. One caveat, though: there's already a book called *The Great Gatsby*, so you're going to need another title.

Your other option is to write down each complaint on a very small sheet of paper and carry it with you everywhere. When you see one of us on the street, hand us the sheet of paper, and we'll stamp it. Ten stamps will get you a free six-inch sub.

If you're out of college, we have no idea why you spent that much time thumbing through this book, but we hope you did it while listening to Bruce Springsteen's "Glory Days" and crying. Next time you want to read something, we suggest a grown-up book like something by Faulkner or Hemingway, or *Garfield: Survival of the Fattest.*

Finally, let us leave you with one reminder: for four magical years, "college" can be used as any part of speech. Verb? "Yeah, I'm just going to college it up this weekend." Adjective? "Dude, that is SO college!" Noun? " 'College' is my favorite noun." However, it works best as a reason screamed at the top of your lungs for every ludicrous act you plan to commit. If anybody asks you why you just stole the sign from outside Kerry Hall, why you just ran through campus naked during a subzero snowstorm, or why you just tried combining Froot Loops and beer, the answer is always the same:

"COLLEGE!!!!!!!!!!!!!!!!!!!!!!!!!!!!!!!!!!!!!!!"

If you scream this at least once a day, you're on the right track.

GLOSSARY

15-Minute Rule The ironclad law that states that if a professor does not show up in the first fifteen minutes of class, the class is canceled.

2-Beer Queer A student who claims to be able to hold his liquor but gets drunk extremely quickly. Distant cousin to the 2-Pump Chump.

2-Pump Chump A man who does not have the ability to last very long during sexual intercourse.

5-Second Rule Principle that food dropped on the ground is still edible for five seconds.

ACT Test similar to the SAT, scored on a thirty-six-point scale, taken mostly by Midwesterners and hillbillies.

Adviser Strange professor you see once a semester to sign your course registration.

Alcoholla Calling on a friend to party with you. As in, "I'll alcoholla ya around nine."

Bangover The terrible feeling following a late night of sex, particularly bad sex.

Bar Scar Refers to ink stamps from bars that should litter both your hands by the end of a night out.

Beast Slang term for Milwaukee's Best, a cheap beer.

Beat Sheet A sheet inserted in between the mattress and bed frame of the top bunk, giving the user of the bottom bunk privacy.

Beej/BJ Slang for blow job.

Beer Bong Contraption involving a funnel and plastic tubing that uses gravity to facilitate the quick imbibing of beer.

Beer Goggles The state of mind in which drunkenness makes members of the opposite sex appear more attractive than they actually are.

Beer Muscles The sudden ability to perform feats of strength when drunk.

Beer Pong Game played on a Ping-Pong table in which teams alternate taking shots at six cups of beer placed in a pyramid at the opposite end of the table. If an opponent hits one of your cups, you drink the beer.

Beer Run Trip to the store to purchase beer.

Beer Bitch The person suckered into making this trip.

Beirut See "Beer Pong."

People born in the thirties named Adolf really got unlucky. Same with people born in the seventies named AIDS.

Bid A formal invitation to join a fraternity or sorority.

Blueberry Muffin Girl whose stomach has begun to roll over the top of her no-longer-fitting jeans. Visualize the top part of a muffin.

Bong Generic term for a water pipe used for smoking marijuana.

Booze Snooze A nap before a night of drinking.

Breaking the Seal Taking your first piss of the night, often resulting in many, many more trips to the bathroom.

Butterface A girl with an attractive body but terrifying face. As in, "Everything's hot but her face."

Carmichael, Lilly Aka the Dayton Delite. Ohio University coed who bravely integrated the sport of beer pong in 1972.

Clowned Out The state of a girl being dressed up with lots of makeup for a party.

Cock Block To hinder one's attempt to hook up.

Crustache Thin, wispy mustache grown by pubescent males seeking to experiment with facial hair.

Dank High-quality marijuana.

Doorknob To be called on someone who audibly farts in public, at which point offender can be pummeled until he/she is able to reach a doorknob. Can be averted if offender calls "Safety" first.

Dormcest An intra-dorm relationship.

I don't know much about Holocaust diaries, Anne Frankly I don't wanna know much about Holocaust diaries.

Dorm Slut Resident of a dormitory who engages in sexual activity with many male members of the dorm.

Double Fisting Actively drinking from a beverage held in each hand.

Drunk Dial To call an ex-girlfriend or boyfriend when intoxicated. Never a good idea (unless he or she lives close by).

Dry Hump (DH) To grind clothed genitalia against each other in simulated sexual intercourse.

DTR "Defining the Relationship." The conversation in which a couple decides if they are exclusively dating.

Facebook Official When a girl changes her Facebook relationship status from "single" to "in a relationship" and her boy does the same. The two are then said to be "Facebook official."

Fake-ternity A non-Greek campus group designed to fulfill a fraternity's position as an exclusive social club, like a dining club or a housing co-op.

Fifth A bottle of liquor containing 750 ml.

Fives Called to reserve a seat for five minutes when getting up, e.g., "I got fives on that chair."

Flip and Fuck A futon.

Floater A half-empty and unclaimed beer left at the end of a party.

Frattitude General disregard for all humanity; single-minded pursuit of beer and hookups.

Freshman 15 Mythical amount of weight supposedly gained by every freshman girl.

If vampires can't see their reflection, how do they do their eye makeup?

Fuck Buddy Two friends who decide to have sex without any emotional attachment. See also: "Any Man's Dream."

GDI "God Damn Independent." Someone not affiliated with a Greek organization.

Granola A hippie. See also: "Tie Dye" and "Wool Socks with Sandals."

Greek A member of a sorority or fraternity.

Grenade The unattractive friend that some member of your party has to "fall on."

Hallcest The regrettable decision to hook up with a member of your hall. Definition is considerably more complicated in the Deep South.

Hall Crawl A party thrown by a hall in which a different mixed drink is served in each room. No crawling is involved.

Handle A bottle of liquor that contains 1.75 liters. Two and one-third times as large as a fifth. So named because it has a handle on the side for easy pouring.

Hazing Abusing new members of an organization as a rite of passage.

Hetero-Hug Act in which two straight men clasp hands, pull themselves together, and pound each other's back with their free hands. Often accompanied by " 'Sup bro" sentiment.

High School Zero, College Hero Person who makes the transition from high school Screech to college years Zach Morris.

HJ Slang for hand job.

HOFNAR "Hard-on for No Apparent Reason." Think seventh-grade Math class.

Hoggin' Occasionally hooking up with a fat girl just for the sake of hooking up.

You can't hug children with nuclear arms. Stop crying, Radioactive Man, you'll learn to express your love in different ways.

Honor Code Compulsory promise to not lie, cheat, steal, or otherwise be a jerk while at college.

Hookup A sexual encounter, either casual or serious. Generally reserved for encounters that go beyond second base.

Last Call Last opportunity to purchase alcohol before a bar closes for the night. Often the time at which hookups are sealed.

Liquor Luge A block of ice through which liquor is run into the mouths of partygoers.

LUG "Lesbian Until Graduation." A young woman who experiments sexually with other women until the end of college.

Mixer (a) A party cohosted by two groups in order for their respective members to meet; (b) liquid used for diluting alcohol for consumption.

Natty Affectionate slang term for Natural Light, a very inexpensive beer produced by Anheuser-Busch.

OTPHJ "Over-The-Pants Hand Job." Common among strippers and girls afraid of commitment.

Paint Pens Pens used by sorority girls to adorn any manner of plastic trinket with paint advertising the sorority's letters and how great it is.

Party Foul Any breach of etiquette at a party, e.g., wasting beer, vomiting in the house, tongue-kissing the bride, etc.

Pledge Aspiring member of a fraternity who is forced to perform various tasks before joining the organization.

Pop a Squat To pee outside, if you're a girl.

"You could swing the wrecking ball a little better." Now, is that constructive or destructive criticism?

Prairie Dog When you have to shit so bad it's poking out. See also "Turtle Head."

Pre-game To get drunk before leaving your house; often necessary if underage and going to a bar.

Puke and Rally To vomit and then return to drinking with renewed vigor.

The Ratio Number of girls at a party divided by the number of guys. Higher is generally better.

Reading Days Days before exam week in which there are no exams or classes. Supposedly provided for studying.

Recommended Reading Reading the professor expects you to do but won't call "required."

Resident Adviser Upper-class student who lives on a hall to enforce rules and handle administrative duties. See also: "Tool."

Rush Process of parties and get-to-know-you events in which Greek organizations pick new members.

Sausage Fest A party with many more guys than girls.

Security Guard Cop with a Napoleonic complex instead of a gun.

Sexiled Thrown out of one's room so one's roommate may hook up.

Shakes/Spins The stage of drunkenness in which the room just won't sit still.

Shocker Sexual maneuver in which two fingers are inserted into the vagina while the pinky goes into the anus. Less demeaning than you'd think.

Curiosity killed the cat. Oh, Curiosity, we never should have bought you that BB gun!

Shot A one-ounce glass of liquor.

Shotgun To drink a beer quickly by poking a hole in the bottom and slurping the beer through it.

Skankersore Blisterlike growth on the mouth of a slutty girl; similar to cold sore.

Slump Buster Large, attainable woman used to break dry spells and promptly disposed of.

Sneaker Chaser A young lady who seeks to date or sexually service varsity athletes.

Sorostitutes Sexually liberal members of sororities. See also: "Sluts."

Spring Breakup Tacit agreement with girlfriend/boyfriend that you will make out with other people on Spring Break and then act like nothing ever happened.

Sword Fight When two males piss in the same toilet at the same time. See also: "Crossing Streams."

TA "Teaching Assistant." Graduate student who aids in the instruction of a class. Deceptively similar to "T & A," but not as much fun.

Teabag To place one's testicles in the mouth of a sexual partner. Popular in the British Commonwealth.

Test Files Files of old exams maintained by fraternities and other campus groups, used as study aids, but never for cheating.

That Guy You know, the annoying guy. That guy.

Tool/Toolbox An uptight nerd who follows the rules.

Turkey Dump Breaking up with your boyfriend or girlfriend before the Thanksgiving Break.

UPB "Unidentified Party Bruise." Often discovered upon waking on Sunday morning.

Upper Decker To relieve one's bowels into the tank of a toilet instead of the bowl.

V-Card Virginity. Usually used mockingly. To be collected (the cool kid's Pokémon).

Wake and Bake To "wake" up and then get "baked" by smoking marijuana.

Walk of Shame The walk back to one's dorm in the morning after spending the night with a hookup.

Wingman Buddy who goes out with you and aids your attempts to hook up.

Work-Study Demeaning yourself for $6 an hour.

Wounded Soldier A beer that is not finished.